"*Lost Orchard* is a testament to higher education at its best, when intellectual curiosity and experimentation create an enduring community—something far richer than a sequence of classes. Kirkland College generated a literary community of astonishing breadth and depth—writers who continue to make significant contributions to contemporary literature. Still efflorescent, this lost orchard has been very fruitful indeed."

—David Fenza, Executive Director,
The Association of Writers and Writing Programs

"The contributions to this anthology are as diverse and interesting as one would expect of alumnae and faculty at Kirkland, the last founded, progressive women's college in the United States. Short stories, plays, and poems cover a broad range of subjects, including breast cancer, dementia of a parent, traveling in Macedonia, recent political events, fantasy, and what it was like being a student at Kirkland. True to the ethos of Kirkland, the collection is not organized by topic or by whether the author was a student, faculty member, or president, but rather in a more anarchic manner—alphabetically by last name. The result is deeply satisfying as a book to read in any manner one chooses, to dip into again and again. And one will want to!"

—Leslie Miller-Bernal, author of *Separate by Degree:
Women Students' Experiences in
Single-Sex and Coeducational Colleges*

Lost Orchard

Lost Orchard

Prose and Poetry from the Kirkland College Community

Edited by

JO PITKIN

excelsior editions
State University of New York Press
Albany, New York

Cover Art: Linda Branch Dunn, Kirkland Class of 1977, "Departure," 2008, 13"h x 16"w, monoprint, collage, stitch.

Cover Design: Amy Stirnkorb

Published by State University of New York Press, Albany

Excelsior Editions is an imprint of State University of New York Press

For information, contact State University of New York Press, Albany, NY
www.sunypress.edu

Production by Diane Ganeles
Marketing by Kate McDonnell

Library of Congress Cataloging-in-Publication Data

Lost orchard : prose and poetry from the Kirkland College Community / edited
    by Jo Pitkin.
        pages cm. — (Excelsior Editions)
    Includes bibliographical references.
    ISBN 978-1-4384-4999-9 (hardcover : alk. paper)
    ISBN 978-1-4384-4998-2 (pbk. : alk. paper)
    1. American literature—21st century.   I. Pitkin, Jo, 1956– editor of
compilation.

    PS536.3.L68 2014
    810.8'006—dc23   2013015941

                        10 9 8 7 6 5 4 3 2 1

For our many teachers
who guided, nurtured, challenged, and supported us
and for those who still believe in the vision
of Kirkland College and its students.

A lost orchard is the road on which we passed
Where a house was with a candle in the night;
And we must go that way still, but at last
The house is by the roadside, but no light.

—Edgar Lee Masters, "The Lost Orchard"

Contents

Preface

We were pioneers. We were innovators. We were independent learners and thinkers. In the 1960s and 1970s, we were among the first generation of college students to study creative writing, American studies, environmental studies, women's studies, and other disciplines. We were drawn to a young college full of promise and unencumbered by traditional academia. Few of us comprehended how challenging this path would sometimes prove to be. In 1968, Kirkland College opened in Clinton, New York, during a time of social, political, and cultural turmoil. As of 2013, it was the last women's college—and the last coordinate college—established in the United States. Known for innovation, Kirkland offered written evaluations rather than grades; interdisciplinary curricula; self-designed concentrations, independent studies, and senior projects. Students governed themselves, made critical decisions about their own course of study, and had an opportunity to pursue an education that, ultimately, was designed to empower women. Yet, after a tumultuous merger with coordinate partner Hamilton College, Kirkland ceased to exist in May 1978. So, how did a literary anthology from Kirkland's diasporic community come about?

In June 2007, I coordinated Kirkland Voices, the first-ever alumnae reunion reading, with Liz Horwitt. A half-dozen readers traveled from Maine to California back to the Hill to read in the Red Pit during the all-Kirkland reunion at Hamilton College. During the reading, many thoughts and emotions crossed my mind. One was relief that a year of planning had finally come to fruition. Another was how seamlessly the readers presented their work—we had never met one another until a few hours before the reading, yet our voices flowed together harmoniously. As I listened to work I had not previously read or heard, I kept thinking, "This is so good!" I wanted to capture and share this moment. At some point between the standing-room reading itself and the reception with chocolate-dipped strawberries and macaroons, I had a notion: Why not publish an anthology so that alumnae who couldn't attend would be able to read this fine work? *Lost Orchard* was born.

Soliciting work from the contributors to Kirkland Voices was easy. But finding other accomplished Kirkland writers would prove to be more difficult, given that for thirty years Kirkland's alumnae have not had a continuously functioning alumnae association, an up-to-date alumnae directory, or a brick-and-mortar (in our case, concrete block) institution of our own to nurture or support us—or, indeed, to connect us. Primarily through the use of social media, the Internet, and word of mouth, I was able to locate many potential contributors and reach out personally.

Facilitating this literary union has been immensely satisfying and profoundly poignant: the project of a lifetime. Selfishly, I wanted to gather the Kirkland community together once again—even if only in the pages of a book—to preserve our legacy. Kirkland's alumnae are finite. We are acutely aware that our history may vanish once the last Kirkland professor and last Kirkland alumna are gone.

Lost Orchard, created to commemorate the occasion of the Charter Class's fortieth anniversary, includes poetry, drama, stories, and creative nonfiction by Kirkland's faculty, administration, and alumnae. It also features work that was read during Kirkland Voices as well as one-act plays written, directed, and performed by alumnae for the 2007 reunion. These contributions encompass a multiplicity of themes and genres yet reflect a commonality of gender, experience, attitude, and age.

Although *Lost Orchard*'s contributors did not all study creative writing, this anthology also provides a glimpse at the vibrant, supportive writing community that Kirkland fostered. Kirkland students had the opportunity to pursue a major in creative writing—one of a handful of colleges to do so. According to the Association of Writers and Writing Programs (AWP), only three colleges—including Kirkland—conferred a bachelor of arts in creative writing in 1975.

Under Bill Rosenfeld's steady direction, Kirkland's nascent Creative Writing Program attracted such talented teachers as Kathy Dewart, Naomi Lazard, Denise Levertov, Tess Gallagher, and Michael Burkard. Many Kirkland students also took workshops at Hamilton with two young poets: David Rigsbee and David Lehman.

Kirkland was a bold experiment in women's education. Although the college only lasted a decade, what a brilliant decade it was! May *Lost Orchard*, in some way, keep Kirkland's light burning brightly.

Foreword

It all comes back to life. The Creative Writing Program with its place in the Kirkland College setting. The workshops at home in the carpeted levels of the Red Pit, the exhibition areas in the List Building, the dormitory lounges, all the learning and living spaces united in purpose.

Above all were the intentions and skills of those purposeful Kirkland students—the people who made the program work, insisted that it function to their satisfaction and advantage. And how hard they worked! Certainly some enrolled to find out what it was all about, several of those from across College Hill Road. (During my first year, a Hamilton enrollee approached me after class and asked, "Are all Kirkland courses this lively?" Such refreshing questions as that give you pause. I couldn't satisfy him with an answer. I just smiled in appreciation, but certainly our workshops were as demanding as they were lively.)

Here's another angle on the same issue: A different student—a genuine Kirkland College citizen—observed in her course evaluation, "In the workshops, there's no place to hide! You're expected to speak up about other people's work, and you have to sit there and listen to your classmates criticize your work—constructive criticism, certainly, as demanded by the faculty, but criticism nonetheless, until you yourself are capable of applying serious standards to your own work." She had specified one of our most important goals: the artistic toil of writing fused to the writer's own honest self-evaluation.

From among all those who joined the writing workshops a surprising number continued to write poetry and fiction. But that aside, all members came away with sharpened skills as readers and critics. By the way, those Kirkland people who went on to graduate programs were invariably noteworthy for their skill at conducting critical sessions. That's the feedback we faculty got, and very gratifying it was.

Also gratifying were the students, some of whom are included in this anthology, who continued their writing in genres other than fiction or poetry but who credited their success in large part to creative writing.

Several of those fashioned double majors and went on to success as editors of law reviews. One who doubled in creative writing and biology became editor of the creative writing magazine attached to her pre-med school. Then there were several who never took a workshop but, influenced by the emphasis on writing in general at Kirkland, pursued writing careers of one type or another, such as creative nonfiction and editing.

As for the faculty's responsibilities, let's not forget evaluations, those end-of-semester narratives in lieu of grades. In the privacy of their offices, they reviewed the semester's work, drafted and revised them into honest, detailed, and balanced summations of each writer's work. Kirkland students expected no less. That was a true joining of skills. I look back over the list of colleagues, all devoted to guiding our hopeful young writers, while they kept their own energies fresh.

Students and faculty alike also enjoyed informal gatherings that brought members of the community together in more relaxed and celebratory moods: the soirées, the end-of semester readings by members of the various classes, the cook-outs for graduating seniors.

In a category of its own stands the Watrous literary prize, founded by Esther Watrous Couper, in memory of her father. It yields handsome annual awards in the categories of poetry, fiction, and essay in criticism. I specify that the Watrous prize still "stands," for it has been carried over for inclusion among the Hamilton College prizes and scholarships as another light beam in the Kirkland heritage.

So far, I've avoided naming individual students or faculty involved in the conduct and progress of the Creative Writing Program. At this point, however, I must say some words about Jo Pitkin's role in keeping the memories and reputation alive. In fact, in addition to founding *Red Weather*, Jo played a part in the very survival of the program. When the merger with Hamilton College had everyone on tenterhooks, she and Hamilton student Scott Klein marched into Dean Gulick's office and made their case for the survival of creative writing. I have no doubt that they helped influence the Hamilton English Department to adopt the program entire. Of course, the Kirkland informal settings and evaluations fell by the wayside, but little else faded.

So we may thank Jo for more than her inestimable energies in bringing Kirkland creative writers together in this splendid anthology, as she did for the group reading at the 2007 reunion. Thanks to her commitment and steady energies, the program thrives today as well as it ever had and remains emblematic of the best that Kirkland College offered its people.

Bill Rosenfeld

Nin Andrews

Star

"Exactly," my first-grade teacher, Mrs. Wilson said, but only once. That day she placed a gold star on my page. The day before she swatted the boy behind me for picking his nose. *(Whap!)* The day before that she sent Anna P. Gibson out in the hall for making squelchy noises with her lips when she dropped pins on the floor. *I can't hear my pins drop!* Mrs. Wilson announced. *But I can hear Anna P. Gibson! (Whap-whap!)* Whenever she looked at me, I stared at my feet. I stared at the dented wood on my desktop, the names carved in it. Leah + Ron. I stared at my black-and-white saddle shoes. My white bobby socks. My plaid jumper. (Why is it called a jumper? I'd still like to know.) No matter where I looked, I felt Mrs. Wilson's gaze on my skin. Sometimes she reached down with red fingernails and pushed my hair from my eyes. Sometimes pushed my glasses up my nose. *I want you to see me,* she said. I saw her. I saw Mrs. Wilson. Mrs. Wilson was a giant woman standing on orange heels with tiny points. I wondered how she balanced there. Whenever I looked back at her, she grew bigger. I was afraid of how big she'd grow.

How the Poem Dies

First there are the calculated deaths, performed with precision and forethought, when I play doctor, sliding on a pair of latex gloves and slicing you open, examining every stanza as if it were an alien or a disease until it is one. Of course you return the favor, leaving pieces of me in another town or time zone, my soul in a sock drawer, my black braids in a hotel room in Peoria where I gaze wistfully at the river below.

Next are the silent deaths when we stare at *The Vindicator* on the coffee table, nibbling blueberry scones, the clink of a butter knife the only sound. We are like those married couples who wish to leave each other but never can. Instead we keep eating and sleeping together, each pretending the other doesn't exist. After a while we become mere figments of one another's imagination. We each think the other is the figment.

At last there are the drunken deaths. I wake the neighbors and howl at you and the moon. You accuse me of infidelity, murder, and theft. (It's all true!) Then we make love until we think we will die from too much sex. We die again and again until even death is not enough. We keep coming back to life, searching for that perfect last line, the one that ends all ends. The one where we die with no regrets.

The Other Girl

It was how the doctor said it, statutory rape, that I remember, his words like cold metal on bare skin, his hands wrapped in latex gloves. The nurse kept saying breathe. *Breathe. Don't scream. Hush.* I couldn't help it, I said, biting my lips. Afterward I took so many showers and walks around my ceiling. I was afraid to answer the phone or see anyone who might see me back. Instead I thought of long lists of things I should have done or said, and that girl outside, the one who knew nothing of this. She who would never see or feel as I did. She stayed outside long after that summer day when the dusk bled all over the trees and the darkness bloomed inside me. I knew why they called it statutory then. Unable to move or scream, a statue was what I was. No matter how hard I tried, I could not step outside. I could not find that girl, the one who used to chase down city sidewalks, racing balls and skipping over the cracks in the cement. The one who would never know the thing inside that hurts and screams and aches even as it wants.

Natalie Babbitt and Samuel Fisher Babbitt

from *Tuck Everlasting*

The following are excerpts from Natalie's Tuck Everlasting *(Farrar, Strauss & Giroux, 1975), which was written in 1973–1974, while we were deeply involved with Kirkland College. It describes the setting of the Tuck's house in the woods—modeled closely on the small house we had in Forestport. It was my—and my family's—get-away place, an idyllic escape to the forest on the edge of a large pond. We spent many weekends there, even getting ourselves snowed in completely one winter—finally rescued by the state police. In the summer, we were there for several weeks at a time.*

Page 47/48: ". . . climb a long hill, . . . see ahead another hill, and beyond that the deep green of a scattered pine forest . . . A wide stand of dark pines rose up, loomed nearer, . . . a rutted path, lumpy with roots . . . The late sun's brilliance could penetrate only in scattered glimmers, and everything was silent and untouched, the ground muffled with moss and sliding needles, the graceful arms of the pines stretched out protectively in every direction. And it was cool, blessedly cool and green . . . . then ahead the path dropped down a steep embankment; and beyond that, a flash of color and a dazzling sparkle. Down the embankment . . . there it was, a plain, homely little house, barn-red, and below it the last of the sun flashing on the wrinkled surface of a tiny lake."

Page 50/51: ". . . the homely little house beside the pond . . . the gentle eddies of dust, the silver cobwebs, the mouse who lived—and welcome to him!—in a table drawer. There were only three rooms— The kitchen came first . . . open cabinet . . . dishes stacked in perilous towers . . . an enormous black stove . . . every surface, every wall piled and strewn . . . The parlor came next . . . furniture loose and sloping with age . . . sat about helter-skelter . . . the bedroom . . . a dusty loft . . ."

Page 52: ". . . on the old beamed ceiling of the parlor, streaks of light swam and danced and wavered like a bright mirage, reflected through the windows from the sunlit surface of the pond. . . . And over everything was the clean, sweet smell of the water and its weeds, the chatter of a swooping Kingfisher, the carol and trill of a dozen other kinds of bird, and occasionally the thrilling bass note of an unastonished bullfrog at ease somewhere along the muddy banks."

Yes, there really was a mouse that lived in the table drawer. And because of those wonderful bass notes, we christened the place "Frogs' Weep." When we left Clinton, we sold the place—very reluctantly—and began a new life further east. Only a few years later, we learned from the new owners that lightning had struck the house and that it had burned to the ground. About a year ago, intrigued with Google Earth, I zeroed in on "Frogs' Weep." I expected to find, if not a new house, then the remains of the old one, and there it was—a concrete slab. But the real surprise came when I saw that the pond itself was gone. For whatever reason, the dam had been removed and now a sickly little stream flowed through the empty basin of what had been our pond.

Spooky.

Nina Bogin

The Lost Hare

Every day a different weather,
weeks without seeing moon or sun,
and a hare I've been trying to track down
these twelve years gone, ever since

I glimpsed it, deep in thought,
in the high grass of the marsh;
I saw the ash-gray tips of its ears.
Seeing me, it disappeared

into blackthorn and wild rose,
leaving its burrows unattended,
the entryways clogging with cobwebs.
In the meantime

my hair has gone gray,
my hands thick-veined, and the lines
of my thwarted quest cross my face
from every direction.

My long-haired daughters have grown,
left for other cities. We tend the fire,
keep the rooms clean, lay the table for two.
And beyond the black door

the sky fills up with stars
shedding their slow light
on the innumerable paths
through the marsh-grass

to the hollow
where the lost hare sleeps
bedded down in the thoughts
and dreams I hoarded there.

The Old World

These towns, these places on the map,
come complete with auras, their names
resounding like chimes. Rivers and bridges,
steeples and the smell of ink.
I look down from the bell-towers
and see them spiraled at my feet:
the vendors in the square, the cobbled streets
where the first editions were churned out,
rainwater flowing through the gutters to the sea.

Flocks of starlings fly up and up, winding me
into their legend, who once toiled in the fields
or, in the back alleys, scrubbed blackened pots and pans,
never learned to read, and long ago
disappeared into an abandoned grave
where the Hebrew letters of my name blend
into the moss-covered stone of the land.

The Orchards

I walked through the orchards again.
The sky came down behind the tree-trunks,

inside the cold branches.
And there was a taste of rain or snow,

almost intimate. Quick brushes of green.
Preparations. I walked down

the line of trees, into the curve
of land and around. Listened

to the wind stop there and stir
the lifted branches,

the gentle hiss along the edge
of grass. A slant

into light. So still, so still,
you can hear the world happening.

Michael Burkard

Planetary Nebula in Vulpecula

Don't talk so closely to yourself
and for god's sake when you decide
to come in out of the rain
remember you are coming in
out of the stars too, the Dumbbell
Nebula, and the super nova, and galac-
tic dust arriving light years after
you and your rainstorm.

Sometimes When the Street Was Weeping

Sometimes when the street
was weeping I would stay
outside late and watch
neighbors—some known
some not—come home
for the evening—I would
light a cigarette and para-
phrase their days out loud,
all by myself, all for my-
self. No explanations were
ever needed or required.
I became a stranger to
myself. One friend in par-
ticular I liked to watch—
as he always looked like
he was about to change
his mind about something
in the evening. He would
hesitate and go half-way
back to his now-quiet
car. Then back again
toward his house.

Thirteen Ways

1
I don't want to look
at anything including
I thirteen ways.

2
One woman cried when
she wrote, cried a
few times, but most
of the time she was
an equipped shadow.

3
Equipped shadow for
anyone who does not
know and those numbers
would be higher today
and higher tomorrow
too and the next day
equipped shadow is
a steal variation from
the poet Wallace Stevens

4
who wrote "Thirteen Ways
of Looking at a Blackbird"
a long time ago. I have
thirteen ways of being
allergic to women, to my
father, and to men if a
certain form of love is
inviolate (if love has
more than one form).

5
Maybe love is a biological
necessity and for some of us
therefore an allergy also:
for those of us who have
never gotten even self-love
"right." It would be more
interesting to get it wrong,
if you know what I mean, but
not in the same way as I have
actually gotten it wrong.

6
It is snowing among my father
and my mother and my many loves.
Some days I would not like the
sun know even how to count how
many creatures great and small
I have loved and how no one knows
this about me because I have never
quite said so and so of course I
to some extent don't know it quite
either for just that slight fear
of acknowledging. It is snowing
among my shadows and my acknow-
ledgments.

7
Within a complex of imaginary
numbers multiplication by i
rotates counterclockwise. The
imaginary numbers have their own
number line and it is perpen-
dicular to the real number line.
The i rotating is in a sense just
what I mean by my I. I first

8
heard of imaginary numbers in
a way in which I mistook: I
thought we sent man to the moon
with imaginary numbers because
the computer models could not
do it with real numbers—so I
assumed or misheard that that was
how/when imaginary numbers were
invented: not so: imaginary numbers
come into being much earlier: and
as I say this I am struck by the
fact that come into being as a
series of words to talk to imaginary
numbers reads strangely and somewhat
wonderfully: it's an unintended notion
of course, sometimes the best kind
although like "wrong" the worst kind
might be equally interesting

9
My sponsor when I got sober and whom
I still stay in some touch with used
to tell me he thought "interesting"
was a kind of code word for me a kind
of non-committal place or sound or word
to hold up. Think he was on to some-
thing as the word as often a preferred
one but maybe more so had a slight
ring to it when I would use it even
I could hear. I don't know if Charlie
heard the same ring or not.

10
I was looking for signs driving from
Charlie's last May and a bird swooped
in front of the car. I do not know if

11
this bird was a sign or not.
Sometimes signs are cheap and
sometimes life feels like a legitimate
allegory.

14

12
A student writes that C. is a bitter
old woman the student says this fondly
but I think exaggerates some of the
bitterness. What I am thinking is
where is C. when she was younger and
not so bitter (the student is more
accurate than I want to admit), where
is eight year old C. or thirteen year
old C.—yes, thirteen, of course
because here we are, just briefly,
in like in the old days when C. was
twenty-six and you could look right
through her or when she was forty-one
and published the incredible Dream
of the Flaming Red Shirt and her
Thirteen Stories. One could almost
be afraid of her but C. would not allow

13
it. As best she could she would sit
you down with herself and ask you to
tell her stories of your life, the real
story, like who are loving now, really,
where do you really want to be, really,
is your heart open and why not?, are you
writing are you coming back will you miss
me like I miss you I left a message with
one friend figuring it would get to you.
Cryptic C., alive in the heart and soul
and with the words floating in between.

Selma Burkom

Recondite Relations

Once I knew a muffled man my
bachelor uncle, Uncle Sam
Sam looked no one in the eye
grown-ups called him crippled-shy
A man no child could hope to know
dead now, long decades ago,
Alive, he spoke infrequently
in memory he talks to me:
words riddling-rich in indirection
intent obscured beyond detection
Older now I think I see
that muffled man lives on in me.

Could I have spoken openly
perhaps you'd not have labeled me
your nemesis, your private bane,
inflictor of some awful pain.
Could I have spoken openly
I would have said, you mean to me—
the type, the modern muse divine
the force that drives my ragged lines,
embodying an abstract light
a flame unflickering down the night.

I'll never know my Uncle Sam
but hope he wasn't as I am,
But as I'm muffled, I can't speak
except in language dense, oblique
my meanings mired in metaphor
myself a moated, hollow core
an empty room with bolted door.

Leslie Cook

A Sudden Vision of Upstate New York as Dakota Territory

I have read in stories about winters like this. The snow
collects itself about my door, the wind
blows mileless drifts as to hinder the sight.
It is a moonless night as wolves howl at grey clouds,
their beards icy against their chins, their fur
matted against the ribs. Soon,
they will come to the house, breathe their wolves' breath
on our frosted windows, in search of. And in the morning
their trail is lost under snow, and more snow,
until the howling is for the roof,
and the pathway at the door is only a dark tunnel.
This is when even sturdy Norwegian men
begin to feel a bit loony, their wives
knowing the endless whiteness even in their souls
have said nothing, but hold in their arms the babies
who no longer cry, and pray prayers to reach no god.
Always in the darkness of their hearts, a woman
who arrived last winter carrying in her arms a bundle
of blankets, and white flesh frozen together, his tiny fingers and
fingernails fisted perfectly as if to reopen, close again.

What of landscapes?

What of landscapes?
That old barn down the road,
near the corner stone where the three
townships meet: Worthington,
Peru, and Cummington, that barn
where we found dried snakeskins
and looked for live ones;

where we found rotting squirrels
and brittle raccoon skulls, empty
cow stalls and 1940 license plates, always
expecting bats crouched
in the dark beams, daring
the dead wood to crack under
our weight when we climbed up
to the loft, eyes wide open.

Once, an old man lived nearby,
kept the tools he tilled surrounding
fields with in a shed across the road;
kept horses and stored hay here
in this barn; set each stone
of its foundation and others
by hand; raised the roof
on the then batless handhewn beams.

New owners, to make room for lots,
and valuing old barn boards more
than old barns and animal ghosts,
tore the siding off, piece by piece
into a pickup and drove out
the dirt road, leaving the frame,
the structure, the form,
to collapse under an unfamiliar open sky.

The foundation, defining
a hole in the ground, is the only
shelter, burying milk snakes and mice
each winter. Only the old friends
still walk with us, the dragonflies
ignoring the toads stiffening flat
on the road, and, restless
we balance on the stone walls down
to the granite marker and back.
It is harmless snakes that startle
in the rotted timber.

Grandfather Poem

There was no Thanksgiving poem
this year. How does one say: a man
has lived a long life, not
an extraordinary life, but a good life,
with a good wife. He has raised
two children, who have in turn, each raised him
three grandchildren. A man,
who listened to Bach
painstakingly from his cellar,
who could speak to you
in Dutch, English, German, or French,
could read Latin, and he understood
the insides of a radio better
than himself. A man, who came
on the boat from Holland
at seventeen, played chess
like a master, and when his grandchildren visited
he would play for them "Mary Had A Little Lamb"
on his violin. How does one say:
a man—a husband, father,
and grandfather—the grandmother,
the aunts, the uncles, and cousins sit
around the table giving thanks
not to God, but thankful. He is thankful
a grandson shook his hand, a pretty girl
kissed his cheek. How does one say: "Grandpa,
you have wet your pants."
"You're at Gerda's, Nick.
You will have to stay wet." The conversation
moves elsewhere. "Would you like some more wine?"
"Karin, tell us more
about the magazine you draw for."
He dabs with a cloth napkin
at his mustache, worried
about the cat Snowy, at home alone.

Nancy Avery Dafoe

from "The Writing Contest"

SCENE: *The curtain rises on a dark, nearly bare stage. The setting, although not distinguishable, takes place inside the minds of the individual characters. The time is contemporary due to references to computers, but a date is impossible to determine. A single spotlight reveals a small, old desk and wooden chair at center stage. On the desk is an antique typewriter. Around the desk on the floor of the stage are balled up wads of paper and stacks of books. Dressed in black, the characters do not appear to be aware of one another except at the end of the play.*

(As the spotlight goes up on the desk and chair at center stage, the audience hears the microphoned sound of mechanical typewriter keys clicking. Papers are scattered around each writer.)

VO: *(professional intonation: off stage)* The Writers' Spa Contest is pleased to announce its annual short story competition. Our contest winner will earn a trip to beautiful Belize and an opportunity to meet with international writers, in one of the most exotic locations on the planet, for a writing workshop and opportunities for publishing your work.

(Spotlight goes off typewriter at center stage. A spotlight goes on at roughly Center Right where SEAN is seated, facing the audience. The rest of the stage remains in darkness.)

SEAN: *(seated, rubs her face tenderly)* Work. Ooooh. My tooth aches. Or is it my computer screen that makes me feel the pain? *(leans toward audience, pretending to read a computer screen)* "You have 0 unread messages?" *(stands up and walks toward Downstage Center.)* Well, that's it! No e-mail. Not a single response from anyone validating my ideas. That in itself is enough reason for the mood I'm in, to say nothing of the cavity eating away my nerve endings.

(She holds her hand to her jaw again, then suddenly hurries back to her chair, leans over, and picks up a piece of paper from the floor, unfolds it, and walks a few steps more toward the audience.)

Word count: 5,313 words. Damn! Editors like the under 3,000 variety. At 5,000 plus, it's too long or not nearly long enough. That's the problem with the way my mind works: 5,000 + word-SEAN; it's like one of those stores, you know, WOMAN, all caps *(gestures to show her large figure)* for the plus-size figure. Instead of skipping lunch or dinner, however, I'll going back to that infernal computer, adding *(exaggerates adding)* words. So, I'll take my last story and close my eyes before chopping it in half, taking out the internal organs, and stitching it back together to see what I've got besides 2,527 words.

(She sits down as the spotlight on her is turned off.)

(Spotlight comes up on BILL, Downstage Right.)

BILL: *(Holding a manuscript in his hands, speaks using various intonations)* Word? What's the word? FUCK. FUCK? FUCK! *(stands up and walks down stairs into aisle of the theater)* I think I got in trouble for that one back in high school. BILL's FUCK story got him a 3-day suspension, but at least the FRATRICIDES no longer wanted to punch in my face every time I navigated those gray hallways. I've graduated *(pauses)* to "Fuck only every few pages" stories in which a character named Gabriel mentally masturbates. Not an ounce of nostalgia. *(pauses, turns and walks back on stage to where he started out)* The one I'll send will be marked by pustules, presenting a photographic image of the highest degree of impropriety that will linger long after the reader closes his or her eyes. *(changes tone)*

(Spotlight goes out on BILL who remains standing in the dark as the light moves to MARISA at Upstage Left.)

MARISA: Eyes her manuscript: *(Gets up nervously, hesitates in her movement toward Center Stage and in her speech: reflective. Holding a paper in her hands.)* If I choose a story that is a straightforward narrative, I could demonstrate technique in an age when the narrative is becoming a lost art. Beginning again, I could use a narrator-agent or go to the other extreme with a nonnarrated narrative. *(exasperated)* It's all MARISA's self-conscious performance. If I present an interior monologue then shift to stream of consciousness, would the shadows be observed? The shades, yes; it's about the grays: the manifestation of becoming. *(pauses and takes a deep breath before looking over her shoulder to rear curtain and back to Center as if expecting someone.)* The question is: Does my awareness of narrative self appear to be uncertainty? Will they read hesitancy rather than self-reflexive narrative and reject the story outright? I'm no A.S. Byatt. Post-Modernism is dead. Is it all an exercise in futility? *(She retreats slowly, sitting back down and looking at the piece of paper in her hand.)*

(Spotlight goes out on MARISA and lights go up on FOX.)

FOX: Futility? It's fuckingly futile. *(Animated, he gets up at Center Left and begins pacing in widening circles, gesticulating as he speaks.)* Changing my name ought to count for something. Crafty as a FOX. Start on the third day—symbolic possibilities right there number 3—and work backward to the moment they all went blind or maybe deaf. *(pause, finding insight)* Mad. That's it. The—blank—they all went insane, non compos mentis, nuts, nutsy, nutty, screwy, teched, unbalanced, unsound, wacky, witless, wrong—choose word later. All I have to do is write it, and they will come.

(FOX does a tap dance then throws out his arms in a wide embrace of space.)

(Spotlight goes out, but FOX continues dancing in the dark. Spotlight goes up on HADIYA.)

HADIYA: *(Stays seated at Downstage Left as she speaks clearly but demurely.)* Come to HADIYA's heart, her soul. How can my words not find a home? My story breathes truth because it is what I have seen, identified as a hummingbird in my palm; *(looks down at her hand)* its neck broken; its wings still.

(Spotlight goes out on HADIYA and lights up CAL who is seated between Upstage Right and Upstage Center.)

CAL: *(Standing, looking at the script in his hand, leaning against the chair.)* Still at it? This is the last one! *(Dramatically holds up the script to the heavens.)*

It's not that I'm jaded, but, unfortunately, I have to make a living. There is, however, no reason to be intimidated by the others. Reticence. I'm more than reluctant. I'm wedged. *(walks around chair, pushes it aside)* Count rejection notices? Hardly, but I have kept track of where I've sent my missives. *(intones another's voice)* "Please provide SASE for notification only. We recycle." Of course they do. They recycle CAL's blood and intestines, stopping only to remove reusable paperclips. They might actually be more useful, however, the paperclips, that is, than the written word.

(Grabs his chair and sits back down, studying the script in his hands.)

(Spotlight goes out on CAL and up on BILL who is still standing.)

BILL: *(Runs to Center Stage and lands on his knees with his arms outspread as if he had just finished a dance number; speaking quickly, sarcastic, intones another voice for the words in quotes)* Words . . . words . . . words. How did Shakespeare do it? My work? No. No. No. "No simultaneous submissions." Right. *(Gets up and walks toward Downstage Center before sitting down on the stage with his feet dangling over the stage.)* I thought I'd just put my life and my writing on hold while you editors dick around. I'll wait six months while you decide that BILL's story is too profane for your audience that just might consist of someone's grandmother who, in all likelihood, would never read your fucking publication even if she didn't need laser surgery on her cataracts. I'll send out my *tour de force* again and wait another six months.

(Stands up again and walks slowly back to Downstage Right as he speaks.)

Let me calculate for a moment—math was never my strong suit in school—If I follow their rules and wait, I'll hit two editors a year on a story, and let's just say that it takes a *(emphasis on "published")* published writer a couple of dozen tries to get noticed; my story has a chance—to see the light of an audience's eyes in about. *(Throws himself down in his chair, pauses, stands back up, climbs on the chair standing up with arms spread out wide, speaking loudly and sarcastically)* 12 years!

(Spotlight goes out on BILL and up on SEAN.)

SEAN: *(Stands and walks around her chair, then to Center Stage)* I've been at this for years, but so far . . . It's not a vanity press. This one might be worth it. A prize of $2,000 and an all-expenses paid trip to the Writers' Spa in Belize. I won't win, of course, but if I did, if I did, I'd have to be ready. So it's a question of choosing the right story, the one that will hit a note with the editors. My 2,527-word sleeker version, but it's not my best story. The story I want to send . . . *(pauses)* No. This time I will send a story that has a prayer.

(Walks determinedly back to her chair, sits back down, and begins to type at an imaginary computer as the spotlight goes off.)

(Spotlight is directed at HADIYA who is still seated.)

HADIYA: It would be sacrilege to pray, so I will hope. From what I know of the customs in Belize, I would be most comfortable there. Yes, I can imagine . . . *(Leans forward as if to stand, hesitantly, but remains seated).*

(Spotlight off HADIYA and on MARISA)

MARISA: *(standing slowly, pacing as she talks deliberately)* Imagine, if I won? Could I really go? Just like that, pick up and fly to Belize as if there were no other concerns in the world? No children to pick up after school, no worries about time off from my job? But an all-expenses paid trip to a place where writers meet and have an opportunity *(pauses)* an opportunity, time, and space, a *"room of one's own."* If I won, would it validate my belief in my writing?

(Spotlight off MARISA who is still standing and on to FOX)

FOX: Writing the scene, he can envision it. *(He acts out the scene of the story he is telling.)* A Hollywood type sits next to ME on the plane to Belize, immoderately talking, stammering, gesturing as I siphon off his words and postures, creating a layered sequence of conversations, not delineated. It's just a matter of selectivity. . . . Meeting industry types and discussing a screenplay after the book contract. I can picture it. Now it's simply a matter of choosing the right vehicle. The winning entry.

(FOX begins shuffling through his papers as the light goes out.)

(Spotlight on CAL who is seated with his hand on his chin and his arm leaning on his knee.)

CAL: *(holding paper)* "Enter Cal. No . . . Exit Cal. If it's going to end, it might as well end with the Writers' Spa Contest. Even in the unbelievably unlikely event that I win, *(stands up and walks toward Center)* they'll probably lose their publisher's backing, cancel the stipend, reneg on the Central America trip. I think I'll title it, "The Last One." They won't even know it's a threat. *(Wads the paper in his hands, lifts, then drops it)* Some threat.

(Spotlight goes out on CAL and up on MARISA)

MARISA: *(Takes out a cigarette from her pocket. Places it in her mouth as if to light it, then removes it, studying it as if asking the cigarette the question.)* Threatening exposure as an imposter. How do I know I am any good? What makes a good writer? Or a writer good? If I could be reduced, analyzed, then synthesized, the sum of my parts?

(Spotlight goes out on MARISA and up on FOX)

FOX: *(Jumps up as if he had just discovered something important. Spins the chair around and lifts it up before setting it back down.)* Parting her red hair! The color of highly polished cherrywood—she secures it with a clip, no, no; it flows over her bare shoulders and down her back, springing from the ends, perpetually pirouetting. *(turns himself)* That's what I notice about her when she walks away from me. *(clasps the chair to stop himself from moving around)* The beginning . . . I'll start with the woman leaving, her back turned toward the narrator. *(turns his back to the audience)* Never, never turn your back to an audience. *(He turns back around)* But she can turn her back because she is walking away from us in the pages of a story. It's a place to start—the subtraction of chronology from the equation. First, next, later, all removed, so we are left with now, now, now!

(Spotlight goes out on FOX and up on SEAN.)

SEAN: *(Her head toward the ceiling, pondering, speaking slowly then inspired)* Now, what to select? What has an angel's chance of winning? A ghost story? My ghost, however, will be corporeal.

27

(Spotlight goes out on SEAN and up on CAL.)

CAL: Ghosts haunt my words. It's never good enough, is it? No, not for the contest. That's merely diversion. Mine's better than the published crap I read every day, but if I'm honest, and I don't want to be; to put it simply, it's not: *(uses another voice to quote from Joyce)* "I go to encounter for the millionth time the reality of experience and to forge in the smithy of my soul the uncreated conscience of my race." GODDDD! When taken together, my words are much smaller—and I'm not talking about quantity—than that one sentence left by that fucking Joyce. One damn sentence that annihilates. I could name hundreds more because I'm reasonably well read. And it stops me. It stops me.

(Spotlight goes out on CAL and up on HADIYA who is seated.)

HADIYA: Stopping sometimes I listen to the bird noise: a low whistle, an incessant chirping, then the owl calling before the dog, and still, I'm surprised at this silence where individual voices are heard and retained before the world takes over again. If I am allowed to sleep and wake to a new moment . . . I never write what I think, but if . . . if I acknowledge the bird song . . . I will keep those words.

(Spotlight goes out on HADIYA and up on BILL who is pacing.)

BILL: Words of inspiration? I've never known it intimately. She's a false promise, promiscuous, making me sound like some jilted fool in the morning, but I'm not. No Muse between my sheets. Give me a flesh and blood perspiring woman groaning with delight in my bed. I'll write without those ethereal Muses. *(walking toward the audience and toward Downstage Center)* I work at it. Surprised? We're supposed to be inspired. What's that quote about the . . . that line about something dropping from the ceiling? My ceiling is metaphysically AND physically solid. Nothing getting through, and yet, I have something on the page at the end of the day. Words I know could strike that collective conscious. Irreverent words and yet . . .

(Spotlight goes out on BILL and up on SEAN)

SEAN: Yet, nothing fits. *(throws a paper to the floor)* I don't know exactly when I realized that nothing was the right size, but I have known for some time before acknowledging it. 350 words on a page that appear to coalesce until closer inspection. That is the secret.

(Spotlight goes out on SEAN and up on HADIYA.)

HADIYA: Secret? The secret is trust. *(smiling)* Once mistrust enters the house, the words evade the host.

(Spotlight goes out on HADIYA and up on FOX.)

FOX: *(Sitting on the stage floor, suddenly he jumps up as if springing to life.)* Hostage to the moment. Notebooks, journals, once on a napkin in a diner outside Scranton. I knew a writer who told me he wrote the lines on his arm when he was filling up his car at a Thruway station, and there was nothing handy to get it down on. *(Writes on his arm, then studies the writing)* Can't read it. *(laughs)* Immediately! Or lost!

(Spotlight out on FOX and up on MARISA.)

MARISA: *(Phone rings. She gets up, distracted.)* "Lost in thought." The interruptions are just what I need to keep from finding out, to *(phone rings again)* to keep from *(rings)* to keep from discovering if the *(rings)*, to keep from *(rings again)* . . . discovering

(Spotlight goes out on MARISA and up on CAL.)

CAL: Discovered the smell? Stale, flat air closed in too long with the heavy bodies struggling in their seats, unable to escape, considering the distance to the exits, but unable to leap up and run. . . . That would be my words you detect . . . dead on the page.

(Spotlight goes out on CAL and up on SEAN.)

SEAN: My page: "She had studied suicide by drowning *(the sound of typewriter keys is magnified)* and was well versed in literary allusions from Ophelia to Mrs. Dalloway. With the method determined, it only remained to come to a decision about the time and the location." *(Typing sound stops.)*

They'll suspect it's autobiographical when I'm not the least bit suicidal although the vision of my death is a presence with which I coexist. *(Looks around behind her and to the left and right as if paranoid.)*

(Spotlight goes out on SEAN and back on CAL.)

29

CAL: It's about existence: "I have been thinking of Salman Rushdie of late, *(sound of typewriter keys)* and the fact that his name Rushdie could be taken as a literal translation for rushing death." I think if I had invented such a name for a character, no one would have believed it. I'm thinking of turning from fiction to journalism as I board the last shuttle to Jupiter." *(Typing sound stops)* If they comment at all, they will say it is too journalistic. Fatalistic.

(Light out on CAL, up on HADIYA.)

HADIYA: A fatality: "Unable to lean forward without accidentally or prematurely detonating the bomb, *(sound of typing)* Nuri bint Khalidah bin Ahmed Al-Khalil retched all over her Jalabiye. It was then that Nuri knew why she had chosen this victim: the Jew, who offered a cloth to clean her mouth, looked like her." *(Typing sounds cease)* It is the story I see.

(Spotlight off HADIYA and on BILL.)

BILL: *(using a falsetto)* "I saw him he is looking at me and Oh, my God, *(sound of typewriter)* what will Kristen say when I tell her No Sarah had better not tell the bitch but that's Sarah so I supposeI can't he's still fixated on my ass thinking I'm a virgin but then I suppose I really am if you don't countKeith and he doesn't COUNT because that one time OK who am I kidding? Those few times were more like an act of generosity or charity with him coming too soon and if she knew about Keith then well, it doesn't really matter, because, Oh, *(laughing)* he's going to fall off that ladder thingy if he doesn't stop staring at my boobs, and if I just move my lips like this . . ." *(typing sound stops; his own voice, sarcastic)* Soooooooooo, it sounds derivative? In any case, they'll start adding punctuation. The point of view incongruous.

(Spotlight off BILL and on SEAN.)

SEAN: "Reversing direction, I heard the crackle and boom of the bolt *(sound of a typewriter)* and the splitting of the tree before it toppled. *(sound of typewriter)* And even though my papa said it wasn't so, I swore I could smell the burning of the man before running into the yard. The vagabond under the tree had been split in two as if struck with the blow of an ax—only without blood because the lightning had burned it away. My mother felt somehow it had been her fault." *(Typing sound stops)* When I'm writing, I hear their voices as if my characters rebelled, left the page, and confronted me belligerently.

(Spotlight off SEAN and on BILL)

BILL: *(typing sound)* "Confronted with the affront, Western man examines the beam in his eye. Discovering John J. Geoghan serially molested . . . the Rose by any other name, in pagan and Roman myth, converted or perverted, the rose becomes one in the blood of the crucified Christ as Geoghan stepped forward and gently touched the altar boy on the back of his pale neck." *(typing stops)* I'll have to change the name, of course; the danger is slipping into journalism.

It's a nasty business, but someone has to begin the revolution.

Kathy Durland Dewart

Grey Fox

Late February.
On the path to the beaver pond
my neighbor found a grey fox,
gut shot,
dead.

No one comes here to kill.
Around here we call each other when we see
the first bluebird,
the first fawn,
wildflowers when they break out
in a small dot of sunlight in the woods.

You were out of your territory.
Maybe a farm boy with his 22,
on the other side of the hill
got you,
a piece of you
and you died
a long way from home.

You and your fur brothers,
the wolf, the muskrat, the mink,
all slaughtered for warmth.
Sailors wore your skin and fur
in the frozen nightmare
of dark and cold,
the Poles,

North, South,
unknown lands of ice
and died of the cold,
a long way from home.

What Is Already Here

I want to be with the red-tailed hawk
as he flies over the dry
grass, the swamp,
the hemlocks.
I walk over the ground
that is not yet
frozen
and imagine the life
beneath me.
Not beetles or bugs or worms
but the mouse people of children's books,
dressed and sitting at the table,
ready to eat dinner
in the hollowed out roots of the trees.

I am not a realist.

The truth is
they are rolled tight and hungry
in their nests of hay and feathers,
delicate, unsafe in the open field.

All winter I fed a mouse
who had taken up residence in a bluebird box.
Sunflower seeds, apples and dog treats.
In the spring he was gone.

At the edge of the woods
I try to be still, invisible.
But I am waiting for something to happen.
A big buck could stomp through the woods
and break the silence.
A flock of turkeys, foraging
over the moss for nuts,
would create a terrible racket.

The hawk cries. I look up.
For him
This is enough.

Each creature,
branch, rock, blade of grass,
knows how to be
with what is already here.
When the day turns to evening
even the sky
is quiet.

Rachel Dickinson

Scotland or How I Flunked Europe 101

When I was twenty, I got on a plane and went to Edinburgh, Scotland, to live for a year. It was 1978 and I had just graduated from Kirkland College and was headed to Scotland because I had won a fellowship from a foundation that wrote me a check for $6,000 and said have a good time. I had to do a project outside the United States and I chose one in Scotland because it seemed more exotic than England and yet they still spoke English. Kind of.

When I left my little village in upstate New York thirty years ago and landed in Edinburgh in the beginning of September I didn't know a soul. I'd never traveled before, and wasn't connected to a college or university so I knew there would be no one to help me make plans or to fall back on when I failed miserably at whatever it was I was going to do. I took a cab from the airport to the university and had the cabbie drop me off at the student union along with my suitcase and my backpack. Three hours later—after making one phone call to a number found on a card pinned to a bulletin board—I was standing in my bedroom in a flat in Morningside, a nice neighborhood of row houses just beyond the university. My flatmates were Phani, a man from Greece who had a brain tumor and was studying political science at the university; Amir, an engineering student from Iran; and Michiko, Amir's girlfriend from Japan. We had varying degrees of proficiency in English from my less-than-perfect use of the language to Michiko, who spoke no English at all. We were an odd lot. Amir and Michiko liked to dress up and go to discos, which were just springing up in the city, where they would dance and drink Carling Black Label beer. Phani—I suspect because his head hurt—drank quite a bit of ouzo and retsina every night and would stumble to bed mumbling and cursing in Greek. I took to frequenting the local pub and developed quite a fondness for pints of stout and glasses of single malt whisky, neat. I met a couple of Canadians and most nights we'd meet at the pub and drink pints of ale and stout and bitters and glasses of whisky and smoke lots and lots of Player's brand cigarettes while trying to figure out what was up with the Scottish people. And every Thursday evening we'd listen to the Dixieland jazz band that played at the pub. Eventually the band joined our table during their breaks and the banjo player, who wore a vest and was a dead ringer for Dylan Thomas, would look at me with rheumy eyes and say in a thick brogue, "Darlin', I'm goin' to get to New Orleans someday and I'm goin' to look you up." And I'd always say that'd be nice.

Edinburgh smelled like a mixture of distillery grain and diesel fuel and every now and then I can conjure up entire sections of the city if a diesel-fueled truck passes me when the corn is being chopped out in the country. I can close my eyes and see the pizza place that sold pizza with shrimp on it and the little truck on the corner that sold baked potatoes. And I see the castle and Arthur's Seat—the nub of an ancient volcano that rises in the city's center and served as my refuge when I climbed it about once a week to sit on its rocky top and get the bird's eye view of a city I felt only a tenuous connection to.

I developed a love of train travel that year and once bought a month-long BritRail ticket and lived on the train and went wherever it would take me.

I traveled to Thurso and Oban and Penzance and London and all the spots in between and would stand in a station and pick the longest haul for the nights when I would curl up on a hard seat and try to get some sleep. I'd get off at a station when I was hungry, find a market nearby, and buy bread and cheese and apples and a can of beer to take with me on the next train out. I didn't care where it was going.

In April in the span of two weeks life in the flat fell apart. Amir—this little Iranian man with the little mustache and love of Western music and clothes—was called back to his country because of the Iranian Revolution. When he left, he looked terrified because he knew that the lifestyle he had come to love was over—Khomeini would never permit it. Phani's brother came from Greece and put Phani in the hospital where he had brain surgery. It didn't look like he was going to make it. Michiko disappeared when Amir left and I never saw her again. And I was left standing there, looking at the empty bedrooms, wondering what I was going to do.

I remember going to the pub and ordering a pint and a whisky, lighting up a cigarette, and then sitting at the table in a daze. My Dylan Thomas banjo player came over and after a moment said, "Darlin', you don't look happy. Go home." I looked at him and knew he was right. I had to leave it all behind—the oppressive sadness and anxiety of the flat, the cold dreary Scottish days, my pints and my whisky, and the diesel-fuel-mixing-with-brewer's-grain smell of a city. And for years after I left I felt like I failed in some basic way—like I had flunked Europe 101. I mean, what did I do beyond survive and learn how to drink whisky? But now when I think back on those gloomy Scottish days, I realize that maybe that was enough.

Carol Durst-Wertheim

Zemel

The word *zemel* brings me back to a summer during the 1950s in the southern Catskill Mountains of New York. My family was visiting with my father's clan. We were all staying in the old, tipsy clapboard house on Uncle Willie's property in Monticello. Willie had been born in the house. Later, he built the solid stone and brick place where he and Aunt Tillie, my father's sister, raised their four sons and daughter.

The "boys" were all married adults by this summer. The three local fellows all came "home" for lunch each day and I watched them slide into the booth seats around the kitchen table, heard them torment my Aunt Tillie until she produced sufficient hot food, perhaps fresh-baked zemel or blueberry pie for dessert.

Zemel is a yeast-raised dough, rolled around cinnamon-sugar and raisins, much like rugelach, except it is not made with cream cheese dough. *Zemel* might be a Yiddish term derived from the German *Semmel*, a sweet bun similar to a hot-cross bun, or it might be an invented word, bastardized from Russian and Yiddish, spelled according to someone's imagination.

Aunt Tillie learned her baking back on the farm, where her parents and Willie's—as well as some 500 other East European farmers—took in boarders during the summer months, starting in the 1920s. My father always told us tales of his work, milking cows, washing up in time to be the waiter serving breakfast, cleaning the dining room and then heading off to town for groceries his mother needed for the next meals. His sisters Tillie and Sadie baked, washed dishes, made beds, and helped their mother set up for the rest of the day.

On a wood-burning stove, before rural electrification was universal, my grandmother prepared three meals a day for 30 to 50 guests, who came up to "the Catskills" for their health. Specifically, they came to avoid tuberculosis and to gain weight. As teenagers, my aunts, Sadie and

Tillie, helped guests do just that, baking a range of homey calorie-laden desserts. But they made items that allowed for flexible timing, so yeast dough could rise while they made up the beds or ingredients could be adjusted, in case my father was late coming back from the grocer's in White Lake. My father's brothers helped with the farm chores and took jobs in transportation—long-distance trucking and taxi services—just as soon as they got their driver's licenses. Aunt Sadie was married by 16 and left to start a family up in Sydney, New York. Tillie married Willie and began to raise her family in nearby Monticello. She developed skills as a baker, learning when the dough needed more flour, more moisture, more time to rise.

Summer weather and an icebox the size of a picnic cooler prevented her from specializing in delicate pastries. She used farm produce, eggs, and dairy items, so there was always plenty of fresh whipped cream to hide a burned spot. Yeast-raised dough with the rich moisture of sour cream was easier to handle on muggy summer days than a more temperamental cream cheese pastry. Since there was no room to store leftovers, everything had to be eaten as soon as it was prepared, or it had to have a purpose when it turned day-old.

I've always thought there must be a family recipe for *zemel*, but my grandma never learned to read or write in any language and what might have been in her daughter Tillie's kitchen was lost when she was moved into assisted living. My mother wrote something down long ago, probably that summer back in the 1950s. She laughed as she read the ingredients to me from her crumbling paper, "a glass of milk (meaning 6 ounces), 5 cents' worth of yeast, ½ glass of sour cream or more, sifted flour, one glass at a time."

My cousin Larry remembers my hanging around the kitchen that summer when I was only three and "helping" Aunt Tillie make the *zemel*. A while back, he began asking me to try to reproduce his mother's treat. As I develop this recipe, now in the 21st century, I send samples to my cousins Larry and Gary, hoping to do justice to their memories of their mother's special *zemel*, 50 years later. The verdict: They are delighted with the tastings and recall the honey glaze that was not in my mother's notes.

I rest my hand on the soft yeast dough on the counter. I have a visual memory of that country kitchen in the 1950s, helping Aunt Tillie sprinkle on more, still more, cinnamon-sugar, tossing handfuls of raisins around. Although I learned professionally to cut rugelach from a circle, like pizza wedges, I remember just how to pat and roll this dough into a rectangle and then cut it into strips and finally the triangle patterns Aunt Tillie had shown me on her kitchen counter years ago.

In my head, I still hear the banter of young men with their mother. I can smell yeast and cinnamon-sugar baking. While Aunt Tillie constantly moved food and dishes around the kitchen, talking rapidly with everyone, all the while keeping an eye on me with the *zemel* dough, I must have stayed in a sweet mood, popping lots of those raisins into my mouth.

Zemel

This is a breakfast pastry, midday snack, or teatime sweet.

Yield: 70–80 pieces
Dough:
1 packet dry yeast
1 t. sugar
6 oz. milk
½ lb. unsalted butter, 2 sticks
1 c. sugar
1 t. salt
1 t. vanilla extract
½ c. (4 oz.) sour cream
4 large eggs
6–7 c. flour

Filling:
1–1½ c. sugar, mixed with 4–6 t. cinnamon
2 c. dark raisins plumped in boiling water for 1–2 minutes, water drained off
1–2 c. chopped nuts (walnuts or pecans) Topping .
2 oz. unsalted butter, melted
1 oz. honey, stirred into melted butter
Cinnamon-sugar

For dough
  1. Combine yeast, warm water and 1 t. sugar until softened and dissolved.
  2. In a 2-quart saucepan, scald milk and butter together.
  3. Add cup of sugar, salt and vanilla and stir to cool slightly. When mixture is tepid, blend in the yeast mixture, sour cream and eggs, although this will remain lumpy.

41

4. Stir flour, 1 cup at a time, into liquids and beat after each addition. Dough will be sticky and elastic, growing "heavy" but remaining too moist to be kneaded.
5. Continue to add flour until the dough begins to pull away from sides of saucepan, somewhere around 5–6 c.
6. Push the dough into lightly floured bowl, cover with clean dish towel and set aside to rise for about two hours. It will almost double.

To make *zemel*
1. Preheat oven to 350 degrees.
2. In a small dish, prepare topping by blending melted butter with honey and set aside.
3. Divide dough into four equal parts. Set one part on a well-floured pastry-rolling surface, incorporating about ¼ c. additional flour so dough can be handled without sticking. Press by hand and with rolling pin into a rectangle approximately 8" × 20".
4. Cover entire surface with cinnamon-sugar—more than you think you should!
5. Liberally toss chopped nuts across dough. Cover surface with generous handful (about ½ c.) raisins.
6. Using a pizza cutter or tip of a spatula dipped in flour, cut dough lengthwise into two 4" × 20" strips, then cut triangles zigzagging across each strip with the wide end about 2" so you have about 16–20 pieces.
7. Starting at wide end of each triangle, press some raisins onto "bottom" edge of dough, which will become center of the *zemel*. Roll up from wide to narrow end, finishing with point of triangle tucked under bundle.
8. Repeat for remaining three sections of dough.
9. Set each bundle onto baking sheet. Using back of a spoon or pastry brush dipped in the honey-butter mixture, lightly touch the top of each *zemel*. Sprinkle tops with more cinnamon-sugar.
10. Bake for about 15 minutes or until light gold in color, browned on bottom, and soft and fragrant.

They are best served warm.

Stephanie Feuer

What Counts

"Girls = Boys in Math." "Girls Measure Up in Math." The headlines were clever and upbeat. Based on test scores of 7 million students, a study published in a recent issue of the journal *Science* concluded that girls perform as well as boys on standardized math tests, reversing the results seen in similar studies over the past 20 years.

Most of the articles invoked the 1992 talking Barbie doll, who, among her other nuggets, said, "Math class is tough." Few passed on the opportunity to recall the controversial remarks made in 2005 by then Harvard president Lawrence Summers, who said women did not have the "intrinsic aptitude" needed for top posts in science and math. None of the articles talked about my mother.

Or your mother. Because Summers wasn't completely wrong. There is something to those XX chromosomes and the fact that counting is the best-kept secret of our gender. Our moms knew.

The study abstract also says that this time the standardized tests did not include questions that measure mathematical thinking. They were a measure of computational ability, not aptitude. In other words, arithmetic. So math may still be hard, but when it comes to arithmetic, it can be said that girls have a natural advantage, a whole lifetime of counting. Our mothers just needed to let us in on the secret.

My mother was always counting backward, although I didn't know it when I was growing up. I didn't know she was reformulating the timing of the major events of her life. She passed herself off as a peer to her younger suburban lady friends; her size-4 figure and impeccable dress ensured that she could trim years off her age. To her, age was as fluid as putting on a new evening dress, and it was perception that counted.

Her mind could go at lightning speed, and she could perform her arithmetic wizardry without looking away from a conversation.

Her memories of Broadway plays, world events and dance crazes—she recast them all to fit the age she was claiming. It's amazing I didn't hear the beads of her mental abacus clacking against one another.

There was a time when she almost tripped up. She was always careful to calculate her age relative to her sister's, since I knew they were born five years apart. My aunt, a onetime budding comedienne, had known Woody Allen, then a neighborhood youngster named Allen Konigsberg, when he was writing one-liners in Brooklyn's Midwood High School. When *New York Stories* was released, a magazine cited details about Woody Allen's Brooklyn roots, including dates that didn't jibe with my mother's retelling of my aunt's brief stage career. My mother distracted me from the facts with the story of my grandfather refusing to let my then unmarried aunt go to California with a producer who'd seen her in summer stock. That's the way it was back then, my mother said. Instead of setting off for a dramatic career, my aunt counted the months until she was old enough to get married.

Girls are always counting. With the onset of menstruation, there's a primal and painful reminder to take life in 28-day cycles. The consequence of failure to count could have a profound impact on the future, as in unwanted pregnancy, or, at the very least, wardrobe-related issues. I lost count and found myself in line for grad school course registration on an impossibly hot day in new, and newly stained, white pants. Before classes had even begun, I'd mortified myself.

One of those classes was a required statistics class. I found something completely comforting in the constancy and predictably of the relationship of the numbers and patterns and rules that were presented—such a contrast to the arbitrary encounters of my single life.

It was surreptitious counting that kept me in spare change when I first graduated. My boyfriend at the time needed an extra for his poker game, and my careful counting of the cards helped me raise my way to winning pots.

I am not alone in finding comfort in charts and counting. Weight Watchers knows this. Their successful program has women, and it is mostly women who enroll, assign point values to their foods and record and tally them on a pocket-sized chart. It's three points for a bagel, five for a chicken breast, and that ice cream cone is seven points charged against an 18- to 37-point daily target. There are bonus points for exercise to add another layer to the obsessive counting, and even a slide rule to help calculate values for personal recipes.

In my quest to have a child, I became a master at counting in nine-month intervals. In September I knew that if I successfully became pregnant that month, I'd deliver in May; a January conception meant an October baby. And when I did get pregnant, as the baby kicked I calculated all the milestones—how old I'd be when the child entered grade school, college, perhaps had a child of its own. I became a master at counting forward.

I never detected my mother's creative counting until she had a minor heart attack. When I arrived at the hospital, too impatient to wait for the elevator, I raced up the stairs (three flights, 2.6 calories of post-baby fat burned). She sat propped up by a pillow, looking pale and frail. An IV tube was attached to her wrist, and she had an oxygen tube resting in her nose. She was sedated and scared.

But when I reached for the chart at the foot of her bed, color came back into her cheeks and lips. "Put that down," she said. "It's a good place, they're taking care of me."

But it was too late. I saw on the chart what she didn't want me to see, what she'd been furtively recalculating all those years. Weeks after we celebrated her 59th birthday, her chart revealed that she had just turned 65.

You have to know what counts. That much is in the genes.

Elizabeth Fletcher

Seagull

Salt dune grass whips in hurricane air,
the sting of each blade enough to make a whale blow

Out at the sandbar where the sea bellows, the
twisted wooden ribs of a small ship lie
swallowed anew by each green and foamy crash

As the waves draw back, a seagull lights,
hunches into the wind and squawks

Weather eye cocked, it searches out crabs
to dash against the rocks

Beach Fox

Sun painted sky
Orange, streaked gold
Pinkwash and lavender drift warm with
the burning red star into the navy rippled darkness
of a cold Atlantic sea
Along the curving shore, driftwood fires flash
Tidewater flows across still warm sand
At the ocean's foamy edge, a russet fox pounces
Fish dangling from his sharp grin,
Up he trots over bright white dunes into full moonrise

Doris Friedensohn

from *Eating As I Go:*
Scenes from America and Abroad

A few years ago when she was visiting New York, my granddaughter Emily, then nine, proposed lunch at a French bistro, La Bicyclette, which she remembered from an earlier visit. "We could eat Italian," she said, "but the restaurant is noisy and you wouldn't like it. Or we could have sushi, but my Grandma Jane took us to a Japanese restaurant last night." Like her parents and grandparents, Emily is a discriminating restaurant goer. Had I pressed her further, she might have suggested an Indian place where the dal reminds her of lunches at home in Kathmandu or a Peruvian hole-in-the-wall where everyone orders garlicky roast chicken. My grandson Sonam, then seven and a half, agreed with Emily. "The French restaurant is really nice," Sonam said, "and I can have *crème brûlée* for dessert."

At Emily's age, I hadn't yet been on a plane. There was no television at home to transport me into remote African villages where women haul water in earthenware jugs and grind millet by hand for the family's stew. The news arrived in newspapers and over the radio. Except for war-induced shortages and victory gardens, food was not considered newsworthy. When I gobbled up my hamburger and mashed potatoes but left the spinach, my parents reminded me of "the starving Armenians." While we were safe in New York, Hitler's army was marching through Europe, slaughtering millions of innocent people. Our GI's were over there, defending liberty. We children could help the war effort, my father would say, by joining "the clean plate club"—no foolish complaints and no waste.

In my Jewish, semi-kosher family, eating was not the path to global education. My brother and I learned world capitals and state capitals as well as the names of mountains, rivers and valleys by playing geography. When we kids were taken out for a Sunday or holiday lunch, the destination was often the neighborhood Tip Toe Inn. I loved the big airy space, the double layer of thick white tablecloths, and the formally attired waiters who presented the menu with a flourish. The place was famous for its not too lean corned beef and its peppery pastrami sandwiches served hot on platter-sized plates covered with white doilies. Choosing between them was anguish.

The "foreign" restaurants I remember from my childhood on the Upper West Side of Manhattan were mostly Chinese. My parents approached them with caution, screening out the forbidden pork and shellfish. Irish pubs dotted the area, but they were havens for male drinkers in flight from women and children, or so we were told. When my mother treated me to lunch during one of our regular shopping expeditions, it was usually to Chock Full O'Nuts for a thrifty cream cheese and nut sandwich followed by a whole-wheat donut and chocolate milk.

I was eleven the first time I ate in a French restaurant, Fleur de Lis, in the West 60s. For years our French teacher had been training us for this peak experience—with every lilting *"bon jour, mes élèves, comment allez vous?"* At Hunter College Elementary School, French and art history were as critical to our training as English and math.

When the great day finally came, I still wasn't sure which *fourchette* to use with *la salade*, but I did know how to ask for bread and butter in properly accented French; and I knew the difference between *boeuf, poulet* and *poisson*. As for *crème brûlée*, it would be another decade before I had my first unforgettable bite. . . .

~

Food is my point of departure. I use food, shamelessly some might say, to reflect on my moorings, my American life, changes in American culture, and my experiences as an American in the world. More than any other theme, I pay attention to eating as it brings people together and keeps them apart. The Jewish food taboos with which I grew up are intended to unite family and clan while excluding all others. I've always fancied myself, naively perhaps, as belonging to the party of inclusion. In food markets and restaurants, whether on the Upper West Side of Manhattan or in the Tunisian village of la Marsa, I struggle to connect with strangers. Around the table—at an artists club in Mozambique, with colleagues in the Republic of Georgia, and at home in Leonia, NJ—I monitor intimacies with new acquaintances, old friends and my closest relations. At the edge of these encounters, and sometimes right

49

in the center, are politics and economics, religion and gender. What we eat figures prominently in each experience. Ditto for where we gather and under what circumstances. All these concerns belong to the social surround of eating, my focus wherever I go.

Let me be very clear. As I travel, food is the occasion for my learning rather than what I am principally committed to learning about. At the end of the road is my reckoning with myself. Perhaps, as I cross the finish line, a well-fed existential accountant will help me tote up the fruits of a wider purview and a fortunate life. . . .

Eating in America, I relish our fortunate pluribus. Still I try to keep this soft multiculturalism in perspective. The hype and slick food ads about eating together mask deep rifts of class, race, gender, religion and national origin. In the parking lot of the supermarket, a man in a torn jacket asks for $2 to buy a coffee. Close to half the children in New York City's public schools are eligible for free lunches. In the rich state of New Jersey, more than 500,000 people depend upon the Community Foodbank of New Jersey and its affiliated agencies for food support. It doesn't require a visit to my local soup kitchen to remind me that eating is not an equal opportunity activity.

Nor is the kitchen (usually) a place of shared burdens or just rewards. Even when cooking is seen in the full context of family life, it remains an arena where routine labor crushes creativity. My own need is to hold fast to the joyful aspects of meal making without turning into a kitchen slave. As I grow older and my household becomes smaller, I am content to shop around for what others have cooked. Thank goodness for feminism—and an adequate income. I can make this choice without apologies or too much guilt.

～

"How do you eat?" the father of my Nepalese daughter-in-law asks me, when I tell him that I live alone. "Friends and relatives come to my house," I say, "and I eat at their houses." True, but only partially. . . . When I first learned that my husband Eli had cancer, I imagined myself eating alone, joyless and bereft. He died in 1991. The plant-filled dining room facing the garden is still my favorite room in our house. Over the years, I've come to relish my freedom to eat (and drink) to excess or hardly at all. Despite the loneliness, living alone has a lovely simplicity. Visitors, while deeply welcome, disturb the peace. Eating alone in Tokyo in a restaurant where no one speaks English, I experience a heightened interest in everything around me—including myself. Eating alone in the suburbs, I reckon with my losses. I also revel, unexpectedly, in the company of strangers.

Elias Friedensohn

from My Lovely Impassioned Students, 1972–73

Since the late sixties students have poured into art departments in such extraordinary numbers that an area once considered marginal has burgeoned into an empire. Some of these are my lovely students. They are, many of them, more impassioned, better students than those in the sixties. In demanding that the arts be an established part of their curriculum and their lives as well, students have understood something about the potential of art.

Our students have experienced since infancy the instantaneous, simultaneous communication generated by the mass media: that rape and bombardment, that blurring of the real and unreal, the like and unlike. They are no longer constipated by the conventions of puritanical literary and intellectual values that for so long have dominated other senses. However, their backs are up against the technological wall. They smell death in the passivity that technology enforces. Will they find a way to use it and dominate it? Will they evade it? Or will they become, like the machine, beautifully, seductively soulless? Their reaction is action. It is, curiously enough, something like ceramics—ancient and of the hand—or a dance—ancient and of the body—that does not lie to them.

Political and social theorists have yet to acknowledge the possibility that cultural forces create the seedbed of change. It is in this arena that discontent, despair, disgust, awareness and anger, joy and celebration are first made manifest. Inevitably, as a crisis grows, artists face the hue and cry of the self-appointed firing squad: "Social utility or die."

The firing squad (which can include artists) recognizes that the arts, in their best and truest form, are inevitably the enemy: they are as much the enemy of the ideals of liberal/radical change as they are the support of authoritarian systems. While political critique may be an important part of an artist's work—and a source of strength—it is, nevertheless, not central. The moment such concerns are imposed from without, art begins to die. Art does not change the world in any immediate sense. But it does create the climate that makes change possible. It does keep alive "impermissible" possibilities by embodying them in a form that is the condition of that experience. It makes that experience believable by evoking an alternative world. The possibilities that art envisions are not necessarily "good" but rather reminders of the full range of being. Recognition is not permission. It is, rather, an acknowledgement of wholeness and balance. It may be that art continuously attempts to address the psychic imbalances of individuals within a given culture.

What so many of our students want is the chance to be generative. They want to move as actors and creators. Poetry, painting, photography and the guitar are closer to them than the rest of our baggage at this moment. These are roads to the quiet center from which structures emerge honestly. It is from creative gestures that critical acumen will grow.

From there students will move to writing and reading. The language of the senses is an enormously significant form of intelligence and understanding. For many students it has become the creative thrust and the primary form of inquiry. It is, for many, the new spiritual center.

We live in a time of painful transition and flux, in a state of heightened anxiety. We live among people who feel threatened; their cherished values and interests, their life's work and commitment are under attack. Let us then admit our anxieties and acknowledge those of our students—particularly since anxiety is one of the necessary components of intelligence and sensitivity. Students speak of being spaced out, hung up, and freaked out. They need to get their heads together. These phrases refer to their anxiety (and ours) in a world that seems to be coming apart. To put it all together is to want wholeness, identity, meaning, self-knowledge.

It is perhaps healthier to play the guitar and make love than to be overcome with anxiety and hopelessness. It is healthier to reassemble the inner self and then to make again connections with structures outside the self. It is not an insignificant part of change to do this. In fact, it is fundamental if the changes we seek are not to be warped and blighted in the process of changing. History has taught us that the revolution eats its children. Thus, it behooves us to move with caution and to search not only for change but for new ways to change.

Nazi aesthetes collected art along with lampshades made of human skin. We remain mindful that there is no necessary equation between the love of art and the love of good. However, some of our students make that equation for themselves. They see clay in their hands as an affirmation of their human center; as a rejection of the tyranny of the machine, of the production line and consumerism, of the beast in each of us. The ceramists, carpenters and guitar players take their places in the commune; they struggle to balance the needs of a life to be spent, at least three quarters of it, in the rat race.

Our students are searching for continuity with the world of nature, materials and sensation that the ancient Japanese craftsman had when he invoked the spirit of the wood before carving it. In search of durable meanings, they are prepared to try everything from Yoga and Lubovitcher communities to Jesus, Zen and dope. They are prepared, if these goal are clear, to submit to disciplines of extreme rigor as they glimpse the relationship between focus and revelation.

Our students are not certain that revelation is possible, but they seek it nevertheless. They seek it in the past, in those places and times that have invoked it. In their innocence, they resist us and our invasions. They do not want to know too much about history or too much about art. Art is a place in which purity of the self can be preserved, they think. To make art is to be active.

It is their rebuttal to hopelessness.

Tess Gallagher

Instructions to the Double

So now it's your turn,
little mother of silences, little
father of half-belief. Take up
this face, these daily rounds
with a cabbage under each arm
convincing the multitudes
that a well-made-anything
could save them. Take up
most of all, these hands
trained to an ornate piano
in a house on the other side
of the country.

I'm staying here
without music, without
applause. I'm not going
to wait up for you. Take
your time. Take mine
too. Get into some trouble
I'll have to account for. Walk
into some bars alone
with a slit in your skirt. Let
the men follow you on the street
with their clumsy propositions, their
loud hatreds of this and that. Keep
walking. Keep your head
up. They are calling to you—slut, mother,
virgin, whore, daughter, adultress, lover,

mistress, bitch, wife, cunt, harlot,
betrothed, Jezebel, Messalina, Diana,
Bethsheba, Rebecca, Lucretia, Mary,
Magdelena, Ruth, you—Niobe,
woman of the tombs.

Don't stop for anything, not
a caress or a promise. Go
to the temple of the poets, not
the one like a run-down country club,
but the one on fire
with so much it wants
to be done with. Say all the last words
and the first: hello, goodbye, yes,
I, no, please, always, never.

If anyone from the country club
asks if you write poems, say
your name is Lizzie Borden.
Show him your axe, the one
they gave you with a silver
blade, your name engraved there
like a whisper of their own.

If anyone calls you a witch,
burn for him; if anyone calls you
less or more than you are
let him burn for you.

It's a dangerous mission. You
could die out there. You
could live forever.

I Stop Writing the Poem

to fold the clothes. No matter who lives
or who dies, I'm still a woman.
I'll always have plenty to do.
I bring the arms of his shirt
together. Nothing can stop
our tenderness. I'll get back
to the poem. I'll get back to being
a woman. But for now
there's a shirt, a giant shirt
in my hands, and somewhere a small girl
standing next to her mother
watching to see how it's done.

The Red Devil

the nurses on the cancer ward call it
because, like acid, if it spills
from the needle onto skin, the patient
has to have a skin graft. Red devil
for how it singes the inside of
the veins, causes the hair to fall
out and the nails of the hands and feet
to lift from their beds, to shrivel
or bunch like defective armor.

Now the test reveals the heart
pumps 13% less efficiently.
Never mind. Your heart
was a superheart anyway.
Now it's normal. Join
the club. Get tired. Learn to nap.
Watch the joggers loping uphill
as if under water, as if
they had something to teach you
about the past, how sweet
and useless it was, taking the stairs
two at a time. They still
call you *hummingbird.*
Sooner or later you'll be flying
on your back to prove
you've got at least
one trick left.

Judy Silverstein Gray

On My Bookshelf

My parents filled our home with a love of words and literature. Not only did we read *Little Women*, but we piled in the car and set off to visit the home of Louisa May Alcott in Concord, Massachusetts. As my mother and I read *All of a Kind Family*, she shared stories of her childhood, longtime friends, New York City trolleys, the Automat, and big bands. She also spoke of losing her own mother as a young child, the Depression, and its impact on her family. She encouraged us to be inquisitive and pursue what interested us most—and not just the attractive or serene stuff—but the stuff that might feel like nails on a chalkboard—politics, the role of women, and the words chosen by those with opposing points of view.

My parents encouraged us to linger over words and their meaning, to develop an imagination, and to take time to ponder. They taught us to celebrate words. At a young age, they made it fun to hear them read books such as *Finnegans Wake*. And they taught us to listen for sounds and emotions conveyed by descriptive words. It's been an enduring source of joy.

Childhood trips to the library were excursions filled with anticipation. It wasn't just the library; it was the squirrels we passed on the way there, the parks where we played on the way home. It was that sense of ritual.

My parents ensured we viewed our books as a passport—of sorts. Helping us select a stack of books encouraged our excitement. We literally begged to start reading the moment we got home. Skillfully steering conversations, they taught us to articulate thoughts about those books long after a story was finished. More importantly, they taught us a sense of wonder about the world. Often, they'd share books taken from their own shelves, and we'd start a family journey to far-flung places such as Mikonos, or the Galápagos' Archipelago. Those virtual outings influenced my sense of adventure, my love of other cultures, and future travels.

I recall our family gathering in the evenings and paging through books. Together, we'd explore the words, carefully looking at illustrations. We scoured the highest bookshelves, requesting the long-spine books so we could linger over imagery of oceans, castles, wildlife with twisted horns, and names that were challenging to pronounce.

Together, we cooked food to delve more deeply into the culture of a place we discovered in a book, at a time when ethnic cuisine was not so easily available. While reading *Japanese Fairy Tales* with its exquisite illustrations and richly woven tales, we donned colorful kimonos, sitting on pillows around a low table, using chopsticks to eat my mother's version of sukiyaki, while lute and kobo music played on our phonograph. Our parents trained our ears and our imaginations. This total immersion was one made complete with delicate paper flowers from the store, Takashimaya, in New York City and my father's expertly folded origami cranes and butterflies.

We learned about Olmsted and Vaux and their vision for creating Prospect Park in Brooklyn. Then we hopped in the car to visit the meadows and rustic pavilions, bridges, and special gardens. Conversations about what we read allowed us to know our parents and the world we lived in. Simply put, it was a family affair.

Outings to bookstores and libraries, even on vacations, were a special treat. I loved finding a special nook to read about the history and nuances of the place we were visiting. For a while, I identified cities and countries by their bookstores. That sense of connection to places and writers continues. As an adult, I still search for local authors so I can get beneath the surface of a town.

When I see familiar books on a shelf, such as *A Wrinkle in Time* or *One Morning in Maine*, I am transported back to my childhood. A book jacket design catapults me to a certain place, inspiring a flood of delicious memories. It's not just recalling the story; it's the feel of the pages between my fingers, and it is why I still favor a clothbound book. I like recognizing the cover with my bookmark poking out over the pages as if to say, "I'm waiting, come back soon." Savoring the connections it makes with memories of learning and being part of a family that encouraged curiosity and connections to the world still feels special. There's also something refreshing about slipping into a place between the covers of a book and shutting out the world for a while.

Books give me something else. In certain circumstances, I've had to shed furniture, but I've always held on to my books. In many cases, they have been the backdrop of my life—reliable old friends with a compelling history. In our current home, my husband and I have created a cozy library brimming with familiar books—and some newer ones too. My books stand shoulder-to-shoulder with those from my husband's life. It's a place where we can both sink into the ritual of thinking, remembering, celebrating and making sense of the world.

Recently, I discovered another unexpected reason to appreciate traditional books. During the past few months, I've been settling in with some of the books in my late father's vast and storied collection. The books have a comforting papery smell. His notes—sometimes in the columns, and sometimes on scraps of paper, make the read seem more like a visit. In most, he has inscribed his name and in what city he was when he started the book. This treasure trove of information inspires so many memories and recalls invigorating discussions. On my bookshelf are family narratives and stories that reach beyond the confines of a page.

My parents taught us that between the pages of a book are unexpected voyages with twists and turns echoing our lives. Literature also gave them a powerful way to interpret and pass along what they had learned. In that spirit, I have been re-reading *My First Summer in the Sierra*, by John Muir. The Sierra Club founder first stumbled upon the High Country of what is now Yosemite National Park in 1869. But my copy, a gift from my father when I was a park ranger just out of college, also contained an unexpected surprise. Nestled between the pages, I rediscovered a sheaf of my dad's writing about his first trip to Tuolumne Meadows. And then, I found another surprise; a letter I'd written my dad thanking him for joining me on my first trip through the High Sierra camps. Not only do Muir's words ring true, but between the pages of his book, my father had chosen to archive our own precious memories.

You just can't find that kind of surprise in a Kindle.

Susan Hartman

Nine-Month-Old Boy

Maybe that's why you laugh, pulling yourself up to stand:
You're like a deer
remembering field. You stamp one foot, the other,
your small body rigid, proud. Two years ago,
in Ithaca, a deer stood in fog, fog
hiding the woods he'd just left.
It was 6 a.m., and the gray light around my shoulders
was turning yellow, turning white. Next to me,
belly to the ground, a friend
touched my arm.
This was why he'd awakened me—
his restless visitor from the city, blue
stamped under my eyes. The deer
froze—catching our odor—his brown throat
arching toward us in the long grass. He imparted
something: Courage
flooded me as quickly
as the fog vanishing around us.
Now, I hold my hands out
to you in our Brooklyn apartment,
encouraging you to walk. Your eyes, darkest brown,
lock with mine—and you stamp, stamp.

Gloria

After Hurricane Gloria, after the sky
dark all day with branches—a peel
of green light. A couple of men come out
and stand in it, hands
in their pockets. Then some kids—
running alongside the fallen branches.
On Flatbush, everyone is walking,
and I see our neighbor, Annie.
She averts her grey eyes
as always, but just before
the storm began,
she rapped loudly on our window,
warning us. I head
into the coffee shop. Eunice, the owner,
pours me a cup, her apron, as she stands
by the black stove, so white. Nearby,
Annie's smoking. A man in his 70s,
I've seen here before, shuffles in:
dapper, cool. "Gloria,"
he drawls, sitting across from Annie. "I'd like to meet her.
Right, mama?" "Mama,"
Annie says, slowly. "I like that."
"I've got 52 grandchildren," he says. "Forty-one
dynamite years of marriage before my wife passed."
Her hand trailing smoke, Annie waves marriage away.
They talk about the old ones:
the Great Hurricane of '38,
which destroyed his mother's small house,
and Carol, which in 1954, swept Annie's young aunt
into the waters off Cape Hatteras.
Then Eunice, anxious to get home, pulls
down the blinds. "See you tomorrow," she says,
and watches us file out
into the late afternoon light.

In the Generation That Laughed at Me

Three days after their funerals, they
went down under the village, three feet below,
and they all knew where to find it.

—André Schwartz-Bart, *A Woman Named Solitude*

Sleeping
under the longest root
of the tree,
I waited
for a woman with my face.

The women passed by
on their way to the market.
Chattering under the branches,
they broke off monkey bread,
sucking it as they walked.

Those women knew me
before I lost face
and went underneath the ground.

When I left the village,
they dug holes
near the roots of the tree
and poured palm wine
down to me.

In the generation
that laughed at me,
the woman with my face passed
with her lover. She tripped over a stone,
and as they laughed
I rose through the roots,
slipped into her small body.

Tapping her lover's arm, I ran ahead.
He followed me laughing.
We re-entered the village.

Martha Hawley

Becoming What You've Always Been: Subsurface Integration

*Dedicated to the late Arves Johnson-Rucker, Kirkland '73,
from Canton, Mississippi. In gratitude for her quiet friendship
and raucous swooning over the music of Otis Redding.*

In the Netherlands, integration means different things to different
people. Most agree that society has been polarized by events at home
and abroad since 2001, and for many, integration is mainly about
restoring harmony between native Dutch citizens and the resident
Moroccan and Turkish minorities. For the Dutch right-wing, now
vociferously represented in Parliament, integration means imposing
tougher laws on the Islamic "tsunami," with restrictions on immigration
and control over local mosques.

Ethnic groups from all over the world are visible in Holland;
most are required to pass an exam on Dutch language and culture.
The test for Western immigrants is more diffuse, especially for the
(formerly) blonde blue-eyed types like myself. An editor at a Norwegian
newspaper originally commissioned this essay; he wanted a personal
comparison of assimilation and integration based on my childhood in
the USA and adult life in the Netherlands. My story, he said, carried
provocative ideas, relevant to Norway, but defied translation.

In the 1990s, I embodied multiple identities while living in Arab
East Jerusalem as a trainer with a European Union media program.
Most Palestinians thought I was Scandinavian. Nobody thought I was
Jewish. The exact opposite scenario was conjured up by the five-minute
walk into West Jerusalem, where I was presumed to be Russian-Israeli
and was addressed in Hebrew. A German NGO had hired me, which

suggested to others that I had a very German face. I had just acquired a Dutch passport (making me a dual national) underlining my Dutch traits for some. In terms of bloodlines, my father was a New England WASP/Huguenot, my mother Canadian of Scottish descent.

I grew up on Motown in New York suburbs: first New Jersey, then Connecticut. My parents' marriage had faced early challenges: the New England family viewed Canadians as a backward folk, while my grandmother in Toronto found Americans* to be ill-mannered ruffians. Part of her civilizing strategy was to teach the granddaughters a phrase in French if one wished to decline further servings of food at the dinner table.

My mother married a Yank, but she remained a fervent critic of the delayed U.S. entrance into World War II. I heard about it often in the years before starting kindergarten. I began school with a touch of my mother's accent (tomahto), but it was teased out of me by five-year olds who understood that the sound was linked to defeat of the British in ancient times, the official start of the big American blend. Other accents were part of the soundtrack—we watched *I Remember Mama* and *I Love Lucy*.

As kids near New York City, we experienced teasing and bullying on my block, but we also shared a feeling of belonging there together, with our diverse surnames and faces. Marching Soul bands were the best part of the St. Patrick's Day Parade in Manhattan. People mocked other ethnic groups, and some people were mean, but everyone was part of the picture, colored by Yiddish words, Sioux Warrior cries, English Christmas glitter, smells from an Italian bakery or Chinese restaurant, the eloquence of Cuban dance bands. We were preschoolers, not yet onto the back-story.

After studying and working in South America and Asia, I came to live in Amsterdam as an adult, where I met Dutch, Brazilians, Spanish, Portuguese, Turks, Moroccans, Chinese, Indians, a multitude of nationalities from Sub-Saharan Africa and the Middle East; as well as people from the former colonies: Indonesia, Suriname, the Netherlands Antilles and Aruba.

Non-white friends described relaxing once back in Amsterdam after experiencing racial stress in neighboring countries; refugees from war or persecution felt safe and cared for in Holland. But the Dutch, enriched by their own emigration to and colonization of the Caribbean and Asia, were used to others visiting and moving on.

With so many foreigners now arriving to stay, old social anxieties have crept to the surface and found a resting place in public life. They didn't have far to go. Modern Dutch society was, after all, built on vertical segregation or "pillarization," with separate schools, work places, newspapers and eventually broadcasting companies for Protestants, Catholics, Socialists, and so on. Assimilation used to mean finding your pillar. We made new ones.

As a non-corporate immigrant, I experienced an intense transition: with lawyers at the helm, I challenged deportation and eviction notices; I grappled with questioning by police and judges while obtaining a residence permit. But for every condescending official, there have been countless individuals who truly helped me "enter" the country.

My first neighbor in Amsterdam, Ida, had "emigrated" to the apartment below ours from her family base ten minutes across town. She missed them terribly. Moving out of the neighborhood was an aberration in her clan, but Ida had secured her own apartment at this address, and in a city with a housing shortage, that was a deciding factor. I noted at the time: "Due to a heart condition, she has, at age thirty-one, been declared permanently unfit for work and receives the corresponding disability payments. She watches television, makes mosaic replicas of famous paintings, and rides a motorbike to visit her mother in the old neighborhood, the sailors' quarter . . . she moonlights regularly with the 'Three Tigers Cleaning Service' . . . run by an aging septilingual ex-candidate for the priesthood." Television advertisements in those days called for kinder treatment of foreign workers, depicted as cleaners, like Ida. But unlike her, they were Turkish or Moroccan, paying taxes from their legal wages.

Ida wanted to make it on her own, and perhaps she identified with me and my Colombian partner because, like her, we were far from home. She accepted my beginner's Dutch without comment. When I spilled tea on her red-velvet couch, she smiled in exasperation and affectionately called me "*oliebol*," referring to an inert, doughy mass, the deep-fried traditional Dutch New Year's Eve symbol of celebration and renewal.

Many Dutch people respond automatically in English at the sound of an accent. Some like to practice; others want to help or show off; still others like the language because they are grateful for the Canadian liberation of Amsterdam at the end of World War II. In the beginning, I devised strategies for prolonging Dutch-language conversation: I lied, for example, saying that I was from Finland and didn't speak English. I worked to expand my vocabulary, eavesdropping on shoppers at street markets and repeating their exact words, no matter how large or small the order.

Learning Dutch in one town doesn't automatically open doors in all others. Villagers on the diminutive Dutch North Sea Islands sustained separate and mutually unintelligible dialects for centuries, and a revival is underway in our times. The 1990's again: when floods affected farmlands in the central Netherlands, less than two hours drive from any point on the country's perimeter, the farmers speaking on camera were given Dutch-language subtitles on national TV news. Native Dutch have staved off full integration with each other with some success.

"Standard Dutch" does exist, and this is the language of radio and TV, but in the hinterland there are voices calling (in a variety of accents) for rebellion against this linguistic and cultural imperialism from the major towns and cities in the western Netherlands.

Newcomers can choose an accent and talk their way into the Dutch version of the big blend, but my current experience with integration and assimilation is ambivalent: at the supermarket or newspaper stand, we foreign-born can become part of the picture to our heart's content, but in more intellectual settings, we may come under the scrutiny of a different view. Roots say it all, especially if you're from the umbrella culture: the USA.

A cultural center in Amsterdam, known for tackling tough social debates, organized a panel discussion on American identity—without Americans on the panel. A few U.S. natives were asked to attend and take front row seats. An endearing presentation was made by Chris Keulemans, the Dutch author of *The American I never was*, about a lifelong identification with American popular culture. As the discussion continued, American-descent shoulders in the crowd drooped under the realization that our own ideas about our identity, however muddled, were not welcome at this event. Live specimens would disturb the process of coping with the symbols. We had been assimilated, if only in other minds.

During my years as a radio producer I was happiest talking to people on the street, and grass-roots integration is good enough for me. I take credit for the fine points: I ride a bicycle with a working headlamp, I love drawbridges and I have become a serious speed-skating fan. Daily life moves faster than panel discussions and policy ratification: TV ads are now also produced by Turks and Moroccans; and a national cultural institute has decided that we non-Dutch speak "World Dutch," a new term for standard Dutch spoken by ethnic foreigners. Officially, I have no ethnicity—I'm a "Western Foreigner"—but I know better. Toma*h*to has crept back into my speech.

In recognition of the North, Central, and South American zones, the author has attempted on occasion to introduce the term Usamerican *for people from the United States. Response has been limited to date, and the term* American *is applied to that population group in this essay*

Alice Aldrich Hildebrand

A Dream of Our Own Imagination

*All depends on keeping the eye steadily fixed on the facts of nature,
and so receiving their images as they are. For God forbid that we
should give out a dream of our own imagination for a pattern of
the world.*

Truth emerges more readily from error than from confusion.

—Francis Bacon, quoted in *New York Review of Books*,
5/10/07 by Freeman Dyson

"Keeping the eye steadily fixed . . ."
A tall order, nowadays,
as the world keeps jittering out of sight;
molecules, atoms, electrons, quarks,
waves, bundles, clouds of probabilities—
back then, in 1600, things within things were at least solid
and generally stood still to be observed;
no anti-matter, no Schrödinger's cat.

Of course, latterly, God had such a firm grip
that all the facts belonged to "Him"—
the priesthood, really, who kept accounts
weighing calamity or boon against offering.
Think of them, feathered or hooded or masked
black robes, white robes, naked under the sky . . .
theirs the power of measurement, the power of time.
Knowing the precise dance of the stars,
the inexorable glide of the moon into shadow and back out
the even more stupefying loss and return of the sun,

they taught hope, discipline, ardor, trust. Superstition?
Think of us, the regular folk, who have always had
to till, hew, gather, fight, love, grieve
in the midst of the celestial game; willingly, eagerly
we create and re-create the pattern of the world.

In Sneek and Menaldum,
my ancestors lived their days
beneath the shadow of the church clock.
No Catholics there, they wouldn't have gone
to Mass, kept Saints' Days;
no popish cathedrals in Friesland,
no one to ring an *Angelus*
not a head would be bowed to a priest.
But the hours belonged to God,
and church-going a religion all of its own
though over Europe, through so-called Christendom,
the footloose philosophers raved.
After them the naturalists, a crazy troop
laden with sketch pads, collecting bags, hand lenses, measuring sticks;
I'm their future, I ride high rejoicing
on the tide of their errors
a poet novice in the world's vast temple
seeking, as they did, to cast doubt on the familiar
to pierce confusion with the simplest of tools, words.

Ask a child, ask an artist;
only the dream of our imagination can find the pattern of the world.

Advent, 2008

I.

"Even so, Lord, quickly come . . ."[1]
Under the apple trees frost heavy as sin
whitens bleached grass, holds dawn.
Gray cloud backlit with peach color
spreads south and one black cat hunched
on the splintered railing,
vigilant for mouse, for fox,
ears twitching at crow call
waits for the sun.

II.

"Hymn and chant and high thanksgiving,
And unwearied praises be . . ."[2]
On a dark day of no particular glory,
over the wet streets of Ellsworth—
where storekeepers have lit windows,
swagged lamp posts with balsam
as if this were any other year—
above the river in flood after storm
comes the matter-of-fact honk of geese
ready to settle. A young man
pulling his fiancée along the path
from the stores to the library
stops and gently
turns her face to the sky.

III.

"Born on earth to save us . . ."[3]
In the cold barn, I reach into a cardboard box
burrow in peat moss to find
carrots, firm, sweet as they were last September.
Rubbing them in my hands, brushing off the dirt
gently breaking the fragile roots with which they still
seek life, I carry them inside.

[1]"Come, Ye Thankful People, Come": Alford
[2]"Of the Father's Love Begotten": Aurelius Clemens Prudentius
[3]"On This Day Earth Shall Ring": Piae Cantiones

After My College Reunion

for Nancy Avery Dafoe and Gwynn O'Gara

Dear Gwynn and Nancy, how was your ride home?
My way back took me through the middle
of New York state, across the middle of New England,
thinking about middles,
about not-quites, about
"not yet one thing nor the other;"
in short, about us, with our careers as
"so far, not famous writers"
who nonetheless keep writing
in between a lot of other things.

A college reunion after thirty-four years;
we only went by invitation, to read our work,
an event for which I managed
to re-awaken the hunting writer-self;
not the tamed animal who says so well those things that others want,
circling the tented ring, perhaps with resignation, but so
adept on the little circus bike.
Not that one, but the one uncaught, still,
who lurks where the words come unawares,
who pounces, makes a meal, feeds hungry scavengers,
can roam all fields at will—that one.
Now will I put the sinewy beast of me back to sleep?
What meaning can this trip to Kirkland have in my life?

Here in my quiet small place after that weekend away,
dizzy from the up-spin of gray highways, the webs of gray cars
I could spend hours attempting to make sense
of this weekend with strangers,
in a once familiar place now so long unknown;
how well you both know, I'm sure, the energy it takes—
first to grab hold and still the whirling ball, the plunging carnival ride
long enough to get a small part of it to write about
then to do the writing in any tatterdemalion fashion at all;
last, to coax it, to smooth it, to make it cohere.
Am I the vampire of experience or just another mammal
who has to kill to eat?
Hope your ride back home was good.

Ellen Horan

from *31 Bond Street*

April 22, 1857

In New York, March turns to April by way of its trees. Apple trees dot Orchard Street, left standing after the Dutch farms fell. St. Marks Church is known for its gnarled old pears. Washington Square is rimmed with cherry trees, the tiny petals cover the pavement like pink snow. In spring, new leaves soften the edges of the limestone edifices, and bricks and paving stones seem a part of the earth itself, with moss, sprouts and worms wedged between the cobblestones. Magnolias bloom in church gardens, and all around the fringes of the city are stretches of wooded riverbank, with coverings of ground pine, wood violets, oak fern, and partridge vine.

Samuel sat on a log in a clearing by the river, scraping the scales off a mackerel. An Indian sat on the opposite log, carving a piece of wood. Samuel watched Katuma, in his dusty blue work pants, whittling away at the tiny piece of willow oak, smoothed into a hollow curl, not much larger than his thumb. Katuma was as tall and broad as Samuel, with skin the color of darkened butter.

There were footsteps from behind, padding along the earth of a beaten path. It was Katuma's daughter, Quietta, in a gingham skirt with a sleek braid swinging along her back. She carried a pile of vegetables in her apron. When she reached the clearing, she emptied the vegetables into a basket and sat next to her father on the log. "Here girl," Katuma said, handing his daughter a carved whistle. "It sounds enough like a bird. Blow it if you see any men riding past the market toward these woods." Quietta worked at a fruiterer's stall at the Greenwich Market on Christopher Street, the westernmost market in Greenwich Village, just blocks from where they sat by the river. She came down to the riverbank in the afternoons, where her father liked to sit and fish. Between the fishing hut and the city street, was two acres of bramble and high brush, and the path down to water passed an old storage shack and a broken down building, now derelict, which shielded this part of the woods from Greenwich Street. Greenwich Street was busy by day with horse drawn lorries and lined with brick fortresses, warehouses that were filled with barrels and crates and burlap sacks—packing houses and manufactories that had swallowed up patches of the old Village. By night, the streets were empty with the workers gone. Down the slope by the river, where Samuel slept each night in the hut, the sky was large and filled with stars.

Quietta took off her shoes and padded in and out of the hut, and got some kindling for the fire. Tall trees enclosed the clearing and the warm sunlight from the late afternoon filtered down in columns. The aspen leaves shook softly. There was a shuffling sound as soft as the wind in the leaves. A boy appeared at the clearing, coming down the path even more quietly than Quietta.

"Here comes the fancy boy," said Quietta, teasing John about the britches and little jacket he now wore, purchased for him by the lawyer's wife.

"We have a bounty," Katuma told John. "Samuel and I caught these fish without a net." The bucket was filled with glistening fish coiled in the bucket, up to the brim. The river glinted through more trees, not far from where they sat, and a raft was bobbing in the water, tied to tree branch at the bottom of the sharp bank.

"Will you take me fishing?" asked John.

"I will take you, eagle, when the trial is over, and you take off those fancy clothes." Katuma called John 'eagle' because he always carried a flying eagle penny in his trouser pocket. Quietta called him bird. "When the summer comes, we'll go to Rockaway. To the Lenape fishing place." Quietta placed the basket of vegetables before John. "First the vegetables, bird. Cut them up." Samuel tossed John a knife he had been using on the fish, a dagger that landed at the boy's feet upright, point first, in the earth. John picked it up, and started stabbing at a beet.

"Father, bird is trying to make a whistle out of the beet.

"You can't cut a beet with a double sided blade," said Katuma, handing John another knife. Katuma lived with his wife and daughter in a proper house on Perry Street. He earned money working as a longshoreman on the oyster barges. Come spring and summer, Katuma, along with his Indian friends, used these tiny huts for weekend pleasure, fishing for striped bass, weakfish, porgies and bluefish from dugout canoes they kept along the banks of the Hudson. It was on this stretch, one summer day, while Dr. Burdell was still alive, that Samuel had first met Katuma.

From him, Samuel gained his knowledge of the waterfowl and shellfish that were so abundant that you could catch them with a stick and a pail. Even though Katuma was a day laborer, living in the city, it was not so long ago that his people reigned over this kingdom. Katuma told Samuel and John stories about his grandfather, the son of a chief who ruled the richest oyster beds and spawning grounds in the harbor, his lands stretching from this spot, spreading fifty miles east into the marshes of New Jersey.

It is always best to hide in plain sight, Katuma had told Samuel, after the murder. He had been right. The northern shantytowns and Negro neighborhoods had been the first places the sheriff's men had gone looking for him, tearing in and out of the shacks and hideaways, and startling sleeping families, Fleeing Manhattan posed a greater danger. A lone Negro wandering through the countryside would be suspected to be a fugitive from the South. A fugitive was a boon for the bounty hunters, more so if a slaver discovered there was a link to a murder.

After the murder, Samuel had first gone to seek asylum at his church and, being told that it was not safe, he came down to the river to Katuma's hut. Quietta brought him some food and drink and during that stormy weekend, he slept, wrapped in furs and blankets. It was February, and when he stepped out of the hut, snowflakes swirled lightly about, falling like a light ash. The ribbon of the broad river was barely visible, shielded by a blanket of white that rolled over from the opposite shore. The bank of New Jersey disappeared under a dense curtain of snow. Looking into the flurry he could see nothing but the snow itself, the infinity of its white flakes thick as the depth of a million stars.

"Did you come from the lawyer's office?" Samuel asked John.

"Yes, they are all busy. The trial is starting soon," said John.

Katuma shook his head solemnly. "Maybe after the trial they will stop hunting for Samuel."

"You are useless with a knife, bird," said Quietta, taking the knife from his hands. The vegetables were chopped into ragged pieces. "Here, go fetch me some water. Try to keep the minnows out." She handed John a pot that hung from a tripod and John headed over to the bank of the river.

Samuel finished scaling the last piece of fish and Katuma placed them in a pan he had rubbed with seasoning. As he was crouching over the pan to start the fire, the Indian paused, his back braced, his head cocked to one side. All of them heard the faint distant scratch of iron scraping against iron.

"Scatter," whispered Katuma. His limbs pushed him upright. He leapt to his feet and Quietta was instantly gone, dashing silently through the trees. Samuel worried for a second about the boy, at the waterside, but he knew that John was hidden by the high riverbank, so Samuel started to run north. In the winter months, they had all talked about routes of escape, and John could run south on the sandy stretch along the river's edge. The boy was faster than all of them.

A shot rang out like a crack. Samuel heard a bullet whiz into the trees. There were voices now, back by the hut. Samuel kept on running, the adrenaline carrying his limbs at a faster and faster pace. Down South, a manhunt was accompanied by dogs, but now there were no bloodhounds, and without the use of scent, these city men were blind, crashing through bushes, without a clear direction.

Samuel kept going, pumping his legs and arms faster and faster. He jumped over a fence, cutting his hand, and he landed in a churchyard. He crept along the shelter of tombstones and then dashed down a lane, under pear trees that were in bloom. Breathless, slowing down to a walk and at other times trotting, he zigzagged through the stable alleys that ran behind the houses, past the little Village kitchen gardens, keeping off the main streets. The sun was still high, and the spring evening had not yet changed to twilight. Better that it was still light—a Negro, running behind the houses in the shadows would create alarm. He bent over, catching his breath, then started again at a saunter, walking casually like a stable hand making his way home. Finally, he reached 6th Avenue, and cautiously stepped into the traffic and crossed the street.

His heart was still beating fast. There was a milk cart standing without a driver, idle at the curb, and he moved to the other side of it. He picked up the horse's brush from its bucket, and started brushing the horse, ducking behind the horse's flank, crouched low, to use the vantage to look around. His heart slowed and he regained a steady breath. Across the broad avenue, he spotted a posse of men on horseback, at the corner of Perry Street, seeming to debate which way to turn. The posse turned and headed north on the avenue and Samuel, hidden behind the milk cart, watched their backsides recede, bouncing in their saddles.

A man hurrying by, wearing spectacles and a black suit, stopped to ask Samuel where to find the apothecary. Samuel pointed him to the apothecary sign, and the man rushed off, tossing Samuel a coin. Samuel saw that not a foot away from him was a poster on a pole: Reward: Wanted in connection to the murder of Dr. Burdell—a Negro, 30 years, tall and strong. The poster had a black face in profile, an etching that could be a caricature of any Negro, with a sloping forehead, tight curly hair, and overly large lips. It so little resembled Samuel, that just about any man of color could be assigned the role before he. There wasn't anyone among the legions of policemen or general population that could point him out as the man who drove Dr. Burdell on the night of the murder. Hide in plain sight, thought Samuel. With the posse fanning out toward the north, he would return to where he had been hiding, close to the riverfront. Katuma and his generations of Lenape, here on this crowding island, understood how to flee. Like fledgling birds, they scattered from a familiar spot, then circled around before coming back again, calmly resettling on their terrain.

Elisabeth Horwitt

Taking Care of Marilyn Monroe

Allison spent her first day on Fire Island clearing her father out of the cottage.

She'd put it off all summer, drawing masochistic comfort from his toothbrush next to hers, his cache of Heath Bars in the cupboard, his beat up corduroy jacket hanging in the downstairs closet. But she was closing up the house at the end of the week, she couldn't leave his personal things to molder all winter. Dad would have said, stop wallowing.

She saved the bedroom for last. Except for the bare mattress, it was exactly as it had been that Sunday in June when they'd headed for the ferry together, expecting to return the following weekend. It was very much Dad's room. Even before the divorce, Mom hadn't come out much, preferring the Hamptons and her trendy New York friends.

Dad's framed photos of Island wildlife would stay, of course, and his classical records, and his books. They were part of the house. Walking resolutely up to the bureau, she opened the top drawer and began transferring his T-shirts into a battered old suitcase. She was doing fine until she came to his favorite Lacrosse T-shirt, dark blue faded almost to gray from exposure to sun and salt water.

A dip in the ocean after breakfast, then Scrabble on the big red blanket, always in the same spot, by the dunes. He'd taught her to play when she was seven. She didn't win a game until well into her teens. When she lost her temper once and demanded why he couldn't give her a break once in awhile, he'd replied, quite seriously: "That would be bad for your character."

"You're a self righteous jerk sometimes, you know that?" Allison told him now. She buried her face in the shirt and finally let the tears come.

Next day was bright and crisp, perfect fall weather. After doing her Yoga on the deck, Allison walked down to the Village Market, pulling a little plastic wagon of the type summer people used because only locals could drive on the island.

On the way home she encountered a stag eating garbage out of an upended can. During her childhood, deer had been a rare, breath-catching sight. Now they were ubiquitous pests. "Scram! Beat it, you stupid beast!" The antlered head came up, dark eyes unreadable. Suddenly uneasy, Allison sidled past quickly.

Mounting the steps to the cottage, she stopped short, hearing high, thin cries from under the house. There was no basement, just a sandy crawl space, her secret hideout as a kid. Peering into the dimness, she made out a moving bundle of fur. Kittens, three of them. Their cries sounded desperate but weak, like they'd been calling for hours. Poor little things, where was their mother? Cats had a tough time on the island off-season.

She took the groceries inside, found a cardboard box and took it outside. She had to crawl on her hands and knees to get to the kittens. When she got close, they blew up into spitting puffballs. By the time she'd captured all three, her hands were covered with itchy, red pinpricks.

She put the box down on the living room floor and got a saucer of milk. They wouldn't touch it, just went on crying. Maybe they didn't like one percent. What the hell was she going to do with them? Maybe they weren't strays.

Officer Davison, known to summer people as Lou the Cop, frowned at the mewing box on his desk. "What'm I supposed to do with this?"

"Help me find the mother," she told him. "Anyone still out here with an unspayed female?" The village registered everything that moved: dogs, cats, bicycles, even the little wagons.

With a martyred grunt, Lou opened a big black binder and ran a thick finger down the page. "Marilyn Monroe. Leiberman, 26 Bayberry. Nasty beast, we had complaints."

Allison thanked him and picked up the box. As she turned to leave, he said, "You hear about the break ins?"

"No!" She felt a chill. Crime was almost non-existent on the island—during the summer.

He nodded. "Couple of summer houses, closed up for the winter. Nothing stolen, but they got trashed pretty bad. I'd keep my door locked if I was you."

He sounded almost pleased, Allison thought, as she carried the box outside. "The locals resent us city folks, but they need our money," Dad would say. "They think we look down on them, and of course, they're right."

Number 26, Bayberry was a glass and metal cube perched on the dunes. Allison eyed it with dislike. Somebody with money and no taste had built this monstrosity, not caring how out of place it looked among the Island's weathered, shingled cottages.

The doorbell was answered by a sixtyish woman in a lilac silk lounging outfit. Weary, mauve-lidded eyes stared out of a face as smooth as wax. Botox, thought Allison. "Ms. Lieberman? I understand you own a female cat. Has she by any chance had kittens recently?"

"Been there, done that," the woman replied in a Lauren Bacall rasp. "She's too old now." The box let out a plaintive mew, and the stiff face came alive. "You have kitties in there? Can I see them?"

The living room was stark white and two stories high. A huge orange cat lounged on the creamy leather couch, staring balefully at Allison. She put down the box on the coffee table, and Ms. Lieberman instantly stuck her face inside. "Hello babies! Come to Mama—Ow, dammit!" She yanked her hand back. "They must be starving!" She accused Allison.

"I gave them milk! They wouldn't touch it."

"Did you heat it up? Oh for God's sake." The silk pants swished through a swinging door, then Ms. Leiberman's head came back out. "Want some coffee?" Allison politely declined.

The kittens finished the warm milk in seconds. "Don't give them any more for at least an hour, they'll just puke it up," the woman warned.

"Would you like one, Ms. Lieberman?" Allison asked hopefully.

"Call me Emma. I'd love one, but Marilyn would get jealous and beat the bejeesus out of it, wouldn't you baby?" Hoisting the huge cat to her chest, the woman cradled her, gazing down with a yearning tenderness that made Allison uncomfortable.

"I named her Marilyn Monroe because she's a blonde bombshell. She's also a first-class B-I-T-C-H, aren't you baby? Mmmm, yes you are!" She scrunched her face into Marilyn's stomach.

"Would you like a kitten?" Allison asked Sally, the cashier at Village Market, next morning. "They're awfully cute."

"No thanks. Hey Joe," Sally yelled over her shoulder, "you want a pussycat?" "I'll take pussy anytime," grinned the man behind the meat counter.

Ignoring him, Allison asked Sally if she could put up a sign.

"Go ahead," the woman shrugged. "Island's crawling with strays, nobody wants 'em."

"Except Jeeter," Joe put in.

"Who's that?" Allison asked.

"Government man, lives in that patch of empty land near Sunken Forest. He takes in strays, must be a couple dozen in that shack of his." said Joe, shaking his head.

"Nut case, if you ask me," said Sally.

"Aaaah, Jeeter's all right," said Joe.

Allison put the box of kittens back on the wagon and, with a resigned sigh, started walking east. Once she'd left the village, the island became wild and lonely, all the summer houses closed up for the winter. The sidewalk turned into a raised boardwalk that ended abruptly after the last cottage. Beyond was a wilderness of sandy hillocks, beach grass, clumps of bayberry and gnarled, stunted trees. She jumped down and began trudging, the box clutched awkwardly to her chest. Blasted kittens. Most people would just dump them, but of course, she couldn't do that.

Soon she encountered tire tracks and followed them into a small pine wood. A sign nailed to a tree said, "Beware of Attack Cat."

The woods ended in a windy clearing by the bay. A black pick up stood beside a neatly shingled wooden structure: a cabin, not a shack, thought Allison. Smoke swirled out of a stovepipe poking out of the tarpapered roof. Several cats lounged on the small deck, soaking up the mild September sun.

She felt like a trespasser in the Appalachian hills where you stood off a good ways and called "hello the house!" if you didn't want to get peppered with buckshot. What sort of a man would choose to live in this lonely spot, with nothing but cats for company? She pictured a grizzled, wild-eyed old hermit.

The door opened and a gangly figure emerged. He looked about thirty, clean-shaven and deeply tanned. He wore his gray-streaked hair long, like many Island men, but no one would mistake him for a local, Allison thought. Too intelligent-looking, too elegant. The Rainforest jacket and the Timberline boots suggested Upper West Side. Probably he'd fled Manhattan for a simpler, less stressful life. He silently watched her approach with the box.

"Hi! I'm Allison. Are you Jeeter?"

"That's right." He looked and sounded wary.

"I heard you take in stray cats." She offered him the box. "Nobody else wanted these little guys."

He frowned at her. "Including you, I take it."

"They aren't mine! They just showed up in my cellar."

The stern face relaxed slightly. "I just get sick of people bringing me kittens because they're too lazy or tender hearted to have their cats spayed." He reached for the box. "Don't worry, I'll look after them."

Allison felt let down, frustrated. Jeeter intrigued her. She didn't want to just turn around and leave. "Could I please use your bathroom?" After a second, he nodded.

This is a real home, Allison thought, gazing with pleasure at the dim, low-ceilinged room. She guessed that Jeeter had made the pine trestle table and the sturdy-looking rocking chair by the iron woodstove. Books and dishware sat neatly on shelves, not a dirty dish or a crumb in sight. The cat smell wasn't bad at all, considering there were at least a dozen furry shapes lounging and sidling about the room, watching her with unwinking yellow eyes.

There was a shotgun by the door. What does he need that for? Allison wondered uneasily. Deer hunting was prohibited on the Island. Turning abruptly, she went over to a beautiful, hand-drawn topological map on the wall. She'd always imagined Fire Island as a long, thin pencil, but the map showed all too clearly where it had been whittled by currents, gouged by storms.

Jeeter cleared his throat. "The bathroom's through there."

When she came out, he was heating milk on the little Coleman stove. She asked how many cats he had.

"Couple dozen maybe, it's hard to keep track. They're pretty independent, except when they're sick." He poured the warm milk into a shallow bowl and placed it on the floor near the kittens.

"You must really love them," said Allison. He didn't answer.

The smallest kitten mewed piteously, crowded out by its siblings. Jeeter picked it up, dipped a finger in the milk and inserted it in the tiny mouth. The kitten began nursing avidly. Watching, Allison felt a warm tickling inside. "When I first came here last fall, there was a whole colony," he said. "Then the winter came, and they began to die." His voice was stony.

Allison nodded. "The summer people abandon them."

"So you know about that."

"I spent my childhood summers here. I couldn't believe anybody would be so cruel." She'd cried when Dad first told her about it, in the too-quiet voice he used when he was really angry.

"The parents probably tell the kids that dear little Whiskers will be so much happier wild and free, not stuck in an apartment." Jeeter shrugged. "Maybe they believe it. People will believe anything to avoid guilt."

"Tell me about it," said Allison. "I volunteer at a women's shelter, and I've met people who've convinced themselves that Aunt Lucy or Cousin Katie will be just fine, living on the streets."

He said abruptly, "Would you like some herbal tea?"

When they were seated with their mugs, she asked how he got through the winters. He said he read a lot. "I head down to CJ's when there's a good game on the tube. And I work, of course."

"What kind of work?"

"I monitor erosion for the Army Corps of Engineers. The cabin comes with the deal."

"Kind of isolated out here, isn't it?"

"I've got the cats to keep me company, and the deer. I birdwatch, too. There's a Piping Plover nesting ground just east of here."

"I know," Allison said eagerly. "I used to go there with my Dad. He's an amateur ornithologist. Was, I mean." Her voice faltered. "He died last spring."

"I'm sorry." He looked somber. She guessed that he, too, had experienced a terrible loss.

They sat by the wood stove, drinking their tea in peaceful silence. Allison took tiny sips, making it last.

"It's funny," said Jeeter. "People abandon cats at the drop of a hat, but not dogs. I think it's because cats don't fawn on them like dogs do."

"Several of your cats are staring at you adoringly right this minute."

"That's because I'm the food man." They both laughed.

Walking home, the empty wagon rattling behind, Allison felt stirred up, elated. She heard Jeeter's harsh voice saying, "Then in January, they began to die." How many men cared deeply about anything besides their own wants and hang-ups? She thought of ways she might bump into him, as if by accident. He was clearly a private person, and she didn't want to scare him.

The following morning, Emma showed up on her doorstep with a plate of plump little cookies. "Found you! Sally at Village Market told me where you lived. Have a rugelach."

Allison accepted one with thanks and took a tiny bite. "Mmmm!" Pure butter. Probably about five hundred calories per cookie. Emma was looking expectant. "Would you like some coffee?" Allison asked.

The woman beamed. "Love some! Decaf if you have it." Inside, she gave a theatrical shiver. "It's freezing in here! Ralph had our place winterized."

"Ralph's your husband?"

"Technically, yeah. We split last July. You probably heard of him. Ralph Lieberman? *The Last of the Big Time Spenders?*"

"He's rich?"

Emma's laugh disintegrated into a smoker's hack. "That's a movie, honey. He directs them."

She shook her head. "Ralph, the last of the big time spenders! That's a hoot. So how are the kitties doing?"

"I found somebody to take them."

"Oh, good! Who?"

"A man who really loves cats." She didn't want Emma bothering Jeeter. Half an hour later, when her guest showed no sign of leaving, she said it was time for her daily jog.

"Good for you!" said Emma. "I got arthritis, so I'm stuck with this." She gave her plump thigh a resentful whack.

Later that day, Allison checked out the TV listings and smiled when she saw that the Jets were playing the Pats.

CJ's was the locals' hang out, open all year round. Allison went over to the bar, ordered a draft, then scanned the room. There he was, sitting at one of the little tables with a stocky little man in an Islanders sweatshirt. She took her beer over. "Fancy seeing you here," she smiled.

Jeeter blinked up at her. "Hi, um. . ."

"Allison. Can I join you?"

"Yeah, sure. This is George."

The other man barely glanced at her, before turning back to Jeeter. "Antibiotics don't work worth a damn. Doctor says it ain't Lyme Disease, what the hell does he know? Friggin' deer spread it like the plague. Don't see why we can't just shoot 'em."

"Now George, you know that's illegal." Allison liked Jeeter's calm, measured response. His companion seemed like a typical local red neck. "There are far more humane methods of population control," Jeeter went on.

"I'll show you population control. Bang! No more deer problem." George looked slyly at Jeeter. "Like we did with the cats."

Allison's eyes widened in shock. "You don't shoot cats?"

"Not anymore we don't. Jeet here put a stop to it, hid in the woods and shot at us. Man, we ran like rabbits." George gave a guffaw, but kept glancing towards Jeeter.

Allison looked at Jeeter uneasily. "He's kidding, right?"

"I fired over their heads, of course." His smile was bland.

"Some of the guys are still pissed," George said. "We all get stir crazy in the winter. Hunting cats gave us a chance to blow off steam."

"Yeah, big kick, killing helpless animals." Jeeter leaned forward, hands pressed flat on the table. "You got any trophies, George? Tabby heads on your wall?"

Allison felt Jeeter's pain and anger like a spreading ache deep inside. Looking from his fierce, finely-drawn face to George's thick red neck and small, baleful eyes she thought, it's like they're two different species. Drawing her chair closer to Jeeter's, she glared at the local man. "You don't give a damn, do you, about the agony you made those cats suffer!"

The local man drained his glass, threw down a five-dollar bill and stood up. "I'm outa here. Bleeding heart liberals," he muttered, stomping off.

Allison and Jeeter's eyes met. She raised an eyebrow. He smiled faintly. "I guess people get a little primitive out here," she said.

"Not at all. They're just regular folks."

When the game ended, they walked outside together. Allison was delighted when Jeeter fell into step beside her, then couldn't think of anything to say. It had to be something meaningful: he wasn't the type for small talk. At the intersection with Midway, she slowed, getting up the courage to invite him up for a nightcap. "Good night," said Jeeter, turning west and striding away. Damn! Thought Allison.

She had trouble falling asleep. She kept seeing Jeeter coolly aiming over the heads of beefy, red-faced locals who yelled and scattered. He wasn't a violent person, she assured herself: just passionate. Compassionate. She thought of the kitten suckling on his finger and got that warm tickling again. He had large hands. Her body stirred under the covers. What would it be like, to have all that fierce intensity focused on her?

Next morning, she woke up shivering. Through the window she saw gray clouds scudding across the sky. Emma came by around eleven with an oversized shopping bag. She looked happy, a little sheepish. "Ralph called me up last night, he's booted out Minnie the Moocher. Time to play the big reconciliation scene."

"Minnie the Moocher?" Allison was amused.

"The red-haired slut he's been screwing. I knew she wouldn't last," Emma said smugly. "Here." She pushed the bag into Allison's hands. "I brought out all these gourmet goodies from Zabar's, shame to waste them."

That night, Allison dined on smoked salmon, mesclun greens and goat cheese. She felt guilty, because Emma seemed to think they were friends.

The TV weatherman's melodramatic voice caught her attention. "Batten down the hatches, folks, there's a nasty Nor'easter coming our way. It should hit the Tri-state area by tomorrow night." Allison cursed, wondering what to do. She'd never been on the Island during a bad storm.

"Do you think they'll evacuate us?" she asked Sally next morning.

"Nah, this is nothing." The cashier looked scornful. Somewhat reassured, Allison bought flashlight batteries, bottled water, and canned soup.

By mid-afternoon, the rain was falling in sheets, hard gusts of wind rattling the windows. Allison lay on the couch under a blanket, trying to read a book about Native American spiritualism, with half an eye on the Weather Channel. Coastal flooding was a strong possibility.

Around seven-thirty, the electricity died, cutting the weatherman off in mid-sentence. In the sudden darkness and silence, Allison heard the ocean's full-throated roar. She told herself that the house had lasted through much worse storms. But it was so cold. Outside was pitch black, all the nearby houses closed up for the winter.

She had a sudden picture of Jeeter sitting in his rocking chair by the wood stove, safe and warm, in his little cabin by the bay.

Allison stood up stiffly, and climbed the stairs. In the bedroom she located her backpack, put in clean underwear, her toothbrush and deodorant. Downstairs, she put on her sou'wester, hoisted the pack, opened the door and stepped outside. Wind-driven rain slashed her face. She bent her head and began trudging. On Midway she stepped into ankle-deep water. She cursed, then laughed, feeling giddy.

"This is nuts!" she yelled at the sky.

When she reached the end of the boardwalk she jumped and fell forward, coating her hands and jeans with wet sand. She blundered through the pitch dark woods, hands outstretched, till with huge relief, she caught sight of a wavery yellow glow ahead. She pounded on the cabin door, shoved it open and stumbled inside. "Jeeter?" No answer. The stuffy room seethed with cats. It stunk of wet cat and cat urine. She shucked her soaked sneakers and jacket and collapsed in the rocking chair.

A few minutes later, the door banged open and Jeeter strode in on a gust of wind. Laying a wet bundle of fur on the sofa, he disappeared into the other room. He emerged barefoot, holding a towel.

Allison smiled gratefully, but he walked past her to the couch and began gently patting the cat dry.

"I hope you don't mind me showing up like this," she said nervously. "I thought my house was going to be swept out to sea!" When he didn't answer, her anxiety increased.

The cat sneezed. Jeeter stood up, stared at Allison as if seeing her for the first time. He gave a faint smile. "You're wet. I'll get you a towel and make us tea."

They sat with their mugs by the wood stove, but the silence didn't feel peaceful to Allison. Her companion's dark, abstracted face gave away nothing. Every time he shifted, her body responded. Finally she said, "Getting kind of late." She glanced towards the bedroom door.

"I'll make up the couch for you," he said. Allison's body slumped, tension draining away.

She lay awake a long time, listening to the wind, pushing off a succession of cats trying to camp out on her stomach. Maybe he's gay, she thought, but she knew he wasn't.

She woke up to bright sunshine. Exiting the bathroom, she heard the truck pull up. Jeeter walked in and set a bag of groceries on the table.

"What's it like out there?" Allison asked.

"Messy. I'm going out again later and look for hurt strays. I'll give you a lift home."

The truck bounced along the wreckage-strewn beach, over broken boards, bits of Styrofoam, dead crabs, dead gulls. Turning inland, Jeeter began driving slowly up and down the walks. At the top of Bayberry, Allison asked Jeeter to stop so she could check Emma's house for damage.

Approaching the front door, she froze at the sight of a draggled heap of fur on the stoop. "Oh god! Oh no!"

Jeeter came hurrying up. "What's wrong?" Then he gave a sharp grunt.

"It's Marilyn Monroe, Emma's cat." Fur plastered to her limp body, Marilyn was a scrawny remnant of the magnificent beast that had glared at Allison and her box of kittens.

"This woman left a few days ago?" Jeeter's voice was terribly quiet.

"Yes, to rejoin her husband. They'd been separated."

"I guess Marilyn Monroe wasn't part of the deal," he said drily.

Allison imagined the cat meowing and scratching desperately at the door, buffeted by wind and rain. What had she died of? A heart attack? Exposure? Emma had said she was old. Tears stung Allison's eyes. "How could she do this? She seemed to adore that cat!"

"She probably did, till it was too much trouble." Jeeter's voice was heavy with irony. "A lot of people are like that—haven't you noticed?"

Allison nodded slowly. She knew plenty of people like that. But Emma?

Jeeter had gone back to his truck. He returned with a long piece of wire which he inserted into the lock and began probing. "What are you doing?" Allison asked. No answer.

With a sharp click, the door swung open. Jeeter gathered the cat's body to his chest and strode inside. This is breaking and entering,

Allison thought uneasily, but she was excited, too. And curious. What did Jeeter intend?

"Quite a showplace," he said, staring around Emma's white living room. "That couch looks like a good spot."

Allison saw what he was up to. Returning next spring, Emma would find the corpse of her cat, a silent accusation. She pictured the Botoxed face crumpling in horror and grief, and felt a second pang of doubt. "Jeeter, listen—"

"Her bedroom would be even better. More psychological impact." He headed for the stairs, then turned and looked at her, waiting.

The master bedroom's huge window showed a turbulent, dark green sea beneath an empty blue sky. Jeeter arranged Marilyn on her side, paws neatly together, in the center of the huge white bed. They both stood silently staring down. Go in peace, Marilyn Monroe.

Jeeter gave a deep sigh. He went over to a group of framed photos on the wall, and removed a picture of Marilyn playing tiger in a forest of beach grass. "No more cats for Emma," he said, and smashed it down on the bureau. Allison yelped. He took down a second photo, smashed it, then walked out.

She stared blankly at the jagged crack in the milk glass bureau top. The sound of rhythmic thumping broke her trance. She raced downstairs and found Jeeter pounding a cat-shaped terracotta planter against the flagstone fireplace. It broke, shards skittering in all directions. He stood up, panting, face slick with sweat, body giving off heat and an acrid, animal smell. Their eyes met. Allison felt a jolt of fear mixed with excitement. What is he going to do?

Almost casually, Jeeter swiped his arm across the mantel. China figures cascaded to the floor with musical clinks. He turned back to her and held out his fist, slowly uncurling his fingers to reveal a tiny china kitten. Allison opened her hand to receive it, flinching when his warm fingers touched hers. For a second, she thought he was giving it to her to keep, to cherish, like a live kitten. Then she saw his eyes.

The tiny creature lay in her palm, paws in the air, so cute and helpless. Cradled in Emma's arms, Marilyn had looked neither cute nor helpless. Emma had gazed down at her with a yearning tenderness that even Botox couldn't mask.

"I don't know," Allison muttered. "Jeeter, maybe we're wrong about Emma. She—"

There was a backwash of air. She looked up in time to see the kitchen door swing shut. A moment later, she heard a cascade of crashes, like twenty plates hitting the floor at once.

She remembered, then, what Lou the Cop had said about the summer houses getting trashed. She began to walk towards the front door, picking her way among the broken bits of pottery. Outside, she started walking faster, fighting the urge to look back.

Bursting through the front door of the cottage, she stopped in dismay. The storm had broken in, shattering a window. Papers were scattered across the floor, and Dad's precious Audubon picture books were soaked. I should have stayed, Allison thought, awash in guilt. It wasn't that bad a storm. She went and got a mop and began swabbing up the puddle. Reaching under the coffee table, she spotted a white rectangle lying just beyond the water's reach. She retrieved it, then stared perplexedly at a cream-colored envelope with her name scrawled across it. Inside was a single sheet of paper.

"Dear Allison, Marilyn has pulled her usual disappearing act. She hates to leave, poor baby, can't say I blame her. So I have a favor to ask: could you leave out food and water for her? She'll only eat Cat Pride Chicken Delite, Village Market has it. You might try grabbing her while she's eating. I'll be back Friday. Thanks a million! Warmly, Emma.

"P.S. Better wear gardening gloves when you grab her."

She must have pushed the envelope under the door, Allison thought numbly. Then the wind blew it under the table.

Oh God, what have I done?

Of course Emma would never have abandoned Marilyn. She loved cats as much as Jeeter did. The difference was, her love had focused on one animal, while his was a matter of principle. Like his anger, Allison thought, with a shudder.

I ought to report him.

He's dangerous, a sort of animal rights terrorist. He judges and punishes people, unfairly and cruelly. Poor Emma, coming back to a trashed house, her beloved cat's body laid out on the bed with deliberate malice, like the horse head in *The Godfather*.

Allison went to the list of emergency numbers on the wall and found the police station. She lifted the receiver, then put it down again.

Jeeter was probably back at his cabin by now. She saw him laying out bowls of cat food, heating up milk for the kittens. She imagined him in handcuffs, being hustled along by Lou the cop. She hated that thought.

If he goes to jail, his cats will die, she thought.

Allison shook her head. Dad had taught her to recognize self-serving rationalizations, especially her own. She knew very well why she wasn't going to turn Jeeter in. And it had nothing to do with his cats.

Deborah Pender Hutchison

Left to My Own Devices

while you are away
I expand to possess this house
   claim your anarchic space
with taut sheets   shut drawers   neat stacks
   a different way to do the dishes
   I'll renounce it on your return
but for now it's mine   all mine

it's not that I don't love you   I do
it's just that   so much
   gets given away over the years
increments   so small
   their departures go unnoticed

I move through quiet rooms
   straightening   tucking   arranging
It's as if I am breathing in
   plates   plants   books   small rugs
      even the telephone
to exhale them remade in my own image

Each day I enlarge my capacity
   soon   the piano   its bench full of music
   the major appliances
   the fold-out couch
     the floors   the doors
   the shingled roof
the walls with their wires   arcing electricity

First Ice

Yesterday,
creased ranks of waves
and shredded snow-spitting clouds
ran before the wind.
The black lake a great lung
puffing pale mist into frigid air.
It's giving up its warmth, I thought, and snow
began to whiten flattened bracken, fill
the curled cups of fallen leaves, delineate
hemlocks' hunched roots.

This morning, I knew
something was different. I knew
while still burrowed under Hudson Bay,
wrapped in my own warmth. I knew
as I prowled the length of my dim lair
before opening the drapes.

It was winter morning dark.
Dimly, out there, beyond,
making silhouettes of shore-side
bench and somersaulted dock legs,
white rest had replaced
yesterday's black commotion.

I stood by the window
as slow light confirmed my
knowing, hands holding
the heat of coffee, face and feet
feeling the seeping cold, and thought
about how every thing contains
within itself its opposite,
the other only distant
by a few degrees.

Lynn Kanter

from *Her Own Vietnam*

Della Brown pushed open her front door and stepped inside. The house felt clenched like a held breath, until she reminded herself that Abby was gone. Funny how the silence of a house where no one else lived felt different from the hush of a house where everyone was out. But there were all kinds of silences.

When Abby was growing up, Della sometimes imagined the serenity of an empty nest. Now she had one, and it took some getting used to. No loud music, no dirty dishes in the sink. No one to talk to. Her knees creaked as she stooped to pick up the mail scattered across the dark linoleum floor.

In the kitchen, she watched blue flame flare under the tea kettle before she clicked on the light. With its butter-colored walls and worn wooden table, the room felt cozy despite the afternoon chill. It was late February. Spring was weeks away from her corner of New York State. Della was wearing a blue short-sleeved scrub suit, and when she ran her hands down her arms, the skin felt pebbled.

She sorted through the mail. A bill. Another bill. Junk mail for recycling. The *Clinical Journal of Oncology Nursing*. A hot pink card inviting Abby to rant and rave at some club. She hesitated before sailing that one into the recycling pile. Abby wouldn't care about a club here; she was sharing a run-down apartment in Manhattan with six other girls, all trying to make it as actresses. Della slapped down another bill. Then she held up a slim white envelope.

It was a letter, an honest-to-God letter. She'd thought they were extinct. The handwriting was familiar, though she couldn't place it. The return address in Boston meant nothing to her. She raised the envelope to her nose, but all she found was the vanilla scent of her own hand lotion.

Della sat in a bentwood chair. Its gold corduroy cushion, which Abby had made in seventh grade, was worn to velvety stubble like the miraculous new hair that emerges after chemo. The fabric prickled against the back of her legs as she slit the envelope and pulled out the single typed sheet.

Hello, Della.

Been a while, hasn't it? I tried to find you so many times, back in the day. Now here we are—well past fifty!—and thank goodness for the Internet.

Here's why I'm writing. My son Will is getting married this summer. Now, this isn't one of those June-moon-swoon kind of weddings. Will is twenty-seven, and his bride is thirty-three. They're paying for the whole thing, and they don't want a big to-do. My husband and I are only allowed to invite ten people. My son said, just invite the ten people who've meant the most to you.

There was something about the way he put it that really made me think. And what can I say, Della, you made the top ten.

Now I know that's kind of strange, since you and I haven't spoken since before Will was born. And I know that seeing each other again after all these years is more than a notion. So I'm not going to invite you to the wedding of a boy you've never met, but I am writing to ask if you will see me sometime. We can meet in your town, my town, or somewhere in between. You choose.

Don't worry, I'm not going to stalk you like that little corporal from Minnesota. Remember him? I bet you do. I bet you remember all of it, like I do. They say time heals all wounds. I don't know about you, but I'm still waiting.

Della, I hope this letter doesn't upset you. If it does, just remind yourself . . . it don't mean nothin'.

Charlene (Johnson) Randall

Della's heart racketed around in her chest. She twisted off the flame beneath the shrieking kettle. She refolded the letter and held it flat between her palms like a prayer.

Charlene Johnson. Her closest friend, her comrade, the one person she had ever trusted with her life. No way was she going to call Charlene Johnson.

It didn't matter that she missed Charlene, missed her with a yearning that had grown fierce and lean from feeding on silence. What mattered was that Della had spent the past thirty years trying to erase the one thing she and Charlene had in common.

Della was twenty-two years old when she returned from Vietnam, twenty-two and broken already. It was only a year of her life that took place ages ago. But the experience still fluttered against her heart. It was like a moth that had gotten tucked away into a box of sweaters. Years later you could reopen the box only to find that the moth had chewed the sweaters into shreds, then vanished in a smear of dust.

"But why did you have to go to Vietnam?" Abby had once asked her, peering down from the heights of adolescence from which she could see that everything Della had ever done was wrong. "Why did you even join the Army?"

How many options did Abby imagine a working woman had in those days, when the women's movement was just a rumor to be ridiculed on the evening news? After high school, Della had known exactly what her options were. She could spend her life in restaurants, as her mother had. She could learn to cut hair. She could be a secretary, or a teacher, or maybe a nurse. But that would take years of schooling, and Della could barely afford a semester.

The bargain had seemed simple enough at the time. The Army paid for two years of nursing school. In return, they owned her for three years. And where did Abby think the military had sent its newly trained nurses in 1969—to Berkeley, perhaps, to care for the injured protesters?

No, ma'am. It was first stop, Long Binh; next stop, Cu Chi. Last stop, forget about humanity and hold on to your sanity. If you can.

Della knew her daughter never would have made such a bargain. She probably would have been an antiwar activist, flinging tear gas canisters back at the police. Abby had a life that allowed her to make choices, even mistakes, secure that there would be a margin of safety to protect her.

But no one could provide Della with that kind of life. So she began her adulthood sweating in a war zone, surrounded by carnage and courage and pure brutal stupidity. Even today, if she thought about it too long—if she thought about it at all—Vietnam could rise from the dead and blot out the sun with its powdery wings.

As she sat at the kitchen table, the letter began to rattle in her hands. It was only fear. Fear was an old companion, and she understood its many moods. This was not the spiky panic that followed a loud sound late at night. It was the deep cold dread that sometimes gripped Della when she began to realize exactly what she was in for. She had felt it after Abby was born, the first time she faced three a.m. with a screaming infant she could not comfort. She had felt it the day her husband moved out. And she felt it now as Charlene's letter threw its thin light on all Della had been refusing to see.

She recognized herself, a trim woman with hazel eyes and chestnut hair dusted with gray, finally ambushed by her own history. Her own anger. Her own nostalgia. Her own bloody shadow, and her nation's. Her own Vietnam.

It was an August morning in 1969, but it could have been any time. Every day was the same festival of hell in the intensive care unit of the Twelfth Evacuation Hospital in Cu Chi, South Vietnam. Soldiers screamed in pain. Delirious men cried out for their mothers in high, staccato bursts of anguish. Doctors and nurses snapped out orders in brisk medical shorthand. And beneath it all, oxygen tanks and respirators cranked up their faithful racket.

After three months in Vietnam, Della was intimate with the frantic rhythm of a "mass-cal," a mass casualty situation. She pushed IV morphine into a post-op patient whose legs had been sheared off by flying shrapnel. His bare chest was pale and hairless against the green hospital sheets; his face and throat were deeply tanned. He had the slender neck of an adolescent.

As she cleaned his oozing stumps with antiseptic soap and packed the wounds with absorbent fluff dressings, Della wondered if he had reached his adult height. Well, he had stopped growing now. He would spend his life in a wheelchair, eye-to-eye only with children. Della bundled the dressings with layers of padded gauze bandage that gave the stumps a pillowy look. She rolled elastic stockinettes over the bulky dressings and wrapped them with ace bandages, then hung a six-pound weight from each stump to keep the skin from retracting.

With the back of her wrist, Della swiped at the sweat crawling down her forehead. She looked across the ward, a long central aisle with a row of forty-five cots on either side. The men in these beds had been charred by flame, lacerated by gunfire, dismembered by explosions, mangled by shrapnel, ravaged in every conceivable way by the technologies of war. Some of the patients were recovering from surgery; others were marshaling the strength to survive an operation. Several were beyond the help of a surgeon's blade. Every few minutes she could hear the pounding heartbeat of the hospital: the *whup-whup-whup* of a helicopter delivering fresh casualties from the battlefield.

Scanning the nearby cots, Della spotted a red stain blossoming on a white dressing. She grabbed the angled scissors from the sleeve pocket of her fatigues and cut the bandages from the soldier's thigh. A few small blood vessels had begun to leak underneath the dressings. Della smiled at the patient, a boy with honey-colored skin, curly black hair and a shadow on his upper lip that was more bravado than mustache.

"Don't worry, this is no problem," she told him, and watched the pucker of anxiety disappear from between his heavy eyebrows. She touched each rupture with what looked like a matchstick, its head treated with silver nitrate. The nitrate cauterized the bleeders, turning the blood vessel gray at the point of contact. She had long ago learned to ignore the sickly sweet odor of the singed tissue. Swiftly she redressed his wounds and moved on to the next bed.

For twelve hours a day, six days a week, this ICU and the doctors, nurses and corpsmen who inhabited it were Della's universe. She knew them all so well—their moves, their skills, their talents, their breaking points, their roles in the bracing choreography of combat medicine. With steady hands, Della received the wounded; with soothing voice she eased them into the primeval world of flesh and pain that would now be their home.

One of her patients today had been injured when a white phosphorous flare he was carrying went off accidentally. White phosphorus was perfect for marking targets because it ignited when exposed to air, releasing dense white smoke. Willy Pete, the guys called it, like a friend who demanded respect. But Della only saw Willy Pete after it had gone wrong. Once it touched flesh, the substance turned savage, penetrating layer after layer of tissue until it burned through to the bone. It was almost impossible to pick every fleck of Willy Pete out of a charred, raw wound.

When Della removed her patient's bandages to change the dressing, his burns began to smoke, the residual white phosphorus reignited by the fresh air. She rushed to neutralize it by pouring on a solution of diluted copper sulfate, as the writhing soldier tried to stifle his screams.

Morning stretched into afternoon. Della ran IVs, changed catheters, turned patients in their beds, monitored vital signs. Still the helicopters thundered in with new casualties. Hour after hour she replaced dressings saturated with pus and blood. She clamped chest tubes and emptied glass suction bottles that had filled with blood and fluids from men's lungs. There was no time to stop, to rest, to eat. The urgency of the work and Della's sizzling adrenaline kept her in motion. It was not until the sun faded and she began to click on the goose-necked lamps that she realized the choppers had stopped bombarding them with fresh bodies. For a moment, the war and the healers had reached a draw.

She hoisted herself up on a gurney and slumped there, elbows on knees, staring past her boots at the filthy concrete floor, awash in blood and gauze and the plastic wrappers from bandages. The other medical staff had taken similar postures of exhaustion, resembling casualties themselves in their bloodstained uniforms. It was like those moments in high school at the end of swim practice, Della thought, when she

95

realized she had given everything to the water and had no strength to meet the gravity of the dry world.

In a few minutes, most of the nurses would begin to clean up and restock supplies to prepare for the next batch of casualties. They would mix IV bottles and do another round of wound care and monitoring. But Della would not join them. Tonight she had a different job. She had been assigned to body bag duty.

Together with a somber handful of other nurses and corpsmen, Della would unfold thick, green plastic bags to take care of the soldiers no one could save. They would not get to bathe the bodies or tidy the bloody uniforms the soldiers had arrived in; they could not indulge in any of the small rituals that sought to sanctify death even here, in its hometown. This was strictly a bag-and-tag operation. They would go through each boy's pockets to itemize his possessions, and they would collide with his vanished life—the photo of his girlfriend in her prom gown, the letter from his dad, the guitar pick he carried for luck.

Even worse were the leftover body parts, the severed legs and arms, now cold and doughy to the touch and shockingly heavy. They would strive to match all the pieces together so that each corpse could go home whole, but it could not always be done. Sometimes torsos had been blown into mush; hands or legs had been left on the battlefield. On days like that, body bag detail was nothing more than a grisly game of mix 'n match. Della had learned this early in her tour by trying to match a blown-off foot with the patient it came from. The task was not just to satisfy the Army's need for tidy accounting: The soldier's dog tags were stashed in his boot. He must have found that the jangling metal disks made too much noise when he wore them around his neck.

The sun had disappeared by the time Della finally stepped through the double swinging doors of the hospital. The sodden heat of Cu Chi wrapped her in the mingled smells of mud, fuel, sewage, and rotting vegetation that she and her friends called eau d' Nam. Tonight Della noticed another, sharper scent—cigarette smoke. She did not have to see him to know who it was.

"Mac," she said quietly.

He was squatting against the corrugated metal wall of the Quonset hut that held the ICU, the sleeves of his faded fatigues rolled up to the elbow. His face was tipped down and covered in shadow, and the overhead light turned the brown hairs on his arms golden. Without haste, he rose to greet her.

She nodded at the cigarette. "Those things'll shorten your life, you know."

"Yeah, I've been meaning to quit." The joke was too familiar to bring a laugh—how long could a chopper pilot in Vietnam expect to live, anyway?—but they both paused to acknowledge the effort.

"What are you doing out here?"

"Waiting for you." He ground out the cigarette against the sole of his boot and slipped the butt into his shirt pocket. "Came to see if I could take you out to dinner."

"What time is it?" Her watch had stopped sometime in the early afternoon, and she'd had to borrow one from a corpsman to complete her shift. Now Della's surroundings gave no clue of the hour. The vast Army base was illuminated in patches of yellowish light that seemed more desolate than darkness. The heavens were no help either; it was the rainy season, and even in daylight the sky looked as low and gray as the arched roof of the Quonset hut.

Mac ambled over to her, his boots announcing each step on the raised wooden walkway that traversed the red mud. "What does it matter what the clock says? It's time to relax, to lay back and let the moon shine down on you."

"Oh, a poet." Della could hear her voice automatically fall into the joking cadence she used with all the guys.

"That's right. I'm the poet of the sky, here to wine and dine you in style. My chopper awaits." He inclined his head in the direction of the helipad.

These pilots—extravagant with words, but they didn't waste a gesture. "You do know the mess hall is within walking distance," she said.

"No mess hall for you tonight. I'll take you to any officers' club you name."

"Honolulu."

He laughed. "Any O club within an hour's flying time."

Della ran her hands down the front of her uniform and felt the crusty stains, the ballpoint pens poking up from the chest pocket. "I'm dressed a little informally. I don't think blood and guts will do for evening wear."

"I'll wait if you want to clean up." Mac leaned in closer. She could see his long, thick lashes, the hollows of weariness under his eyes. "But you look beautiful to me, Della."

Back in the World, that line might have moved her. But here, surrounded by thousands of young men, she heard it a dozen times a day. "Beautiful" was just a synonym for "female" or, more likely, "available."

And if there was anything Della was not, it was available. She studied Mac: his tousled brown hair, his heavy-lidded green eyes, his muscled forearms, the light glinting off his watch. "Well, you look married to me."

He took a quick step backward. "How does someone look married?"

"By rubbing his thumb across his ring finger, like you're doing now."

The pilot slid his hands into his pockets. "I'm not married." His grin revealed a slender gap between his two front teeth. "No one's married here."

"I've noticed that."

"C'mon, Della." Even with three feet of space between them, Mac had a way of crowding her. Maybe it was his voice, low and confident and sliding over her skin like suede. "Tonight will be something special," he murmured. "I'll take you to a place you've never been."

"Oh, really? And where might that be?"

He said it with reverence. "The sky."

In fact she had flown in a helicopter. She knew about the thrilling ascent, the shudder of the rotor lifting her far from the animal clash of war. She had seen a fresh green planet spread out beneath the dangling boots of soldiers who perched in the open doorways and trained their rifles on the ground.

It was the other journey Mac offered, the journey of skin and breath and heat, that Della had never taken. And now it was too late. How could she lose herself in a man's flesh after she had seen so many butchered?

Footsteps clattered toward them on the wooden planks. Della recognized the rise and fall of women's voices—Charlene and Mary Grace, two of her roommates in the nurses' quarters. A rush of relief took her by surprise.

"Hi, guys," Charlene called out.

"Hey, Charlene," Mac replied, defeat already in his voice.

Mary Grace scooted past them, her hands clasped in front of her as if she had captured a small, wild creature between her palms. "I can't stop to chat," she said, her eyes fixed on her boots. "We've been doing lap tapes, and if I don't get in the shower within the next ten minutes I'll just have to kill myself, which shouldn't be too difficult considering where we are."

Mac turned to Della. "Music for lap dances?"

"Not even close. In the operating room they use lap tapes to soak up the blood. Usually they throw them out, but when we're short on supplies they have to reuse them. The OR nurses boil them in big tubs."

"Why would Mary Grace freak out about doing laundry?"

She left it to Charlene, an operating room nurse, to explain. "Have you ever seen your mother make chicken soup?" Charlene asked Mac. The brown skin of her throat glistened with sweat.

"Yeah, I think so."

"You know how she has to keep skimming off little pieces of fat and skin while the broth boils?"

"Got it." He whistled lightly through his teeth. "You nurses must have balls of brass."

"That must be it," Charlene said. "I'm heading home. It's been a rough day."

Mac nodded. "Roger that."

"Della, you coming?" She turned away. "Johnnie's waiting in the hooch."

"Be right there."

"Wait," said Mac. "How about dinner?"

What could Della tell him? That she was twenty-one years old and still believed in the possibility of one true love? That she hoped to God the one for her was not as doomed and luckless as a soldier in Vietnam?

"Maybe another time, Mac. I'm beat."

"Della, who's this Johnnie guy?"

She smiled. Here, at last, was something she could give him. "It's not a guy. It's a bottle. Johnnie Walker."

Finally Della knew what time it was. Time to drink.

In the bright yellow kitchen, Della ran her thumbnail down the crease where Charlene had folded her letter. It made a noise like the sweep of a broom, and Della realized that Charlene must have heard the same sound just a few days ago. Charlene had handled this sheet of paper, she had flattened it into thirds, she had released it into a mailbox. She was real.

For so many years Charlene had been a confidante, someone who could hold Della's most searing thoughts and never get singed because she was only a memory. Now Charlene had touched her with this handful of words and Della didn't know what to feel. How lonely would she be once Charlene was no longer a presence she carried in her head, but a flesh and blood woman with demands of her own? How long before Della failed her once again?

Della stuffed the letter into the envelope. Her family would be over for dinner soon, and she was nowhere near ready. She hurried to the bedroom, shoved the letter in the back of her underwear drawer, and yanked off her scrubs.

She was standing under the shower when she felt it—the familiar homeless ache that hid somewhere beneath her bones, a thump of pain like a chord played on the lowest keys of a piano. Della had never found a way to describe or explain this hurt, so she hadn't told anyone about it.

It was like a phantom limb: You wanted to press the injured spot, soothe the damage with your hand, but there was nothing to hold. The bones of a phantom limb could never be set, its muscles never eased. Nothing could heal a part of you that was already lost.

Peggy Dills Kelter

Solitaire

When the weather outside is frightful, play Solitaire. When dementia threatens to isolate you from your loved ones, play Solitaire. When life seems too insane, play Solitaire.

Solitaire has saved me on more than one occasion. I learned this card game, also known as Klondike, when I was a kid. In order to play, I had to first learn how to shuffle cards. I played many solo games of "52 pick up" before I learned how to successfully manipulate a deck of cards between my two small hands. The day I conquered shuffling, and heard the soft lovely rustling sound of cards orderly collapsing from a bridge into a neat deck, was a benchmark moment in my life. Forty-five years later, I still find shuffling to be a pleasurable meditation.

I play with old cards softened by thousands of games. Each card has a hole through it, evidence that this deck was once used to deal blackjack at the Spirit Mountain Casino. When my mother moved from assisted living in McMinnville to her home in Hood River, the discarded gamblers' decks came with her. I've tried to play Solitaire with a new deck of cards. They slide too much, and carry too few memories.

My mother is the reason I play Solitaire so much these days. Every afternoon we play Double Solitaire, sometimes for hours. Each time we begin a game, my mother asks me how many cards she needs to place on the table. Each time, I patiently tell her "Seven." I often wonder why so many card games are played with seven cards. Is the reason mathematical? Religious? Or purely arbitrary?

Though my mother, who suffers from dementia, may not remember how many piles of cards to make, she remembers everything else about the game. She can be ruthless. Her quickness and agility with the cards amazes me. As she sneaks her three of hearts down on the shared pile just before I slam mine, she smiles with a Cheshire cat grin. She has beaten me once again.

Many ethical decisions confront us as we play. As children, my siblings and I had a strict code of Solitaire ethics. The rules were clear. Only one card may be placed on the central piles at a time. No double-handed play. Three cards at a time must be pulled off the deck. And absolutely no peeking at the concealed cards.

My mom no longer has such delusions of propriety. She'll stack three cards together and place them on the central pile, use two hands, and look at her deck one card at a time if she feels like it. Even so, the cards beat us as often as we beat the cards.

The only thing that interrupts my mother from the Solitaire game is her need to use the restroom. Her caregiver helps her up from her chair. My mother asks, for the thousandth time, where the bathroom is. We direct her there, holding her oxygen tubing as she shuffles with her walker to the bathroom.

When she returns to the card table, she is exhausted. Her trip to the nearby bathroom has left her winded and shaky. She collects herself, eases down into her chair, and begins asking questions.

"Where's dad?" "What am I supposed to do?" and "Where am I?" I answer "He's gone," "You're supposed to play with me," and "You're home." Of my three responses, the only one that eases her anxiety is knowing she has someone to play with.

We put the decks of cards away and bring out the tin of dominoes. As with Solitaire, she asks me how many tiles she should start with. As with Solitaire, I answer "Seven." We play the simplest dominoes game we know. The harder games look interesting, but learning new rules would be an insurmountable obstacle for my mother. Even this game, which she's played thousands of times before, can confuse her.

My mother has been known to play dominoes for 5 hours straight. At her assisted living center she often played with other residents until deep into the night. She doesn't remember that she's been playing for hours. She only knows that the round cornered white tiles keep sadness at bay.

Until recently, my mother was an ace Scrabble player as well. Each time we began to play, she'd ask how many letter tiles to take. As with Solitaire and dominoes, I'd answer "Seven." I'd scrutinize my tiles and come up with words like "dot" and "eat." She'd place words like "ingot" and "query" directly over a triple word score. Even in her diminished mental state she always slaughtered me.

I no longer play Scrabble with my mother, but my daughter has inherited my mother's gift for word games. This past Christmas she received a game called "Bananagrams" in her stocking. We spent many hours inside playing with words while outside, in the bitter cold, the snow accumulated.

"Bananagrams" is a delightful variation of Scrabble. Players take 21 tiles (hmmm, a multiple of 7) and begin building their own collection of connecting and intersecting words horizontally and vertically. Players can rearrange words as often as desired. One person wins when all of the 144 tiles have been used and there are no leftover letters in his or her arrangement.

The first time I played "Bananagrams" I thought "Oh, mom would love this game." Then I remembered. She would have loved this game years ago, but today, the unfamiliar rules and unrecognizable package would leave her confused and agitated. Instead, when I visit this afternoon, I'll pull the lovingly worn cards out of the drawer, make us cups of tea, and settle in for another afternoon of Solitaire.

In England, they call Solitaire "Patience." Indeed, I am learning patience from these long sessions of cards and my mother's relentless repetition of questions. Years ago, she taught me how to shuffle cards and play a game. As the deck falls softly and orderly into my hands, I realize that today she is teaching me something profoundly more important.

Naomi Lazard

In Memoriam

*To love animals as well as humans increases one's capacity
for suffering; sometimes I have envied those who are
indifferent to other species than their own.*
                                                    —Gavin Maxwell

Yours is the summer where it beats
the hill to heart again, and if you will,
these auburn moons. The bones will know,
loosened now by fire.
        Gavin, I hear you are
resting near the otters you loved.
Up there in the far west, near the shore.

It was shyness made my letter late
and death forestalled an answer.
But I believe in powers, not in death.
I believe the spirit of your animals
is stronger than I am, stronger
than your death. You loved them.
I loved them too. And so I come
to you, Gavin, in my trouble, flying
without wings to Scotland.

First I saw the kitten on the step,
the one with a sick eye. I bought him meat
and watched him eat, a small scout
stuffing. I walked away, dragging
my steps. He was so weak, crippled by that eye.
The street was terrible with traffic.

104

The lady of the boutique
assured me, settled among gowns embroidered
in Morocco, answered my questions
with a smile. Yes. the kitten
had a mother, home, yet made
the doorstep of her shop his daylight post.
Always fed by someone. But he was so thin!
Thanking her I left, even a bit abashed
to have made myself infirm
over such a small issue.

Some hours later I returned
simply to have a look. Dusk already.
I saw the paper that had held the meat
and saw the plastic garbage bag
someone had stuffed the kitten into.
Only the tail emerged, and the stiff legs.
Oh, dead, all dead. I stopped still
as a tombstone on that street.

Gavin, I don't ask forgiveness.
It wouldn't help anyway. One lives
alone always. One lives alone
in a kind of madness, remembering
the one small half closed eye
and the way he ate that meat.

You understand Gavin.
Your ashes will know.

Elegy to the Twenty Skiers

After the accident it was clear
the pilots were zooming
through the high valley, practicing
low level flying for combat, that is, a war.
They were machine-gun bullets
zapping in and out of the thin high clouds.
Maybe the twenty people in the gondola
whose cable the plane snapped
because the pilot was hot-dogging maybe
those people who fell three hundred and sixty feet
to their death, were also practicing.
    In a war there are, of course, always victims,
    the random selections of fate.
The only difference is this: the dead
are never informed in advance
their participation is necessary.

Notes for the Recording Angel

Matins, the hour of the wolf, just off Sunrise Highway,
behind Home Depot and Office Max
the Price Club watchman sees headlights slash
the darkness, eighteen wheelers trundle into beds.
Men in purple overalls bend their knees to lift
the night's haul, a gross of cartons, sarcophagus-size,
from the truck-bed to their appointed place
in the Price Club. Here other hands take over,
drag out the inner boxes, place them accurately
in the dignity of proper display.

Lauds, before first light, when the trees
are the black scribble across a searchlights glow,
and no trains run. The Paumanok moraine treads lightly,
ghost of the primeval forest that winds
along the shore, braiding feathers of gulls
into its long black hair. Clandestine ships
drop anchor in the island's northern bay.

Prime, the forest primeval is long gone, chopped down
for heat, cabin walls, for rolling stock.
Let us pray for strength. This is the hour
when the Price Club lights open their thousand watt
eyes, the hour of resolve before the work begins.
In the sanctuary between three gallon yellow mustard jars
and twelvepacks of assorted dry cereals,
someone listens to traffic, and finds it good.

Terce, the early birds are trudging down the aisles,
ample women dragging children between towering
displays of salted pretzels the size of concrete blocks.
Their faces are rinsed in kelp-green light,
light from jars full of half-sour pickles.
They are dressed to code, tights and baggy sweater,
Nike, Adidas or Converse, or any of the lesser names
in active footwear. They are looking for necessities,
and maybe some of life's finer things at a discount.

Sext, noon whistles scream that time
is leaving us behind. This is why the women,
dragging children behind them, or carrying them
like groceries in the giant carts provided,
step up their pace. They are buying in bulk
for the long haul because it's cheaper that way,
and it's comforting to have a full larder,
to know you have four dozen frozen pierogis
and a ten pound carton of Velveeta.

None, the Price Club is built like a hangar,
you could park two jumbo jets, wing tip to wing tip,
and still have a little space to play around with.
You have to be strong to make the pilgrimage;
you have to be single-minded. This is a place
where you won't find anyone in a Drop Dead silk suit.
These women don't have it all, don't dress for the office,
don't rush home, put a meal in the oven, take a step class,
change into something black and fragrant,
        sit down to a candlelit dinner,
        a few camellias floating in a Waterford bowl.

Vespers, formica tables and stools all fastened to the floor,
inviting as any of your institutional spaces
prepare you for a tête-à-tête in the jailhouse.
There is something about being surrounded
by mountains of products that brings on stupefaction,
        and a desperate desire to sit down.
The women and children take nourishment
from what is offered: hot dogs, pizza, coke and Pepsi.
The children are little, below school age, restless.
        Some of them squirm and run.
The mothers tolerate this for a while, then call them:
"Courtney!" "Tiffany!" "Linley!" "That's enough, Caroline!"

Compline, elegant names like these summon wealth,
estates on the east end, dressage, horses
to be ridden in the mornings, sailboats on the bay.
These names are aspirations, each one a prayer
that the child may leap out of Massapequa or Yaphank,
supersede the lives of the parents, enter
the class for which their names prepare them.

Denise Levertov

The Footprints

Someone crossed this field last night:
day reveals
a perspective of lavender caves
across the snow.   Someone
entered the dark woods.

Hut

Mud and wattles.   Round almost.
Moss. Threshold: a writing,
small stones inlaid, footworn.
'Enter, who
so desires.'

Floor, beaten earth.   Walls
shadows.   Ashpit at center.
By day, coming in from
molten green, dusk
profound.   By night, through smokehole,
the star.

'Life Is Not a Walk across a Field'

crossing furrows from green hedge to hedge,
rather a crawling out of one's deep hole

in midfield, in the moist
gray that is dawn, and begins

to hurt the eyes;
                    to sit on one's haunches
gazing listening, picking up
the voices of wheat, trail of other
animals telling the nose the night's news.

To be at the hollow center of a field
at dawn; the radius
radiant. Silver
to gold, shadows
violet dancers.

                    By noon the builders
scream in, the horizon
blocks afternoon, a jagged
restlessness. To be
an animal dodging
pursuers it smells but can't
see clear, through labyrinths

of new walls. To be mangled or
grow wise in escape.
To bite, and destroy the net.

            To make it maybe
into the last of day, and witness
crimson wings
                    cutting down after
the sun gone down in wrath.

Kathryn E. Livingston

Chance of a Lifetime

I always thought my breasts were absolutely perfect. I can't brag about my thighs or waist, but I've never had a problem with the size, shape, or appearance of my bust line. I got my first bra when I was eleven, and I developed at a brisk but normal pace. I nursed three babies with my breasts (seemingly forever) and had fountains of milk. My breasts were neither too large nor too flat; they seemed as invincible as adolescents who think they can never be stopped or injured (though that's certainly untrue).

So I was more than shocked to learn, two weeks before Christmas, four years ago, that I had invasive breast cancer. As I left my doctor's office—after a mammogram led to a biopsy, which led to the discovery of cancer—three words echoed in my mind: "This can't be." How could a mother of three sons, who exercises and eats well, get this disease? Not only were my breasts imperfect, one was so flawed that I might pay for its hidden defect with my life.

Like one in eight American women who must confront this diagnosis, I assumed that breast cancer would change my life (if I were lucky enough to keep it) forever. I was right about that, but not quite in the way I expected. I surely didn't foresee that breast cancer would turn me into a more positive person, or teach me how to live in the present moment.

When my cancer was first diagnosed, I began to follow the drumbeat of every potential tragedy and horror that might await me. As soon as I stepped out of my doctor's office, my dear childhood friend, who was with me that grim morning, warned, "Don't go down that road." But I was already on it, preparing for every possible setback, from how sick the chemo would make me to how devastated I'd feel if the cancer spread. The very word "cancer" left me paralyzed with

112

fear of the future: I wanted so much to see my boys all graduate from college and marry, to one day hold my granddaughter in my arms (a special wish of the mother of sons). Instead, I envisioned my family going on without me, and yearned for all the milestones I would miss.

The truth is, I've always been a glass-half-empty sort of woman, even though I appear easygoing and positive on the outside. Inside, I tend to follow the premise that if there is bad luck to be had, it will be mine. This feeling was magnified four years earlier when my own beloved mother was diagnosed with amyloidosis, a rare, and in her case, fatal disease. If my mother could be felled by an uncommon affliction we'd never even heard of, then why couldn't I succumb to something as widespread and unfortunately fashionable as breast cancer—a disease that everyone is talking about and too many women seem to be getting?

Like so many, I didn't even have any of the so-called "risk" factors. It seemed, instead, that my breast cancer was very much about flukes, chances, and plain bad luck, and as I continued down my rocky road, I found that the medical community appeared to agree. If the sentinel node was clear of cancer, then the chance that it was in other lymph notes was very slim. If I scored low on a particular lab test (which, thankfully, I did) my chance of recurrence was slight; therefore, after the lumpectomy, I could proceed directly on to radiation without undergoing chemotherapy. Hormone therapy pills held the chance of unsavory side effects, but this possibility was counterbalanced by the chance that the pills would be helpful in the long run. There was the chance that microscopic cells had invaded other parts of the breast, and so radiation was recommended. Everywhere, it seemed, I confronted a statistic or prediction that either raised or dashed my hopes.

But there was one place where I did not hear about chances. About a year before my diagnosis, I'd begun practicing yoga with a wonderful young teacher who believed that nothing happens by "chance," so when I learned of my cancer, I turned to her. As we discussed my fears for the future, I realized something vital not only about having this disease, but also about everyday life: Yes, there were chances, but there were also choices, and these were my own. I could sit and brood, imagining what might go wrong, or I could start looking at life in a fresh and different manner. I decided that instead of approaching cancer as an unfortunate fluke, mishap, or tragedy, I'd see it as a doorway to knowledge. Perhaps this was not so much about chance, as about finding meaning, even in an experience I never wanted to encounter.

At first it was difficult to be positive. The surgery was frightening (I'm the sort of person who faints at the sight of a Band-Aid), and the preparation, which involved injecting a dye into my breast, was brief but shockingly painful. Later, getting to treatments every day was irksome, at best. And the very first time I went to the hospital for my radiation "simulation" my arm fell into such a deep sleep (actually more like a coma), that I couldn't even wiggle my fingers. But then, slowly, I began to turn my thoughts around. I tried to redirect my attention toward my radiation therapist, a sweet, pregnant lady who positioned me with such care and tenderness. I began to think about how lucky I was to benefit from radiation, and about how grateful I was that I'd gone for a mammogram when I did.

But my deepest epiphany arrived one morning when a yoga classmate asked me how I was faring. I replied that I was waiting for the results of one test or another, waiting for my next visit with my oncologist, waiting to see what would happen. After the initial jolt of panic, waiting is the worst part of the cancer experience; you just want to reach that moment when a doctor proclaims, "You're cancer-free."

My classmate replied, "Don't wait for life to happen. Life is happening now." Her words rang so true they early knocked me over, and I couldn't get them out of my mind.

That night, after I settled into bed, I spent a long time gazing out the window, watching the lights flickering in the distance, and listening to the wind rushing through the pine trees. My gaze followed the spindly outline of my hanging spider plant, moved along the white lace edging of my curtains, and then traced the tangled branches of an immense oak planted more than one hundred years ago in the yard next door. As I watched the moon rise in the tree branches, I listened to the sounds in my own house. My fourteen-year-old was strumming a lyrical song on his guitar, and the notes trickled through his closed door down the hallway. I could hear my seventeen-year-old chatting on the phone with his dearest friend, a boy who was also diagnosed with—and beat—cancer that year. My husband, a classical musician, was playing his clarinet downstairs, and I could also make out the gentle chiming of church bells across town.

I could vividly hear, see, and feel the beauty of my own life all around me. Yes, I had cancer, but I was also surrounded by love. I decided that I would dwell in that beauty and love in the coming months. I would not allow my life to be guided by the possible misfortunes that might await me, or by chances, statistics, or future predictions. I would replace fear with gratitude whenever I could.

After that night, a strange thing began to happen. No matter where I turned, I found beauty and light. I began to live the way I had when my babies were newborn—when every gurgle and sigh and blink seemed like a gift.

As the days passed, my friends called from far and wide, and appeared on my doorstep with flowers, food, and support. My three sons—teens caught up in their own destinies—were suddenly acting in an outrageous manner, tucking me into bed and kissing me goodnight. My husband was both a source of strength and a compassionate shoulder to cry on. In the midst of cancer—a disease I've dreaded all my life—I had far more to be happy about than to regret.

No, my breasts are not perfect anymore, but my slanted narrow scar gives them character (don't ask me why, but my husband now calls my post-surgery breast "the pirate"). Like the wrinkles that have begun to appear on my face, my lumpectomy scar is evidence of experience, tangible proof that I'm both a "survivor" and a celebrant. Before, I appreciated the extraordinary value of every moment well enough, but I didn't revel in those moments, I didn't honor them, the way I do now.

Today, when I spot a redheaded woodpecker in my bird feeder, flopping awkwardly in the tray among the small brown sparrows, I know that his presence is not just a matter of chance. He's here to remind me of all the glorious moments in every day—from the way my eldest son grins in the morning when I offer him a plate of scrambled eggs to the ping of the raindrops on my windowsill in the late afternoon. That woodpecker is a living metaphor for the way I embrace all my days now. The glass, as I see it now, is neither half empty nor half full, but simply overflowing. I'm not waiting for life to happen; I'm scooping it into my arms moment-by-moment, redheaded woodpecker and all.

◆

Donna French McArdle

How Surf Works on Soul

I step in side-to,
chin-up to take the
heave of surf, and when
it comes, I jump and
let the surge slap hard.
It lifts and floats me,
then drops me askew
on beach unsteady
and shifting under
my feet. I scramble
on slipping pebbles. The
sand shifts. The tow drags
me toward deeper
water. The pull is
near unbearable.
To get away from
the worst, I must go
deeper, where before
it crashes, the wave
rises, hoisting me
trough to peak. Top the
swell I look down on
sun bathers slouching
in folding chairs while
others stare, perched on
coolers, looking to
the horizon. This
perspective moves me.

My Daughter's Sketches

She draws unicorns and
treasure maps and butterflies with faces.
For fairies, she pastes glitter, and around
a swamp of muddled finger paint, she glues grass.
I sign us up for nature drawing class.

Realistically
as I can, I draw pinecones, feathers, weeds;
acceptably angled, photogenic
glances I've seen in some magazine, maybe.
My daughter strokes, smells, looks up at the bush.

Then what she draws is
undeniable: Flowers veined like spray
from her warm shower and leaves cottony
as bed sheets. Her page so sensuous, so
true, it takes my breath away. How could she

know this? If she sees
this, what about our adult disguises? Masquerades?
They must be sheer to her, a joke
about hiding in plain sight. When I turn
her drawing upside down to study it,

she laughs. I do too.
Driving home, I see her in the rear view
drawing. "What is it?" I ask. She shows me
two faces both with giant smiles and tears
the size of coat buttons. "It's us," she says.

Penelope's Work

She is unweaving again. Oil lamp balanced on one hand, she brushes
the other over the last small corner of the shroud.
Highlighted so, these threads are heartbreaking,
searing into her memory the moment
she slipped her practiced shuttle into that pattern, the moment
the wind shifted mingling the scents of sea air
and the old, polished olive wood of her empty bed,
the moment she turned from the sunlight
drifting like a net over the Ionian waves
(but catching nothing, certainly not Odysseus)
and watched her son climb the hill to her house
now in such disrepair. In him she sees herself, his father, her past.
Her fingers hesitate. She holds the threads.
She whispers, "Just this. Can't I keep just this small piece?"
She can't, of course. She must remake every last corner, although
she leaves the warp threads in place.

It is a trick (maybe a cruel one), this daily unwinding.
Who, but she, could see her life in this yarn;
she has twisted it delicately so the full garment will weigh only
as much as a few days in summer wasted with crying, drinking,
and staring at the sea. Even studying it, no one could see more than
the quality of her work, a section with heavier yarns woven in,
and some threads draw over others at odd angles. Years ago,
(maybe more once) she worked a scene in which
Odysseus arrives, old and broken, wrapped in a filthy sheepskin.
Missing the sound mind of the prankster and smelling
of his own mindless piss, he bends over a cane, unable,
as husband or king, to protect her. Years ago, she allowed herself (only once)
to twist the threads around his death on a battlefield,
javelins whizzing through the air above,
and the wool from her blackest sheep pooling under his body.

And now she is weaving again. She has turned from her dining room,
filled with the rudeness of bodies, of intruders, turned
to her own chamber to listen to the pull of threads, song
of the sirens. She has heard the rumors—
how you must fill your ears with wax—but she lets
the song wash over her, listening for her name, her fate,

and writing a story into the shroud she would drape over Odysseus
so that as he trudges the field named Forgetful, and drinks
from the river called Unmindful, he could show it
to the next lost soul, and wonder, "Who am I?"
and "What is this tale?" and maybe,
unless he has drunk more than necessary, he might remember,
uncertainly, as if it were a story from his childhood.

She knows the threads are measured exactly, that the past is spun,
the present measured, and she must write the future as it comes to her:
the rosy-fingered dawn's coolness leaving the air, a
stroll with Laertes through the vineyards,
the taste of goat cheese, the slaughter cry
of a goat kid for the guests' meal, the warmth of a heated bath
poured slowly over her shoulders to lessen her weariness,
the fragrance of lavender-scented oil rubbed into her elbows and heels.
She weaves the sensation, right now, of wool on her fingers, lanolin
softening her fingertips, letting her touch gently the past, claim
whatever is coming, because unless this day
Odysseus walks back through the door, this story will not be told.
She will silently dismantle it tonight, and tomorrow,
she will start once again, with just the warp threads in place.

Victoria Kohn Michels

Spring in Clinton New York

Do you remember
that April evening

under the pines,

a small wind
cooling the sweat,

as we lay quiet
for some time?

Lights from
any oncoming car

might have
spotted us there.

Do you remember
how we didn't care?

At The Brooklyn Botanic Garden

Is there anything more beautiful
than The Cherry Esplanade,
bursting with pink joy,

pure enough to make you jump
like the Duke & Duchess of Windsor
in the Halsman photograph?

If only to veil myself in the
hundreds of petals, and
soar with the Redbirds.

They fly through the branches, sing,
chirp, whistle and sing some more.
Birds really do twitter, call out

in crazy codes, skip frantically from
branch to branch with spectacular fury.
Not unlike 11-year-old girls:

*I love you   I hate you   Come
here   Go Away   Leave me
alone   Don't you love me?*

Exasperated, I listen
for her song,
one petal at a time.

Just like the cherry blossoms,
my girl slips through my fingers
like pink snow.

Abilene

In another time
I am in Wellfleet with my father.
I am too young to understand that life
is a gift he gave me. On the beach it is dark.
Frightened, I reach for his hand.
He tells me a joke about Texas. He hates Abilene.

Years later in an orange hotel room in Abilene,
I know how travelling kills time,
and why strangers touching hands
would appeal to you. Father,
you are still a child, afraid of the dark.
What has become of your life?

As a boy, your photograph appeared in *Life*.
"The most beautiful boy in Abilene."
In your white summer suit, your eyes looked especially dark,
like your mother's and mine. After all this time,
you still cannot forgive her, or your father
for not speaking as she hit your face and body with her hands.

I always fall in love with men who are left-handed.
The same thing ruined my mother's life.
You didn't drink, unlike her father,
and you were determined to leave Abilene.
To please her, you began to pray for the first time.
But loneliness is as bright as a lighthouse in the dark.

~

The sound of the ocean in the pitch dark
is like the whisper of lovers touching hands.
I never used to think about misplacing time,
or the possibility of carrying a life
inside me. There are no oceans in Abilene.
I am one year younger than you were when you became my father.

Sometimes I think I may never find a father
for the child I want to bring out of the darkness.
There are painful secrets in Abilene
that were handed down to you and you have handed
them to me. There is sadness on the edges of my life.
Nothing will free me from you except time.

One dark winter night in Abilene,
my father was reading *The New York Times*
when suddenly, he took life by the hand.

Liz Morrison

The Meaning of Meat

If you crawl underneath the picnic table in the backyard of my Aunt Rivka and Uncle Herb's house, you'll find my initials carved in the underside of the table. I don't think anyone else knows they're there. I was twelve and it was the first of many times I would hear Aunt Rivka tell the story of how she and Uncle Herb met Marilyn Monroe in Niagara Falls in 1955. The story must have lulled me into an artistic trance because next to my initials I carved three flowers and the words Flower Power.

Sitting at the picnic table with Aunt Rivka and my mother, I reach underneath to feel my roughly carved artwork from a few years back.

"Ruthie, did I ever tell you about the first time your Uncle Herb and I went to Niagara Falls. We were on our honeymoon and we ran right into Marilyn Monroe, right there on the street.

She was walking along just like a regular person. I even had my picture taken with her." I didn't want to listen to this story again.

"I need to use the bathroom. Start it without me." I try not to let my eyes meet her skeptical gaze as I slip away from the picnic table and walk towards the house.

Aunt Rivka and Uncle Herb live in what my mother used to refer to as a modern house. All one story, clean, flat lines, big windows. I walk through the sliding glass door, through the den, past all the bowling trophies and photos of flushed faces at boozy parties. Aunt Rivka's hair is always perfect in these pictures as if she's managed to add a few spritzes of Aqua Net before each shot was taken.

I see a picture of our whole family, my parents, my brothers and me, taken about five years ago. It's shoved way in the back of the shelf, covered with dust.

Ever since my parents divorced, no one mentions my father very often. Now, when we all get together as a family, it feels unbalanced like a car travelling on three wheels.

Instead of going to the bathroom I pick up the photo, go into their kitchen, open the refrigerator and take out a can of beer. Pabst Blue Ribbon. Christ, what a class act these two are. Not that I have much room to complain. I'd just spent my freshman year at college drinking the cheapest crap I could get my hands on. I open the can, take a long swallow and lean back against the counter. Why in hell did I come home for the summer? I could have stayed at school, worked part-time and come home when I felt like it. I could have taken a couple of classes. I could have spared myself this dose of reality.

I think about all my friends who are staying at school for the summer. Right about now they'd be sitting in the tall, damp grass by the reservoir, smoking a joint and eating Hostess cupcakes.

"Ruth, Ruthie!" My mother's shrill voice brings me out of the tall grass and back to the kitchen. "I'm in here, Mom." I shove the photo behind my back so she won't catch me looking at it. Mom's not one for reminiscing. My mother walks into the kitchen wearing espadrilles, a peasant blouse and a pair of floral print bellbottoms that are way too short.

"Why are you in here all by yourself, sweetie?" Her look is more accusatory than sympathetic, like I may have stolen the coffee maker and stuffed it into my shorts. "I just needed to get out of the heat for a minute."

"Well, we miss you outside. Rivka's telling that silly story about when she and Herb ran into Marilyn Monroe in Niagara Falls on their honeymoon."

I roll my eyes. "I've heard it only about a million times."

She glares at me. "We've all heard it a million and one times. It gives Rivka pleasure to tell this story. You know how she loves an audience. Don't ruin this day for me, OK?"

Here it comes, I think. Here comes the reason I should have taken summer school classes. "I'll be right out, Mom. I just need to pee, OK?" I start to walk towards the bathroom.

"And don't use language like that, either. Nice girls say 'tinkle' instead."

I wait for my mother to close the screen to the sliding glass door before I return the photo to the den and go into the bathroom. Aunt Rivka's powder room, as she likes to call it, looks like something out of a New Orleans brothel. The wallpaper is green and gold with sketches of men and women dressed in some sort of peasant clothing. In some scenes, the men are chasing the women, and in others, the couples are engaged in what appears to be foreplay. In all the sketches, the women are very busty and are bursting out of their clothing. As I sit on the toilet I contemplate the various couples and try to make the correlation between foreplay and using the bathroom. I wonder if the wallpaper in Aunt Rivka's bedroom has drawings of people sitting on toilets or brushing their teeth.

The toilet has a fuzzy rug on top of the tank with a matching rug on the floor around the base. Both rugs are harvest gold and match the hand towels and the shell-shaped soaps arranged like a still life in a shell-shaped dish on the sink. There is an overwhelming scent of air freshener coming from a dispenser, disguised as a vase of flowers, sitting on the top of the toilet tank. The smell makes me sneeze a few times as I flush the toilet and quickly wash my hands.

I open the bathroom door and hear Aunt Rivka through the screen telling the Niagara Falls story. I walk up to the screen door and peek out at everyone sitting around her at the picnic table. As she opens her mouth to speak, I close my eyes, remembering another time she told this story. I was about twelve years old and my father was cooking the steaks with Uncle Herb. They were making fun of Aunt Rivka and her obsession with rattling on about Marilyn. My father was laughing. We were all having a good time. We were balanced. Aunt Rivka's voice brings me back to the present.

"So I walk up to Marilyn and ask her for her autograph but it's clear she's had a couple, you know what I mean, and she can hardly even hold a pen for God's sake. Herb told me to forget it but you know me, I couldn't just let an opportunity like that pass me by. So I say to her 'Miss Monroe, I know you've had a busy day but would you mind terribly if I asked you to sign this napkin?' I had a cocktail napkin from this little joint on the Canadian side that served the best Manhattans. Remember that bar? What the heck was it called?"

Not waiting for Uncle Herb's answer, Aunt Rivka holds up a photo album to show a scrap of yellowed paper, with some kind of scrawl on it, sticking out of the plastic sleeve. Next to it is a faded black and white photo of Aunt Rivka with her arm around a squinting and grinning Marilyn Monroe. Aunt Rivka's hair is perfect in the photo, despite the mist coming off the falls.

I walk back into the kitchen and prop myself up on the counter to savor my beer and my solitude. I could lip-synch the story from start to finish while Aunt Rivka tells it. In fact, I could lip-synch almost any story that any one of my family members tells. We seem to pride ourselves on repeat performances, as if we all have some sort of memory disorder where we forget a story as soon as it's told. I finish my beer, take a deep breath and head out to the backyard.

My three younger brothers have set up a croquet court and are slamming the balls into the redwood fence that runs along the perimeter of the yard, paying no attention to the location of the wickets. My mother and Aunt Rivka are on the side of the house, drinking scotch from plastic cups and sharing a cigarette like a couple of sneaky high school girls. Uncle Herb is cooking several large slabs of meat on a charcoal grill. He's wearing one of those aprons that says "Kiss the Cook" and has a very satisfied grin on his face.

"How do you like your steak done, honey?" Uncle Herbs asks me.

"I've stopped eating meat." I practically whisper my reply, as if this is the first time I've said it out loud. It occurs to me that I hadn't bothered to tell anyone.

"What do you mean you've stopped eating meat? Since when?" My mother's ears have picked up my signal like a short wave radio on a clear night. She marches over to where Uncle Herb and I are standing.

"I just don't like the taste of it anymore. It's no big deal. I can eat all the other stuff here." I point at the picnic table laden with potato salad, ambrosia salad, Velveeta slices and Ritz crackers. I know my mother considers this latest dietary change a personal affront, like it's all about her. I think quickly how to build up my arsenal of answers for the upcoming interrogation.

"Are you hanging out with weirdos at school? Are you spending time with musicians and women's libbers? Are you becoming one of those health nuts?"

My mother has a strange way of lumping groups of people together. "Mom, it's not like that. I told you I just don't like the taste of it any more." I can see that she's not buying my simple explanation.

"This is about your father, isn't it? You're still blaming me because of the divorce, aren't you? If he were here tonight. . . ."

If he were here tonight I'd be eating the steak just like I always have. Dad was the one who made the steaks, Uncle Herb made the drinks and my mother and Aunt Rivka would sit on lawn chairs in the corner of the yard and gossip. That's what I remember. That's how I want it to be.

Uncle Herb tries to soothe my mother. "Betty, don't get all worked up about this. It's probably just a phase she's going through. You know how kids like to try new things in college." My mother looks at me suspiciously. "Sometimes I just don't understand you, Ruth. Your uncle is making us a perfectly nice dinner and you are acting so disrespectful."

Uncle Herb tries to ease the tension by changing the subject. My mother stomps off to discuss my rebellious behavior with Aunt Rivka, giving me a disgusted look as she turns around. Uncle Herb calls me over to him.

"C'mere Ruthie honey and tell your old Uncle Herb about your first year at school." Uncle Herb and I have never been close. He and Aunt Rivka didn't have any kids and he's always treated my brothers and me like he's trying to sell us something.

"It was OK. Exams were hard." I hear the words coming out of my mouth but I feel like I'm not really there.

"So how are your grades?" I can see he's trying to make casual conversation. He flips one of the steaks and I listen to the sizzle of the meat as it hits the grill.

I look up at him and instead of answering his question, I ask him this: "Do you miss my father?"

Uncle Herb seems startled by the question.

"Of course I miss him, honey, but you know the situation."

The smell of the seared meat makes me dizzy. Uncle Herb puts the spatula on top of each steak and presses down on them one at a time. The meat sizzles angrily. Wiping the sweat from his upper lip with the back of his hand, he checks the steaks as the silence hangs over us like smoke over the grill.

"Sometimes I don't feel like I belong here anymore."

Uncle Herb takes a long drink from his highball glass and looks at me like he's going to tell me about human reproduction. He sighs deeply.

"I know how you feel, honey. Sometimes I feel the same way."

We watch the steaks cooking for a few minutes, deep in our own thoughts. "I'm feeling kind of dizzy. I'm going inside to wash my face." I walk away from Uncle Herb and go back into the house.

This whole evening feels wrong without my father. I find the family picture I saw earlier and take it back into the kitchen. The photo looks like it hasn't been dusted in years. I take a paper towel and clean the dust from the glass, my heart pounding as if I'm about to uncover a secret.

My father looks happy in the picture, we all look happy. I study the photo trying to find some sort of clue in my parents' eyes but I only see blank, smiling faces. I return the photo to the shelf, walk out to the backyard and sit down at the picnic table.

My mother, my brothers and Aunt Rivka are crowded around Uncle Herb waiting for him to cut the steak. I pick up a paper plate and walk towards the grill.

Ilene Moskin

High School Prom
From *Remembering My Mother's Childhood*

The stockings hook up
to contraptions built like paperclips—
her shoes are hand-picked,
evil and thorny-heeled.
And on the dress, lime chiffon,
my mother autographs her breast
with the scrolling of his white corsage.

When they dance, he will aim
his white silk handkerchief toward it.
Later, he will press it
for remembrance
in his palm.

Her father will be waiting,
his lap beneath the newspaper.
He will deliberately avoid
the orchid's evidential tilt.

She will feel, as love,
a petal drop inside.
She will mark, to keep, that place.
Eventually, I will lie
my own white face against the target.

My Mother's Body as Territory

My mother's breasts were ominous
released from the underwires—
round and cupped like parentheses.
I would lay my head between them
to insulate my thoughts
from the anger of our usual words.
I would slide my ear
to hear her dinner break down
to its molecules, a squalling process
I equated with my own gestation
played somehow in reverse.
Her whole body seemed to me
an inscrutable chamber
in which things were made and unmade.
But it was better to be stifled there
than to find my body reflected in her eyes,
the tiny figure trapped
in her most silent and boundless places.

Poem

"I have always felt my entry into the world was the beginning of an irrevocable fall."

—Kasper Hauser, as quoted in "The Mysteries of Kasper Hauser"

I should have been content while the mists were at my feet,
the icy spires rising in a clear light.
Before the bones, the chatter of empty hands,
before color roused the heart to its seasons.

In that place, before hair and teeth to bite with,
I wanted eyes and ears, the nudge of sense against them.
I wanted birds waking up under the skin.
I wanted the conspiracies of night.

Beauty was a mutable wave, no, a billow
like skirts, that would not break or disappear.
I even had some in the way of a walk
like a shine across the water,
a round and rolling light.

I should have kept those paler dresses.
I should have worn the irreducible elements,
the smoke and ashes, the grey approximations.
I should have loved that other world instead,
instead of leaping from the gates to be born.

Isabel Weinger Nielsen

She Might Break

The baby came in a glass box. At least they put her there soon after she was born. For warmth. To keep her alive. She was very small. Born in the seventh month. Seven is somehow an important number in the baby's life. Her parents were married seven years before she was born. They never thought they could have children.

It really doesn't matter what the baby's name is. She could be me. Her parents could be mine. But I'll call the baby Aviva. It means life. It's appropriate. The baby has two grandmothers, some aunts and uncles, and many cousins. She is the first girl in a long time. The first granddaughter. The first niece. They all gave her presents.

Mom looks at the baby through the glass box. She can't hold her. She can't nurse her. Only look. The baby is so small. As delicate as glass. Mom reaches out to touch but the glass is cold. She pulls her hand away.

It's Mother's Day. May. The baby isn't big enough yet. She was born last Monday, but she's lost weight. Hospital food isn't very good. Not as nourishing as mother's milk.

"I brought you some flowers. Roses. They're pink."

The father is kind. He still can't believe he has a daughter. A girl. She wasn't supposed to be here for two months. Grandma says she should have been a Moonchild. Now she's a Taurus. But that's okay. Taurus people are strong. She'll live.

The mother hands the roses back to him. Her voice catches.

"I'm not really a mother. I'm not a mother unless I have my little girl here with me. It's Mother's Day. And I can't even hold her."

The baby is all in glass. The mother can't hold her. She stops coming to the hospital to see Aviva. Father stops on his way home from work. At least someone should be there. Even if she's too little to know. She's too little. He's glad he can't hold her. She might break.

The doctor said, "It's better this way. You've got to give her time to grow. You can watch her but don't touch her. She'll get strong. She'll be all right. It's better this way. Just give her time."

The mother's name is Lucy. She has a dream. The dream is about a doctor. A doctor in a hospital. There is a Lucite wall between Lucy and Aviva. Lucite so it can't be broken. So it can be seen through. Lucy watches Aviva. Aviva is having trouble. She doesn't know what to wear each day. She's overeating. Lucy wants to help. The doctor says no. She might break.

She keeps doing things to hurt herself. The doctor says, "It's better this way. You've got to give her time to grow. You can watch but don't touch her. She'll get strong. She'll be all right. It's better this way. Just give her time."

~

The story can begin. I'm a mother. I've always wanted to be a mother. There's nothing wrong with that. I love my children. I have three only children. Each is special. But Aviva is extra-special to me. She's my fulfillment. I couldn't be a mother without her. My other daughter and son are the topping on the dessert. Aviva is twenty now. She's just started her junior year in college. She's a writer. I think she'll be happy there. She's lost a lot of weight and feels better about herself. And she'll be living with her friends, one a painter, the other a dancer. She'll be happy. She's been calling me a lot. I don't quite understand it.

The doctor tells me she'll have to come home. A doctor knows these things. She keeps calling me a lot. But she doesn't cry. I don't understand it. If she's so unhappy, why doesn't she cry? We'll just go up and see how she is. Though she didn't have a very good summer. Her job was boring and she didn't say much. Though she met a young man before she left. A graduate student. Very nice. He goes to Yale.

Let me tell you about this dream I had. Aviva is small and very far away from me. I can't touch her. I can't hold her. I don't know if she's crying though sometimes her face gets kind of twisted and she looks like something's hurting her. Like she's surrounded by a balloon and there's a little person inside that pokes her and pricks her with a stick he has and tells her something but I can't hear. Her face twists whenever he comes near her. But she doesn't push him away. She just lies there with her body all curled and he dances around her and opens and closes his mouth.

She doesn't respond. I want to go and help her but there's a wall that stops me. A clear plastic wall. It's very cold when I touch it. I wonder if Aviva's cold. I can't hear her. I can only watch. She kicks in the incubator as if she wants to get out. She looks strong enough. But the doctor says she has to get stronger. I want to hold her. That will get her strong. I want to nurse her. Hospital food isn't very nourishing. And oh how I want to have her, not just watch.

My husband says at least we should go see her at school. She doesn't seem to be doing well at all. She keeps asking lots of people for help and they take her to the infirmary. And she doesn't want to take any pills. She's scared of them. But she can't sleep. And she won't eat. And she keeps doing things to hurt herself. Like cutting up her fingers. She's done that before. She did it last year around Thanksgiving time. She was very depressed then.

The doctor says she'll have to go into the hospital. She's been home three weeks. She spent three weeks in the incubator and she got stronger so I thought three weeks away from school would help. She seems to be going farther and farther away from me. I can't hold her anymore.

When I put my arms around her, her whole body goes stiff. Yesterday she sat on the floor of the kitchen and cried because she was eating a piece of celery and didn't want to gain weight. But she wasn't really crying. I couldn't hear her crying.

I told the younger kids that their sister really needs me now. I'll have to give her more of my attention this time. They understand. Each of my children is special. Each is an only child. But Aviva is extra-special to me. Especially now when she needs me. I have to take care of her. Though her whole body goes stiff every time I put my arms around her. The little man is poking her with his stick, telling her to stand up straight, to ward off warmth by her stiffness. I read her the story of Rumpelstiltskin once and she asked me to read it over and over again and I think it's him, dancing around her, calling out her name.

Maybe that's what would have happened if I brought her home with me the first time in the hospital. I'd have put my arms around her and she'd have gone stiff and died. The doctor said she'd get strong. It took awhile but she did. It took awhile but he told me to be patient. Even though my arms were empty. Even though my arms were so empty. But at least I have her now. Even though something's wrong. Though not terribly wrong because it often happens to people this age. The doctor says her core is solid. She's just going through a difficult time. Maybe I'll have to stay away from her awhile. Stay and watch and let her grow. If I touch her she might break. If I touch her, she might go farther and farther away from me. So I'll stay away. That way we'll have the same distance to walk when it's time for us to meet again.

She called me the first night in the hospital. Or maybe it was the second night. She was crying. I haven't heard her cry for a long time. I was afraid she'd never cry. It's good to cry. Maybe that's why she was getting all those headaches. Because she never let anything out. She called me to tell me that she couldn't stop eating. They had a kitchen in the hospital that you could walk into anytime and she couldn't stop eating.

I called the nurses but they laughed at me. Because a mother would call and be so concerned. I didn't want them to think that of Aviva. Most of the people in the hospital didn't have people to care about them. But they laughed at me. So I'll stay away. They want her to grow up. To grow. To take on her own responsibility. But she's sick. I want to take care of her. The doctor says no.

I resented the fact that my mother worked. She was never there when I wanted her. Always working. At least Aviva's got a father. The doctor says it's okay for him to visit. That's because they're both men. The doctor says it's okay for Dad to visit for awhile. But not me. I stop coming to the hospital to see Aviva. Dad stops on his way home from work. At least someone should be there. But he can't hold her. She might break.

He tells me about the strange conversations he and Aviva have. That she can't stop talking about being at college. That she keeps telling him she would have been better off if she stayed at school. It's good that I don't go see her. She tells him she wouldn't be sick if she had stayed there. She tells him that being sick is my fault. That I told her she was sick and wanted to bring her home because I like taking care of her. Well I'm not going to feel guilty. I saw her lying on her bed at school, not able to get up because she was so tense and her fingers were bleeding because she kept cutting them. When we asked her if she wanted to stay or go home she couldn't talk. She couldn't shake her head. She couldn't move. And after we had packed all her things, she couldn't get dressed. I had to dress her. And help her walk downstairs. She didn't say anything for three days. I couldn't have left her there.

I went to college in the Midwest and only saw my mother and sister Christmas and summer, and my mother worked, anyway, so I didn't see much of her then. She worked all the time. She worked in the shop that was in front of the house and did people's hair and manicured their nails. When I came home on vacations I swept up. But she didn't talk to me because she had to talk to her customers. When I was away it was too expensive to call, and I promised myself that I'd never do that to my children. And then I got married and found out I couldn't have children unless I had an operation, but most doctors are screwed up anyway and I wouldn't let them. And then I finally had Aviva. All on my own with no help from them. She's my fulfillment. I've always wanted to have children.

The doctor says he doesn't know how long she'll have to be in the hospital. As long as necessary. I can't feel guilty. There's nothing more I can do for her. But I keep having this dream. She's behind a plastic wall and I can't come near her. The doctor says it's better this way. The doctor says I can watch her but can't touch her. When she comes home on weekends I put my arms around her and her whole body goes stiff. This weekend I didn't go near her at all. My husband picked her up at the hospital and he took her to a crafts show but she had to hold onto him as they walked around. She sat down a lot. They've really got her tranquilized. I don't like pills, but I want them to help her. I want her to be well.

This weekend is my birthday. Birthdays are a big event in our house. On your birthday you get breakfast in bed and presents. Tomorrow is my birthday. I don't think Aviva will remember. She's groggy and sleeps a lot. I didn't think she would remember. But before she left she gave me some plastic things hanging on a red yarn. She had made them in OT. One was a sun and the other a butterfly. The sun had a face on it and she said it looked like me. I told her I'd hang it on the kitchen window. Then I hugged her hard. Her body went stiff. Like the little man was poking her and telling her to stand so straight that she couldn't feel any warmth. Because if she hugged me back we might all think she was well. I don't know whether she is. Maybe she's making all of this up.

I don't like it that they're giving her so many pills. My grandma took two aspirins every morning but these tranquilizers aren't a good idea. How can they find out what's wrong if they've got her doped up all the time? I don't understand it.

My mother cries all the time. That her Aviva is in the hospital. She'd get better at home, she keeps telling me. Home is the only place to be. Only a mother knows the right thing to do for a child. I'm not so sure. I brought her home and couldn't help and now she's in the hospital and there's a plastic wall between us. I keep knocking and knocking but she can't hear me. Her body's all curled up and she can only hear the little man. He tells her that she's stupid and fat and ugly and I keep banging on the wall yelling no no but she can't hear me she can only hear him and her body tenses so much she can't move. He pokes her with his stick until finally she curls up and pulls the sheet over her head and holds her breath hoping she'll die. I keep breathing for her and the nurse is watching the incubator and takes the cover away from her and Aviva looks up in the empty room and cries and cries. Then she throws a glass jar and cuts herself but the nurse tells me she didn't do a very good job of it and the doctor says it was a stupid thing to do anyway and not to worry.

She came home on the weekend with big gauze bandages wrapped around her arms and I didn't know what to tell her brother and sister. She didn't say anything all weekend. Just kept going into the bathroom and when I asked if anything was wrong she said everything was okay. She kept saying she hadn't taken anything. I don't think she'd lie about something like that. She kept opening and closing the medicine chest thinking I wouldn't hear.

My husband doesn't say much about the whole thing. He doesn't like to deal with psychological things. When we meet with the doctor my husband doesn't say anything. I'm always the one to ask questions. The doctor tells me that her core is solid. That she'd probably be okay if she went out and got a job and kept busy. She's not ready to go back to school yet. "She has a mountain to climb first." But he doesn't see anything particularly wrong with her. "Cutting her wrists was just a childish thing to do anyway." They can't concern themselves with that. There are too many other people in the hospital who need real help. A lot are undergoing shock treatment. Maybe that's what Aviva needs. Maybe the electricity would kill the little man who keeps poking his stick at her. The doctor says no. Her core is solid.

The dream repeats itself again and again. Maybe she should come home. Hospital food isn't very nourishing. She keeps eating and eating all kinds of junk and she has an infection now and her cheek is all puffed out on one side. She looks lopsided. She doesn't seem to mind except that she has to take different-colored pills and she doesn't like that. She says they'll never find out what's wrong with her if they keep giving her pills.

When she was in the incubator I kept making the doctor check to make sure everything was okay. She might go blind. Lots of babies went blind from the oxygen in the incubators. The doctor said she didn't need any oxygen. She'd get strong if I didn't touch her. If I didn't hold her. If I watched. If the plastic wall was always kept between us. Well not always. They took it away for awhile while she was growing up. But that probably wasn't the best thing. Because now we have to have the wall again. Now we have to have the Lucite wall that's cold. And sometimes I think the oxygen did make her blind because she can't see me standing at the wall, at least hoping to give her a look of warmth. She can't hear me either. She's in her own little world and the little man hands her sharp things to cut herself. Someone always takes them away. He's Rumpelstiltskin and he conjures up things over and over to give to her. Scissors to cut herself. Nail clippers and glass. He keeps dancing around her. He dances and dances.

Premature babies shouldn't be isolated. There are all kinds of magazine articles coming out now. That their mothers should be able to touch them and nurse them and hold them close. They grow faster that way. And stronger. But the doctor says no. And he won't let me come near her now. Not even when she's so fragile. She might break. When my husband and I went to pick her up at school and she wouldn't move or talk I was going to shake her. But that probably wouldn't have made a difference. She was so quiet. Maybe she would have started screaming. She would have started screaming like she did when they put her in the incubator. Just cried and cried and the doctor would have had to put the wall between us then. At least I had her home for three weeks before she went into the hospital this time. At least I got to hold her for awhile even though her body always did go stiff.

I don't remember my mother holding me much. She loved me a lot. I know that. But she didn't have time to hold me because she was always working. I guess she held me when my father died but that was so long ago and I don't really remember or understand. At least Aviva's got a father. At least Aviva's got a father who loves her although he doesn't hold her very much. He doesn't hold her very much but he loves her. She wants him to come to the hospital. She doesn't blame him for her being home or being sick. She never blames him for anything. Always me. Because I talk more. Because I plan things. Because I'm the mother and am around more often.

She's so out of it now. Half the time I talk to her and she doesn't even know what I'm saying. She just tells me that she can't stop eating. Or doesn't say anything at all. She doesn't have the patience to read. She can't even sit in front of a television long enough to wait for one commercial. She started a needlepoint thing in the summer and it takes her an hour to make one stitch. She won't do anything in the hospital but eat and sleep and cry. The doctor's not worried. But Aviva thinks that if she does something they expect her to do, they'll think she's well. And how can she be well if they haven't found out what the matter is yet?

My husband doesn't say anything about the situation. He's very good about taking care of the financial matters though. About getting the money back that we paid for school. And making sure the medical insurance takes care of everything. I wish he would put his arms around her. I wish he would go on the other side of the plastic wall. The doctor was wrong not to let me hold her when she was in the incubator. The doctor was very wrong. She would have been strong now. If I could have held her when she was a baby. If I could have nursed her. She would have grown strong. She would have grown strong and wouldn't have to be in the hospital now. Cold. Behind the plastic wall where I can't touch her. Where she can't hear me. So very cold. And her father won't even put his arms around her. She's lucky to have a father. They're very much alike. They have the same coloring. He doesn't like to deal with psychological things.

My mother still cries over the phone. It's getting worse for Aviva but I won't tell my mother. It's getting worse for me but I don't say a word. It's the third week that Aviva's been in the hospital. She isn't getting better. Or any stronger. Maybe if I stand up against the plastic wall long enough it will get warm and finally hot and melt and there'll be a lot warmth. She'll be well. The little man will suffocate. I can put my arms around her and she won't go stiff.

Barbara Elizabeth Nixon

Chemo

Medicine for a cure
Hardly medicine
But a promise that some
will drink poison and
not be harmed.

My Comfort

Not eating. It is hard.
Nothing but disappointment
I'm trying.
But it is difficult.
Softening produces results
and there is hope.

Gwynn O'Gara

Fallen Apples

She forgets to put on earrings, to comb her hair
she goes out into the perfumed air
and soaks in the sun with the fallen apples

Vagabond Sky

I

The housewife remembers
the guinea pig must eat,
folds the towel after rubbing her arm
along its velvet crop.
She dispenses her son's medicine,
yet another antibiotic she's noticed
the need for, making sure there's a cup
of sweet juice to absolve the bitter.
She mends a rend at his knee
wondering how she'll touch him
when he's sixteen.

She's already being scolded for kisses.
Six, he wipes each smooch off his still soft skin.
He tells her when he's done something naughty,
he's that innocent. She can only give thanks
silently. He tells her when he's mad at her
and a shadow covers her like a bruise.
Fewer and fewer are the casual leanings,
the unannounced settlings into her lap.
He's leaving soon—kindergarten starts next week—
so she hugs harder, kissing him despite his protest.

II

The house overwhelms her some mornings
like her husband with his demanding appetites.
The sun reveals one too many flecks of missed food.
Her son urges "Mom!" one too many times.

She remembers the wash, the dishes, errands and
gardening she forgot long enough to dream
of solitude, Venice, work as compelling as her husband,
demanding and satisfying as her child.
This isn't the little apartment that sang with the sea.
This is a house, rooted as the apple tree,
solid enough for vacuuming and spider webs, a
haven, digging in, a burden, an end.

143

Pressing a lavender spike between her fingers
and sniffing, she thinks back to the little place
they rented and left, its quick cleaning,
the impossibly long stairs up to the view
of boats and bay, the sense of traveling to
new worlds the outlook gave them.

Here she's under trees,
sequestered beyond hedges
not sailing on a breeze.
Animals come to her to be fed,
plants tended, thrive
attracting bees and butterflies.

She knows to water down low,
to leave her husband alone
when he's fuming,
to give her son warnings.

III
She watches the apple tree and chatters to the birds.
When she finds a jay's feather, she knows they're kin
circling the brave tree looking for food.
When the heat comes she watches for red stripes,
eager, yet loaded with foreboding for the endless
sauces and pies, cobblers and breads.
Only one tree yet it fills her life.

The hammock under the redwoods calls her.
Too much to do though her life is not troubled
or flecked with health or money worries.
Too much to do in the kitchen, the house,
the yard, tending husband and son,
welcoming friends, arranging things,
while the rope couch of daydream
and doze calls her to look up
through branches to the vagabond sky.

She waits for the time she isn't the center
of need and desire, when she can tell her men
to feed themselves, and take long walks
without returning on a schedule other than her own.

When the stove gets lonely
and snails take over the garden
sprawling in lawn chairs
after sliming the deck
in a calligraphy of ownership.
And the house sits quiet
and weeds return the garden to meadow
and berry canes strangle the phone
and thistles imprison the mail
and the house is an empty nest
instead of a bear to be tricked.

Let Me Be Beautiful Like Sea Glass

Let my edges that cut be stroked by sand and salt
Let my slick surface coarsen till it's beaten to bits
Let my colors soften as they scrape the bottom
Let the waves love me in their rough way
Let me be changed by that love
Let me not forget I held another
yet fully inhabit my particularity
Let me be smooth enough to be rubbed by small fingers
and slipped inside a pocket or a bowl
Let me prove that beauty is born when something breaks

Gwynn O'Gara, Nancy Dafoe, and Nicole Dafoe

The Kirkland Experience

SCENE: Dark stage. Five women are standing on the stage, apparently unaware of one another. The women represent the students who have attended Kirkland College, the scene beginning in the past with the voices of young women in the midst of their college experiences in the 1970s. The tone shifts as the contemporary voices speak next, finishing with the voice of a Hamilton College student who hears the echo of her mother and the Kirkland women before her—those women who continue to imprint college life on the hill. The voices are joined by a single word that flows from the last word spoken by each character into the first word of the next speaker. The spotlight goes up on KAREN, a young Kirkland student who is in the midst of changes even as the country is embroiled in the Vietnam conflict. She is wearing a leotard, sweatpants, and leg warmers. She is located at the back right of the stage. After her monologue, the light goes out on KAREN and up on MAXINE who is standing back left. Then the contemporary, adult voices of JULIA, standing front, right, and ADRIENNE, front left, speak in reflection on their past, finishing with the contemporary voice of GABRIELLE, front, center stage. As GABRIELLE finishes speaking, the women appear to notice one another as the lights go up, and they move toward one another to center front stage, joining hands at the center.

KAREN: (*practicing her ballet moves*) I don't know why I try. Every teacher says I started too late. Well, most of them don't come out and say it; they don't have to. Except the ballerina from hell. Yesterday during class while we were at the barre, that witch said my best feature is my feet! I'll show her. I don't care. I love to dance. Dance used to be holy. It wasn't about mirrors and who has the longest legs and thinnest waist. It was about gratitude and offerings and welcome. I'll work so hard I'll get into a company after I graduate. The only reason I stay in this god-forsaken place is my parents. All that they ask of me is that I graduate . . . It's so cold. I never get warm. I have three pairs of leg warmers on. It's always snowing. Last year it snowed in May! Yesterday when I went to the library, the wind blew snow into my lungs. Ugh! I thought I was going to die. I couldn't breathe. Suffocated by snow. Lung freeze.

I think I'll try that parsley diet. Supposed to knock the pounds off and completely cleanse your system. Maybe I'll fast for a few days. I have all those carrots, I should make juice first. Carrots like being cut on the diagonal. They told me. I'm going to the dance on Friday. I don't care if those Hamilton lugs look at me like I'm from another planet. Where'd they come from, anyway? A time warp from the 50s? I never knew so many people were into drinking. It's like my parents and their friends except at the fraternities they puke more. I'm so lonely. I'll never get laid. I love having the studio to myself. Even if I have to wait till after midnight. I think I'll try that jazz routine a few more times. Olive! What are you doing wandering around at this time? Come here, doggie. Want to dance? Give me your paws. First this way, now that, now this.

(MAXINE, a Kirkland student in the '70s, wears black tights, blue-jean cut-offs, t-shirt, and cowboy boots. She is peering through a huge magnifying glass.)

MAXINE: (holding up a book) This book says it's from the Ming Dynasty, but I don't think so. Something's off. Could be the glaze or that weird base. If I could see it in person, I'd know. I'm surrounded by 42 types of apples, but what I want to study is 400 miles away! Why couldn't I just be obsessed with cows? Sometimes I wonder what I'm doing in this meshuguna place? Every time I turn around, there's more snow, more mud, and at least one new teacher. I've lost two clogs in the mud! Sucked right off my foot. My father says all I do is cavetch but I tell him, You worked so hard that I should get lost in a snow drift? How did a city girl like me get here? And don't tell me I took the train. Why did the Kirkland student cross the road? To ruin her shoes? No. To see how low she would sink.

I hate the winters here. I've howled at the moon so much, it howls back. When's Charlie getting back? I need to get this done tonight. He said he was bringing me a surprise. Where is he? Maybe he'll drive to New York with me. We could make it by 10. The Met doesn't open till 11. I could be back by 6. Turn in my paper half a day late—and it would be conclusive, revolutionary! Stevens would give me full credit, I think. Damn, it's after midnight. Too late to call him. Where is that bag of cookies? Shit! I ate them. I hope Charlie brings me something to keep me awake. And I don't mean his one-eyed wonder. Time to go back to work. (*Picks up the magnifying glass.*) I'm going to prove this isn't a Ming vase if it takes me all night. I've always had a good eye.

(Light goes out on MAXINE and up on JULIA.)

JULIA: (*with a briefcase in hand*) I arrived at McIntosh without an awareness of Millicent, without allusions, the result of a somewhat flawed high school education, I discovered, not a faulty mind. At the time, however, I was not at all sure. Joyce, Faulkner, Eliot, Pound, and all those incisive, male Modernists who seemed to control the language in ways that left me feeling like a recent immigrant on the shores of our language, were confounding revelations, not exactly damning ones—but damn close—not the "Shakespeare would have loved us all tonight" kind. Pound was across the road, lacing his words with arsenic and ancient tongues while we found Virginia Woolf walking through Root Glen on the Kirkland side; arriving at neither balance nor stasis, settling for apprehension—pun intended. I loved Kirkland immediately and was sure the choice had been a disaster, the contradiction, hers and mine, apparent in everything from her pedagogy to her funding sources. It was only later that I would gain a political awareness of the impossibility of her turbulent existence. The audacity of a dialogue rather than a grade!

I arrived and left in the middle—which would seem mathematically impossible to do—since Kirkland life would span only ten years, but I was aberration in the midst of that anomalistic association, a transfer student. I recall my professors, across the road as well as in McEwen, and the path both up College Hill as well as to enlightenment. The best were easy to distinguish, Sam Babbitt, President and professor who taught me, whether he intended to or not, that Faulkner's *Fable* resonates in the container of the soul before being lifted to the mind. Fred Wagner, across the road, welcoming, offered a hearty laugh and heady conversation that kept me up thinking about Eugene O'Neill's family rather than my own on more than one occasion. I'll judiciously omit the names of those less-than-cherished teachers and experiences I would just as soon forget but am unable to banish from the vernacular of memory. I will not forget Hart Crane's *The Bridge* for the all the wrong reasons. I don't think I could have survived, however, without

Bill Rosenfeld. He offered the greatest gift of any teacher I have ever known, not the generous breadth of his own considerable knowledge but helping me to discover my own. I met my friends through Bill and my future is now linked to my past.

ADRIENNE: *Past* tense. What is over is over. So what if I don't like looking back? I hardly recognize the girl with the long skirt brushing about her ankles and the peasant shirt handmade. She was a poet who still believed that possible. The turbulence of a war in Vietnam wrapped around us even as we insulated ourselves in the forest. A young man in my class read a raw story that jumped off the page, his experience as a former soldier shattering the room. I walked with him once, surprised to find him gone at the end of the semester, a casualty who haunts me if I allow myself to remember. If I remember, I will recall love, not flowery and romantic but sobbing, translucent like the dew drops on the leaves in the Glen. Changed by the experience. If I remember, Kirkland had more than a little to do with who I have become. Confident, unafraid, demanding, decisive, but a human being with a social conscience too rare in the world today.

GABRIELLE: Today I am about to graduate from Hamilton College and walk across the stage, and they're giving me a walking cane? I'm sitting here sweating, and it strikes me as odd how badly I want that stupid cane, how much I want it to be mine. I know it just represents another one of many Hamilton traditions—the ones where men carried those high polished sticks—still, it seems like proof, proof that I, too, can stand amongst them if I choose, that Hamilton is my school, too, an academic institution incapable of simple definition. That or at the very least I'll have the same swanky cane as a bunch of elderly white men—including Ezra Pound. God, my whole family is here, and this graduation speaker is talking about robot wars? I can't believe that I'm almost done with my formal, undergraduate education. It was just moments ago that I was trouncing across campus in the snow. I was just eighteen, making my way through snow drifts past academic halls that towered above me. I would cross the bridge as the path's tiny lights became dimmer and less frequent on the Dark Side, the name a vestige from the Kirkland years that I feel strangely connected to. I know the "dark side" was intended to be insulting, but like reclaiming slang, I feel some sense of pride whenever I say it. I'm going to miss the Dark Side. Those dreadful cement block dorms. I always thought they looked like cozy prison cells. As a freshman, I thought each window looked like it held a different story with charming intellectual characters, characters far different from the story I had grown to know on the other side of the road. There is my freshman year roommate right across stage. She looks healthy—not starving herself anymore, I think. God, freshman year, I thought every Hamilton woman was attempting to starve her body while she fed her mind. I never could have imagined the strength of the women I've met here. The sadness of some, yes, but also the resilience, the fight, the incredible self-assurance they will leave with. The assuring tone of Professor Bruce's voice encouraging the class to read their poems, their "narratives of power" aloud to an all-campus invitee crowd. It was these women who buried my disillusionment with Hamilton. It was these women who represented the great tension of Hamilton, the great success of Kirkland even after she closed her doors. This is truly the secret that only a student here can discover. Woven into this intricate blanket of academia is the fabric of wealthy youth with a powerful underbelly of collective rebellion. The complicated Hamilton of today. The real Hamilton, the one that now has a Kirkland heart. Yeah, I want that cane.

Joanne Papanek Orlando

For many of us in the earlier Kirkland years, the Vietnam War was very much a reality and a worry. Our Hamilton friends went through the draft lottery. For those who would graduate and lose their student defer-ment their numbers meant a great deal. In 1971, the Vietnam Veterans Against the War (VVAW), led by John Kerry, attempted to march from Concord, Massachusetts, to Bunker Hill in a reversal of the march of the British army during the American Revolution. As a young woman, raised in Lexington, I joined them.

To the VVAW (after Lexington)
5/30/71

3 years ago

A march took away

My voice.

Last night

You gave it back.

      (I sang
        "We Shall Overcome"
           Again)

Thank you.

Jo Pitkin

The Lakehouse

A boy and woman. Many days they have taken with them. Somehow when it is written or spoken the dry stalks fold up and don't touch my feet. The boy was very sad and tried opening his mouth for several days, words were staying in, the food he touched dried against his lips and the kiss stayed within. A red morning told him to walk and not stop. And he walked until his legs stayed within and his black hair kept his balance, held him up, until the wind held him up. There was not one small bit of wind, stalk, or hair to hold me up. I began my fall after his. We did not fall together or even discuss it. We were falling separately, not entirely wanting to fall at all. There was the time at the lakehouse. We rowed our boats, not together, out to the farthest points, circled around for a while. We rowed until our oars stayed within the boats. He escaped the flash of a fin under the lake. It was easier than walking or eating. I just wanted to walk. He dreamed that orchids fell on his hair, his breath made orchids. I dreamed there were strangers and was sure we were going to die. Two men found a way to save us. I dream we are together at the lakehouse.

Loss

I have lost a bird. I have lost a tree.
I have lost a city. And a state.

I have lost money. I have lost land
with a blue heron and a green pond.

I have lost flat fields and mountains.
Lost a river. A sea.

I've lost a father, old friends.
A child. A husband.

Now, I must lose the memory of you.
I nearly have it. Your crisp edges slip.

It's almost done. There. No, not quite.

The Mollusk

The mollusk we find in Scituate
where the sea flattens and releases
is not Ponge's oyster but is, as
his is, a world stubbornly closed.

On a far strand bitten with wind,
you pry and pry. That viscous
mass you cannot see does not yield.
Its curved, hinged lid stays shut.

As you clutch its whitish valves,
I see you not as you are, apart,
but as you once were: observant
boy, determined boy, galled boy

scooping, cupping, keeping
the shallows, who will not let
anything go. Not the sharp stalks,
the yellow marsh, the turn of the shore,

not the heavy rope of surf.
Not the awful beautiful
pearl of the possible born of
want, water, grit, salt, luck.

Clare Guzzo Robert

Tea Ball Mind

During my first meditation retreat in 2003, I was intimidated by the tea balls. They hung in little groups, three or four to a hook. They called to me to use them but reminded me that I did not know how. I stuck to tea bags and instant coffee. Thankfully, these required less attention, and no mechanical dexterity.

Tea balls are made of aluminum. Spring-loaded like a large safety pin, the slender wires connect to two little mesh half circles, framed in metal. They face each other to form an airy globe. Pushing the wire handle together will cause the balls to open wide to fill with enough loose tea to brew one cup. This movement requires gentle strength; otherwise the spring will break if forced too hard. It also requires patience and time. To hurry means that tea will be scattered over the counter, perhaps on the floor.

Last February I decided to sit a seven-day retreat, my fifth in as many years. I arrived late, just as the group orientation was ending. When I got to the retreat manager's office to register, I was told to sign up for a yogi job. My past experiences with dishwashing, vacuuming, and pot scrubbing led me to hope for an easy task—dusting, perhaps, or watering the plants. As I looked over the list, the manager said to me, "It's the rule of this retreat that you take the first job offered, and not make a personal choice."

The first job posted was cleaning the tea balls.

I reported for the training as instructed. I was to clean the tea balls after lunch and ready them for the last meal of the day, the five o'clock tea. I was told that it was particularly important that, for this meal, all the tea balls be in place, because so many people would use them at this time of the day.

The next day at lunch, I saw that my fellow worker had not cleaned up the tea balls that had been used between meals. She had done the breakfast ones, but had left me a pile waiting to be cleaned and hung. As I ate my lunch, I was sure that everyone was looking at the tea balls and criticizing me for not having cleaned them.

After the first few days, I saw that if more than half of the tea balls were still unused, I could relax a bit, because that meant that there would be enough for the duration of the meal and I would not have to interrupt my meal to wash them. Each time I passed through the dining hall I would check to see how many used tea balls were piling up, and how many were ready to use. I had tea ball mind for much of the retreat.

When I became aware of what I was doing, I realized that the tea ball was the perfect instrument of mindfulness. All my obsessions about doing a good job were caught up in my practice of washing the tea balls. My perfectionism was full blown. And the physical act of cleaning the tea balls served as a focus for meditation. I could hold my mind on the task of washing, for that was physical. As I sprayed the little leaves of tea out of the ball into the sink, my obsessive mind eased a bit.

Watching my own anxiety rise as people drank tea was also interesting. I could not keep up with the incessant use of tea balls and my desire to have them all hanging neatly in a row. I was helpless to make impermanence permanent. The movement and flow of life was caught up in the little mesh ball on the wire handles.

I willed people to choose instant coffee or tea bags, but they did not hear my silent pleas. Each time I attempted to finish the job, someone else would come by and want a cup of tea. I wanted to say, "Stop, you are messing up my idea of how things should be!"

I began to see the humor of my predicament. I could not stop the tea drinkers, the pile of tea balls, or the flow of time. All of this was out of my hands, despite my desire to control the events happening before my eyes. I had to surrender to the wisdom of the tea ball, the wisdom of impermanence.

At the end of the retreat I asked the kitchen manager if I could take home an old tea ball, as a token. I chose a rusty one, slightly dented. It now sits on my mediation table, a bit battered but elegant, an eloquent reminder. Endlessness, impermanence, the ever present flow of life, thy name is tea ball.

Irma Rosenfeld

Pavane

She had tried to sing
but her voice grew louder
with every rising note.
She did better when she pulled
a string tight between her spaced hands,
single and knifelike, thinning
sound to a whisper.

That small triumph came to her mind
when she contemplated the ladder,
an absurdity filling out
the picture of herself, all weight,
hobbling in an old woman's shoes,
one of these broader than the other
to follow the shape of pain, unbalancing
a solid, housebound woman.

It was time to call the priest;
if he was out, wasting her need
with the merely sick or dead,
she could, in any case, flutter
the pages of her Bible
and stop anywhere.

Instead she settled on a memory
to set beside the melodious,
well-tempered string: a moment
at the Bolshoi Ballet performing

in the high school auditorium,
when she had dreamed
the dancers sat beside her,
equal victims of gravity, fit
to rise only when she did.

The ladder had been there too,
not so much a slip of her mind
as that of a careless janitor.
Climbing it would prove that heaviness
could be beautiful, better than flying,
pulling at her while she went higher
without any shrillness.

Antique

We never knew the relative's name, sex
Or proximity, only that there was some hollow
Opening behind trees, and gates
Beyond the narrow snout of a wolflike dog,
Somewhere perhaps on grounds rich with arrowheads
That some of us had said we found
In public woods; out of that veil
Of privacy had come perhaps the bride,
Perhaps the groom.

                     The rites demanded
The church which old accident had
Placed on a thoroughfare; that brought in
Geography, which took ceremonial
Back to a time before the Roosevelts
Had been dynasty: Old Dutch
Was nothing then, not the manor, the tasteful warp
Of over-aged carpeting, nicks that
Barons and governors had put in undated furniture,
Which was then only private.

                          But the wedding
Went back to the clearing and the publicity
That gods and their children got,
Almost at the vow, for rearing and conceiving.
I never saw the bride and groom; the large audience
Was an accident, the product of rumor,
Behind the store fronts,

                    All on the same street—
The church, the butcher and the school teachers
With double vowelled names rooted
Outside the Episcopalian church
Whose catlike gray and religion
Were almost hidden by the tailored trees,
Whose ministers had names easier for us
To pronounce than our parents' real ones.

When Mrs. Roosevelt came out, all that told us
Was a rustling like the trees around the church,
All that was left to us was wonder
That she had so related herself to us, and then
Evanesced among the chosen few before we stopped
Believing that we also had been invited.

William Rosenfeld

Astronaut

Circling in a strangely certain track
I try to fix on what was once called thing
Out here in place of what we once called space,
Called that to denote lack of any thing
—Denotation is itself a name
Which means to fix, by minds themselves reflections
Of abstracts, lacks, that is, of thing-ness,
Tracks of thought. Space was once not-thing
Between the things we knew to be in fact;

But what was once denoted space is now
Much closer to definitive than this
Essential lack of element in which
I lean, lie, stand, float, an alien
From whatever definiteness once
Seemed true to minds trained truly for an art:
To drift with swiftness far beyond what was,
And take their pleasures jotting on black slates
White tracks of thought which surely did predict
White jets which served to place me where I sit.

And here, with a mind itself so highly trained,
I try to trace my thoughts far back to thing
And fix to it significances where
No old thing now can stand against the new
—Especially where new is not yet true—
And actually fear lest I should fix
A new dimension which itself predicts

Some fearsome need for newness nearly known,
But once known true shall contradict, deploy
The premises which do themselves destroy.

And what when I return, when circling back
In circles smaller, inwardly I move
Toward a world in blackness sadly unillumed
By frequent sunrise, miniature days?
Once there, fixed surely on the orb, on loam,
Will I look back to orbit, where to roam
Through circling thinglessness—will that seem home?

At Shishevo

The words were nothing by themselves. I would buy only one picture, would pay only eighteen instead of thirty-six dinari. Then his look, the abrupt turning up of his eyes, the play of his brows. A striking similarity to the restored Byzantine frescoes I had come to see in this remote Yugoslav monastery. I had of course read much before coming to Macedonia, so I knew something of the suffering imposed by the conquering Turks, and then the Bulgars, to say nothing of resisting the Nazis during World War II. If I needed an image to capture the combination of suffering and endurance, I found it in his face. "Only one?" In that instant I wished that I had purchased both pictures, spent the extra dollar. But, ironically, by withholding the dollar, I had paid for the agonizing expression. "Ah, yes. You will come again, buy more next time."

"But of course."

He and I were both sure of it, just as certain as he was about the dates he attributed to the original frescoes, even though he was approximately one century off. And the names of the saints adjacent to the Virgin Mary "on her dead couch," as he put it.

"Sveti—you say Sent—Sent George is here. Here Sent Michael. This is Sveti Grigor . . ." What did it matter? I couldn't read the Old Cyrllic print above their respective heads anyway, couldn't fully make out their countenances, and even less so the other figures that ascended into the shadows toward the top of the little dome, from where Jesus looked down with that peculiarly Byzantine sternness of the Father's Son, the Judge. A fixture was centered in the forehead to hold the long lantern chain—I remembered it distinctly from the catalogue I had examined earlier. Standing there, of course, I couldn't see all that because the scaffolding was still in place to aid the restoring artists, and no one was working, this being February and cold, and the lamp chain detached. The hewn timbers of the scaffolding, parallels and cross braces, cast fusing shadows, a counterpoint to the tight curves of the inner dome. Those shadows and interposing timbers ensured an obscurity growing upward to the center of the dome. It was appropriate to the mystery of faith—knowing what is up there without quite being able to make it out.

"You must come back in May. Then they will let you climb up to see their progress." I gasped at the audacity of his proposal, actually to climb up into that shadowy dome with no special dispensation, directly toward the brow of Christ.

"Well, but of course." I lied for the sake of being kind. Even if my inclination to return had been stronger, something else happened along my retreat from that tight notch of a valley that made any thought of return impossible, not because of legality but of delicacy.

He walked out of the church with me and waited while I scanned the valley. From no one spot could I see its entire length. I examined the most distant point observable on the opposite valley wall. I could have stared at any one spot, and yet I knew that others just as inviting awaited examination. I fantasized climbing to some, to niches exactly right for perching a lean-to, accessible only by a difficult path, for a place to read, to think, alone. Never mind how to get water up there or the other fundamental comforts. Never mind what other persons might pass by. I drew in one great breath and let it out slowly as I scanned the ridge to what looked like a brief landslide opposite where we stood.

"Is that a wall?"

"You might want to visit Sveti Nikola, too."

"Oh?"

"It's just there. Where you are looking. You cannot see the buildings from here."

"What's it like? Is the church similar to this?"

"Oh, well, it is not so rich in its frescoes. I think not. But, you know, you might wish to go."

He was straining to be fair. But there it was on an inviting ridge that had supported my recent reverie. I am certain that originally the two monasteries were all but inaccessible to each other, let alone to the outside regions. For that reason, no doubt, their holders had built them in this place—"To flee the Turk!" Still, why two in such proximity? Had they communicated more readily back then or had tradition passed down the reticence of my present informant?

"Is the monastery active?" I looked over my shoulder at the former dormitory of Sveti Andrea, now a modest cafe.

"Oh, well, yes. But mainly people wait to go there until summer. There is a small cafe, very small."

"Can one stay there? I mean on a visit, for a few days?"

"Oh, I think. But now is not comfortable. Too cold, you know. The rooms, they are not, you know, not heat."

"And there is a path?"

"Oh, yes. Very steep. Is better to go by Shishevo, by the bell-tower path."

"That's the village across? Below the dam?"

"Yes, yes."

"What's there?"

"Oh, it's nothing. A small place. Nothing."

I remembered it as more, like the several I had seen in these Macedonian mountains. The usual random pattern of orange tiled roofs and white stuccoed walls, the handsome minaret standing as it usually did in these villages, the proportions always just right, and the mosque at its base nearly always just right.

I didn't recall the bell tower, but on my way back below the dam I made it out. The sun was full on both of them, the minaret centered in the village and the bell tower, topped with a cross, at the slope of the valley entrance. The village lay along broad, tillable bottom land, its edgemost houses slanting up the easy hillside. Thus both the tower and minaret took a full day of glare whenever the sun broke through the clouds that wound about the highest slopes and gave the region its beauty and its mood. Should I take the path up there, or had I enough recollections to carry away? I had many more famous landmarks to visit. Yet, what a temptation, and what would a slight change in itinerary matter? I might gain much.

In five minutes I reached the turn-off for Shishevo. I pulled to the roadside to examine the bridge across the River Treska. A troupe of cyclists passed, grown men pedalling home from work. All looked at me. In my recollection, their curiosity seems refreshing, but at the time their stares strapped me to my seat. Being in the car, I had courage enough to give a nod to the middle of the group. None acknowledged it. I was wax to them, I suppose, from which anything like a gesture was inappropriate. When they took in the fact that I had stared back, had actually volunteered a communication, they reset their gazes on the ordinary business of negotiating the deep ruts and ridges of the roadway. Their reactions and the road condition discouraged me, but I felt assured of a special summons to get up to Sveti Nikola, so I pulled onto the bridge and trailed after the cyclists. Their pace was fine, for I needed to deliberate every ten feet to avoid gouging the bottom of my rented auto.

Across the bridge, the cyclists swung right into a lane of poplars. My concentration on the road and the pace of the cyclists had filled about twenty minutes of manipulating steering wheel, clutch, and brake. The bicycle pack dissolved into the several village streets. Just as suddenly what had been a travelogue composition of tiled roofs became lifesize peasant actualities, a series of lots and layers, mud-brick walls with whitewash yielding to springtime splatterings and other eroding forces. Up close the white walls turned pale-dung. The car began to fishtail across the slippery ruts and growl through the heavy mud channels. I rocked and slid past gateways that opened into courtyards and a medieval arrangement of porches, hanging laundry, woven grain cribs, tool sheds, huge harvest baskets on donkey carts, and an appropriate mixture of pigs, geese, oxen, donkeys, and dogs.

Even my steering wheel seemed to slide through my fingers, and I rolled up my window against the mixed fumes. Children, adults, and livestock examined me. They surely would know anyone or thing that had a place in the village, and more than a notion struck me that I was stranger to them than they were to me. As I entered their view, they simply stopped whatever they were doing. When I passed groups, all eyes followed me, as though orchestrated. I felt no hostility in the stares but I knew that more than simple curiosity directed those eyes—the arrested postures, the open mouths. Had I been watching a screening of this journey projected from the anonymity of a TV set, I should have thought "Fascinating! Imagine such villages still existing." But here the gap was closed. The houses, their mustiness, the grainy surfaces, the sucking mud, the people slogging through, all were there directly with me. More than that, the scene itself was not the focus of attention. I was.

This village was at the road's end, the reason for the existence of these unlikely potholes and ruts, the eyes and the arrested postures. They set the limits of my conscious universe. Staring and being stared at closed out any speculation or communication other than Who? Why?

Weaving among these perceptions, my own phantom voice told me, "Turn around. Go back to the main road." At the next wide spot, I would stop, shift, back around, shift ahead, and leave. Toward the end of the next wall I thought I saw my clearing. But at the corner it narrowed to a recess behind which the mosque arose. From its base the minaret shot past the top of my windshield. I automatically stooped forward to see its top, at which instant a cluster of old men in long black coats and pinched pant-cuffs emerged, as if hewn from the deep shadow of the doorway. Then their white-wound heads picked up the sunlight and each became an individual. All moved with shoulders rounded from bearing centuries of piety through low doorways. I was immediately aware that my posture over the steering wheel approximated theirs, although mine was bent from travelogue curiosity. But more than this superficial similarity joined us. Again it was eyes. Whatever they had been talking about was stopped, and as they stood, so did they stare at me, some straight ahead, others sharply over their shoulders, and as they stared, their shoulders rounded more. And even more intensely, I felt the split consciousness of observing and being observed.

I recall that group of ancient worshippers as a handsome picture. But during the actual experience I calculated that in order to turn the car I would need to steer directly toward them. Plenty of room but psychically impossible. So I straightened in my seat, shifted gears and kept driving past, my eyes ahead, theirs still on me. For all I remember of it, the next span of the road was smooth. I do know that I tried hard to concentrate on my destination, which seemed inaccessible only because I could not remember what it was. At the next bend I remembered that I was looking for a place to turn the car. A large, open slope marked the end of the village, and as I turned up toward it, my original intention returned with the image of the bell tower and at its base the path leading to the valley wall beyond.

The tower was simple, two vertical beams of wood with a shorter one between them at the top holding the bell, and a wooden cross rising from that. I stopped again to examine the cross and a pattern leapt into my mind—it proved to be wrong later. The cross appeared to me to be of Roman form. Then the reticence of the custodian at Sveti Andrea, "Oh nothing, a small place, nothing. Not as nice, I think, as this." The penetrating stares of the villagers, the Muslim worshippers. Now they seemed hostile. And why not? Sveti Andrea is Orthodox. Here in the village are the "Turks," and ahead the Roman Catholic monastery of Sveti Nikola. From their mutually excluding commitments, why should any of these worshippers encourage a tourist to visit the others? What might any of them be willing to communicate to the others except "Stay away!" And what was I? Each of them might wonder. What symbol fixed in any landscape, dull or dramatic as theirs, had a rightful claim on the loyalty of my soul? I did not, after all, know what I wanted here, where I was going. Up there? Among the rocks, like a mock Levite, to seek some belief? Perhaps, but was I well enough attuned to others who knew the value of being left alone in their landscapes, at various levels, various depths, like those remarkable museum-case landscapes of mountain sheep poised ten thousand feet above the base eighteen inches below? Very likely that was it, the safety and comfort of a foreshortened panorama, enough to engage my wonder without disturbing my picnic piety.

Finally the whole business came down to a tourist who knew a little from guide books, who had a passing good liberal education, and who needed to fabricate some dignified justification for gawking at people whose real interests and innocence prevailed.

And appropriately enough, the children ushered the truth. They were playing near the bell tower, and when they heard an auto engine in this unlikely place, they came to investigate. The oldest, a girl, led the others not only up to the car but against it with their simple wanting to know. Her face stopped two or three inches from mine, the glass between us. The others peered from along the fender, through the rear window, some from behind her. All were on my side of the car. Only their eyes moved. My hat, my face, my sweater, the jacket next to me on the seat, my hands, back to my face. If asked what they looked like, how they dressed, I would have to answer, "Well, like villagers, in the peasant mode." Intent on making my visit seem like no extraordinary thing. I pretended to concentrate on the tower.

When the girl spoke it was my turn to stare. She repeated something and the others chanted it, until the words separated and became comprehensible. "Od kade ste?" I was finally certain enough to answer. "America!" I watched for a reaction. The others looked at the girl, and I continued my role in the catechism, "America! American. Jas sum Ainerikanetz." Still I could take hold of no response in them. The entire encounter took little time, if measured that way, but in my recollection each detail is deliberate. The leader took her eyes off mine, looked at my mouth, straightened and looked at the bell tower, back to my eyes. Then she turned her head—not her eyes—and commanded no one in particular. I couldn't catch her words but she obviously sent them to notify others—children, some adult? "Come! Quickly! A stranger in an automobile! An American!" I would have to wait to see. Or I could merely drive away.

But as the children ran off toward the houses, someone else approached. Two men walked along the road I had recently driven, and the children who waited at the car parted for their approach. The younger of the men was perhaps thirty-five. His boots came down firmly on the uneven ground as he supported the ancient man at his side. With the last two steps, the younger man removed his hat and pressed it against the rope that bunched the top of his black woolen trousers. His other hand held the old man's elbow. The old man had been to Mecca, as signified by his privileged wearing of the white winding on his fez. As he stooped further to look at me, I could see that he had enough of a task simply to turn his head. His eyes were still clear. His skin was marvelously weathered, and the many lines across his brow joined into ruts that curled past his cheek bones, deepened along the sides of his nose, and played out in the spare flesh under his open mouth. Behind his diminished lips, his teeth were worn to brown stubs, and the question of his breath made me realize at once that I was protected by the closed window. But here was one for whom I must roll down the cold, transparent partition. How deep and secret a cavern my gesture opened to him I can never truly suppose. But the significance of my presence and my own monumental uncertainty struck me then as it had not earlier. As with the children, I had nothing to offer him except to answer his guide's inquiry with "America." He kept his eyes on me. He seemed to attach some echo to the word. America! As if hidden in it were the faintest clue of some purpose that loomed from below their valley but remained a mere breath further than their grasp.

169

From America! His cogitation seemed palpable as he ran his eyes along the ceiling of my car. The gesture vibrated with his pondering. "What has come to us? On this beautiful day, what has God appointed me to discover for my people in Shishevo? From America!"

Now, I expect that I was as wrong about that as about everything else, without the slightest grounds for such a construction except my self-appointment. I was merely unusual. If food for surmise were to be furnished this old man, his assistant, and especially the children, then they deserved more than such a flawed visitation. Perhaps if I had reached Sveti Nikola. . . . But even that last murmur of special significance died without the slightest reverberation. So I shifted gears, strained a smile, raised my hand, "Hvala," and pulled away from all of them. Why I thanked them, I don't know.

When one of the ruts in the road scraped the car's muffler, I realized that I was driving from the village with less care than when I had entered. But my deposit and the insurance would cover that. I had to get back to the hotel, pack, and continue on to the coast, stick to my itinerary.

During the drive back to Skopje, I began to regret my abrupt departure, let alone my abandonment of the impulse to climb to Sveti Nikola. Perhaps I could adjust my schedule, drive back there tomorrow with some sort of gift, some memento of my visit. What might be appropriate? A picture of myself? Something more readily identifiable as typically American, something through which I might represent my own countrymen. A book. But who could read it? Money? More accessible to translation, but ephemeral. Surely someone might be found to translate a brief note of appreciation. "Dear . . ." Who? What? But I was already entering the acrobatic traffic of Skopje. Better left with what we had among us—that old man, his guide, the children. Each of us can go on designing previsions of what it all might have meant. On the flight to Dubrovnik I opened my phrase book to: TRAVEL WITHIN THE HOST COUNTRY. III. Around the Countryside: "What village is this?" *Koi selo.* . . . "Have you a restaurant?" *Dali e imate ristorant?* "Your village is beautiful." *Vashyot selo e ubavo.*

Deborah Ross

Frommer's Historical Guide to
Upstate New York

This past July, my boyfriend, Dan, won the famous Boilermaker 15K race in Utica, New York. Amazing, really, considering that this race is always won by the same three Africans, who are always so far ahead of everyone else that it's hard to even think of them as participating in the same event as the others, who by comparison look like some obsolete version of humanity—Persons 97 or 2003. My boyfriend isn't one of these Africans; he's a sort of Person XP: still functional for most applications, if you don't mind waiting a bit.

Okay, the truth is, when I say Dan won the Boilermaker, I don't mean he was actually running. He hasn't run in any race or marathon for over ten years: too hard on the knees. I'm talking purely about his performance as a spectator. A bunch of us were there watching this race in order to cheer on our old friend Peter, who does it nearly every year. From past experiences, Peter had a pretty good idea about what time he would pass the corner of Oneida Street and the Parkway, where he had told us to stand. What he hadn't told us was what he would be wearing, or how massively he would be surrounded by almost identical sweaty middle-aged men. Nor had he been able to tell us, because he didn't know, that because it was extra hot and muggy that day, and because he hadn't trained very seriously, he would decide fairly early on that walking was fine, that he deserved applause just for showing up, and that therefore he would pass our corner about an hour later than planned. Imagine one of those Where's Waldo pages, only animated, and without the telltale red striped shirt, and that's what it was like trying to find Peter before it was too late to cheer. There we were, scanning the faces on this side and that side of the street as runners passed, slower and slower as the race dragged on, which was helpful, but also in bigger, more homogeneous-looking clumps (nakeder, wetter, redder in the face), which was not. We didn't dare blink, our necks and backs got strained and sunburned—my God, that was one tough race! We were all so exhausted afterwards we had to take a nap. (Peter, on the other hand, showered, went to a family picnic, then drove five hours home to Brooklyn, got up the next morning, and went to work.) But Dan was the hero, the first among us to spot Peter in the crowd, to catch him just in time so we could all yell "Hey!" What stamina!

This performance was impressive in part because even at the time I could see that it would not be only Peter I would be desperately seeking during this trip. It was all a big strain on the recognition software, an extended exercise in finding things that for one reason or another didn't look the way they were supposed to. I was born in Utica but have lived most of my adult life in Hawaii, having moved here when I was still too young to realize that I would need to go back from time to time, and that not being on a fast track to wealth, I probably wouldn't be able to. This was my first return trip in ten years, and the first time Dan had ever been there. Peter, with his five brothers and their children and grandchildren all still concentrated between Albany and Buffalo (we often tease him about the great Evans diaspora), often has a reason to drive up for a weekend. But most of our friends are long and far gone, along with the stores and restaurants and bars of our youth.

Why have I felt so starved for these places, especially now that I supposedly live in paradise? One plausible answer is that people have to revisit the past to see where they went wrong—and most of us do assume, for some reason, that we probably missed a turn somewhere onto some better path. My first step down the wrong road must have happened in Utica, which must be why in my sleep I so often go back to retrace my steps, perhaps toddling up and down the aisles of the old Grand Union grocery store, where I must have once lost my mother, and looking up over the butcher's counter at the giant decorative cow horns, which some jocular adult had told me had come from the proverbial "bum steer." The Grand Union and its whole little shopping center has passed on, but on this trip, dragging Dan with me, I walked over its bones as, searching for signs, I literally trod the two miles of sidewalk leading from the house I lived in until age 13 to the slightly more upscale neighborhood we then moved to. Sure enough, as I looked at the almost familiar houses—closer than they used to be to the derelict and boarded up emblems of a town with plenty of real estate but not much capital—and tried to see them as they were when the Bensons and the Freeds and the Davises and the Tofolos lived there—the former colors, the different gardens, without the added-on attics or garages—I did find the specific place where I think my parents went wrong; the block where things began to look newer and "nicer" but not really better.

But that's their story. What I needed to discover was what went wrong once I was old enough, allegedly, to choose my own path. For this I would need to find Utica 1972, which of course no longer exists. Or does it? Isn't it there, under Utica 2011, waiting to be excavated? This was the task that lay before me: to stare at the present hard enough to make it reveal, like an upside-down rake in a tree in a Hidden Pictures puzzle, some partially remembered vestige of the past. It would probably have been easier to run the Boilermaker.

Guidebooks in this regard are useless. We had plenty of those, and maps, since Dan always likes to be prepared. But how, where, do you look up the name of that mall of factory outlet stores that used to be in that refurbished old cannery somewhere in East Utica? The place is full of malls that everyone thought would breathe new life into the dying economy by attracting people from nearby dying towns; malls that were a great sensation for a few years and soon had few stores and fewer customers. Unless you're with one of the village elders, you have no way of recalling the names of these shopping centers or even where they were, though you will sometimes see a sign someone forgot to remove leading to an empty lot or to a new loop back onto the freeway. Peter knew the outlet mall I was trying to think of—Charlestown—though apparently it went under more than a decade ago. But Peter had his own anxieties about memory and our vanishing past. He has been trying for years to find someone to verify a glimpse he thought he had in the late sixties of a concentration camp mark on the arm of the father of our old acquaintance Jeffrey L. I couldn't help and couldn't even think of anyone else still alive who would know. This is the problem. The village elders are, well, pretty eld at this point and can't be expected to pop out names like Charlestown much longer.

My best human resource on this trip was my Uncle Stu, a living chronicle of Utica big and small businesses from the days of my grandfather's dry goods store to the present: where each one used to be, where they moved to, when they closed, how the owner of this one was related to the owner of that one, on and on. He's especially good at restaurants; the whole family, what's left of them, in fact talk about little else. Our first night in town, Dan and I were invited to dinner with Uncle Stu and Aunt Lois, along with Stu's sister, Aunt Elinor, and found ourselves immersed in a seemingly perpetual discussion—with an occasional historical side-gloss for the benefit of outsiders—about which is the best Greek or Italian restaurant, what you should and should not order where, where Tuesday is a bad night, where the chicken is always dry, whose sauces all taste the same, whose owner or manager or waiter or waitress knows the family and honors them with their best tablecloth.

The most useful piece of information I gleaned from all this dizzying dialogue is that the Tony's restaurant where I used to eat often as a kid has now moved to, of all places, Lenox Ave. in West Utica, where probably no Italian has ever lived, and that it's still the best place to get cheap, authentic, tasty Italian food. Before we left we did indeed take the family to dinner at Tony Speragna's, which really did seem to have landed in a foreign country, next door to and across the street from crowds of bewildered non-Italian children on buckling wooden porches, watching bug-eyed as extended families with high-heeled grandmothers got out of Oldsmobiles and Chryslers, carefully locking them, to go in and celebrate someone's birthday or anniversary. And we got to join in and even hold our own in a conversation about whether the hat-shaped pasta was better at Tony's or at Grimaldi's, where we had been advised not to go because a waiter there was once unkind to Aunt Lois, but where we naively believed we had had a very good meal.

Unfortunately, Uncle Stu is considerably elder even than Peter and myself, and it worries me that there is no written chronicle of everything he knows. What Utica needs is something in guidebooks that doesn't just tell you where things are, but also where they used to be, and what's there now instead. Niagara Falls, now, they know what I'm talking about. Tourists there are bound to feel that almost everything listed in the brochures and commemorated with plaques hasn't actually been there for years. The celebrated Cave of the Winds, for example, is a "sight" not to be missed on any trip to the Falls, though I believe no one now living has ever seen an actual cave at this locale. The whole place, spectacular enough as it really is, you would think, is plastered all over with pictures of its former self.

Utica needs to develop a similar historical self-image—all the more for its lack of any present splendor. What we need is a guidebook that combines the attributes of the *Oxford English Dictionary* and *Videohound's Golden Retriever*, with its exhaustive alphabetical cross-lists, to enable searching any attraction present or past not only by its name but by the name of the proprietor (in case one can remember only that the person who owned it was the brother-in-law of the Bosnian refugee that used to clean Aunt Elinor's house), or key word (in case one can remember only that it contained a display about the history of cheese). Still, I suppose even a tome of the magnificence of the *OED*, complete with magnifying glass, wouldn't be able to include minor exhibits such as Jeffrey L.'s father, so even the most scholarly of tourists to Utica would still have to spend a lot of time driving around in rental cars, staring, trying to sort out the new from the merely misremembered, the deterioration on the outside from the deterioration in their insides.

As kids none of us would ever have imagined how hard this could be. We could see things adults couldn't then, effortlessly, even unwillingly. On this last trip I drove past my grandparents' former house and from the road I could not quite make out, except in my mind's eye, Papa's former rock garden in back that once led to a screened-in porch containing stacked up musty lawn chairs and rusty tables. No one ever sat out there. My cousins and I knew it was haunted and never went around that side of the house, even though it was the shortest way to the living room. We knew it was haunted because we had once or twice caught glimpses there of our grandmother's ghost (though Nana was still very much alive). Officially this specter was the cleaning lady, but we knew she was really Nana's ghost because she had the same first name, Florence, but was much, much thinner and paler. We knew it, but we knew enough not to say anything about it.

Late one afternoon, I was sitting on the carpet in the living room, building walls out of old mah jong tiles, when I suddenly heard a loud, low moan outside the window. The adults didn't react; evidently they couldn't hear ghosts any more than they could see them. But then it came again, and it was so clearly the kind of sound that was real to grown-ups that I had to ask about it. My grandfather—probably, now that I think about it, also the source for my "bum steer" in the Grand Union—explained that it was the sound of a camel crying, because the last straw had just broken its back. Once again, the joke was lost on me. I'd never heard either the cliché or the voice of the wind through big trees, and so I could only conclude he was serious. And sure enough, when I looked out, past the haunted porch, just over the rock garden, I saw a huge camel spread out over the horizon, its head lowered in misery.

I was horrified beyond endurance at the thought of this animal's agony. Yet my parents were completely unconcerned. Something was obviously wrong here. Either adults were heartless, soulless monsters, or this was some different kind of camel whose pain didn't matter for some reason—a symbolic camel, maybe. And so, I decided, it had to be the one on the cigarette package. And to this day, whenever I hear a moaning wind, I see the humps of that big old gold camel against the skyline, as real as the Ko'olau Mountains.

At some point during my childhood—after the onset of puberty, it must have been—it got a lot harder to see things, even when they

175

were right in front of me. Although I have missed Utica horribly ever since I left, I can't say I was happy there. I was just uneasy anywhere else, like a blind person who wants to stay in her own house where she won't trip over the furniture. Near the end of my years there it began to seem to me that my friends were so bored that they rejoiced in other people's misfortunes, including mine, like the Bible salesman in Flannery O'Connor's "Good Country People" bragging about his collection of wooden legs and glass eyes. I started noting a tendency among people from my high school to commit spectacular suicides— driving down Genesee Street at 100 mph and crashing into a building, or blowing their brains out in a public rest room—and began to wonder how the others had pressured them into providing them with this sensational entertainment. I should have been glad to escape such a city of cannibals or vampires, as I began to imagine it. Yet after I left I never stopped boring my friends in Hawaii with complaints of homesickness and nostalgia.

Near the end of this last visit, Dan and I went to see my old friend Bob. Bob had always been there. I'd known him in high school, and still saw him all the time even after graduation, since I chose to go to college only ten miles away. He hung around with nearly every significant boyfriend in my life, and at least knew those less significant. When no boyfriend was present to contradict him in our habitual bars, he liked to imply that we were together. He was the best man at my first wedding. He introduced me to the disastrous boyfriend after my first divorce. In short, the melodrama of my Utica life could hardly have gone on without his sardonic face looking on, or looking down, from atop his skinny, six-three frame. He was an historic landmark, like the Bank with the Gold Dome, defining the downtown skyline.

Nevertheless, I was nearly at the end of this last trip before I went to see him. I couldn't make up my mind. When I finally decided to call it was too late to hide the fact that I had been in no hurry, so he was understandably lukewarm about having me and Dan drop over for a chat, though he did agree to receive us. We sat on the couch in his living room and heard news about his new girlfriend and looked at pictures of her house. We heard about how he had bought the building that used to be his father's hobby shop and converted it into the apartment we were sitting in and one for his sister and her dogs upstairs. We heard about his nieces and their majors and their jobs. At one point there was a pause, and Dan, whom Bob had never seen before, said, "And so, Deborah, why don't you tell Bob what *you've* been doing?" I couldn't think of anything to say, and Bob asked no questions of either of us, and after about fifteen minutes, we left. In the car, Dan remarked, "Your friend Bob isn't really interested in you."

Once again, Dan had won the race: he was the first to spot the truth in that confusing landscape of names and faces from my old life. And as I thought about it, I realized, what he had said was true of almost everyone I chose to spend time with during my last years in Utica, people who even at the time I was aware didn't really like me. Bob, for instance, had not only introduced me to Boyfriend Disaster. He had watched me sit on the floor and be fed from his plate, like a dog, a few scraps of the breakfast I'd been awakened at 3 a.m. to cook for him and his friends. He had kept quiet about the fact that everyone but me knew this man was cheating. Then, when I was finally dumped, he had made a grab for one of my breasts himself, just for the heck of it.

Not everyone in Utica treated me this way. My cousin Rick had admired my singing voice so much he wanted to record it. My aunt Lois, his mom, had taken the trouble to show me how to make truly invisible blind hems. And Peter, hero of the Boilermaker, had once cheered me up at a ninth-grade party, when the boy I liked wouldn't notice me, by putting on James Taylor's "You've Got a Friend." It should also be noted that Peter's response to the detonation of Boyfriend Atomic Bomb, unlike Bob's, was to sweep me off into the mountains and onto a canoe on the lake and let me talk, talk, talk him to death.

Why, then, did I spend so much time trying to get people who just weren't interested to listen, to look at me? Why did I go to a college so close to home that I wouldn't have to deal with nice, new people, and could just keep hitchhiking back every weekend to the same old rat holes? Couldn't I tell the difference between a head-on and a sidelong glance, between eyes full of interest or concern and the back of a head? At least on this trip some instinct prompted me to delay Bob. On the other hand, it was a thrill to see Peter, on our very first morning in town, when he called my cell as he and his partner, Jim, were getting off the Thruway and within ten minutes had joined us for breakfast—at a new restaurant, one recommended unanimously by Aunt Elinor, Aunt Lois, and Uncle Stu. And they, too, I felt sure, had been really glad to see me after all these years. It showed in their faces. Maybe my eyesight was finally improving.

On our last day in Utica, Dan and I went to the zoo with my old friend Dorothy. Her life over the last thirty years couldn't be more different from mine: living near the transcendental meditation center in Fairfield, Iowa, spending as much time as possible in the still space between breaths—a space I avoid by keeping my mind as busy as possible. We still connect, though, through mutual respect for each other's way of being, and a shared, hopeless, Will-and-Grace sort of devotion to Peter. So she was willing to time her annual visit to her mother and sister (and Peter and Jim) to meet up with me and Dan.

The zoo had changed quite a bit in ten years. They had put in a nature trail with cages in the woods for pheasants and wolves and even a rare snow leopard. So natural were the habitats that these animals were nearly impossible to spot. We watched a few family groups stop in front of an enclosure, pause a while, and move on, not saying but allowing each other to believe that they had seen something. It was like the Emperor's New Zoo. Once again, Dan was the first in our group to locate and point out every hidden creature behind the logs and foliage.

There was a new lookout, where we could see all of Utica far below, nestling familiarly in the Mohawk Valley just like on a map, the old red brick buildings from this distance hardly showing their crumble. As we stood there marveling at the long view, I glanced directly down and saw—I swear—an enormous camel. It was the mother of the smaller one we had seen earlier in the petting zoo, which itself was as big as a full-grown horse, and with the added effects of vertigo and foreshortening, it was truly the biggest animal I had ever seen, bigger even than the elephant fought over by the six blind men in the story. But this one, stretched out on the ground, humps glowing golden against the late afternoon sky, was real—as real as the Adirondack Mountains, or the face of a friend.

Betty Sarvey Salek

from *The Fish in the Mirror*

"The town of Lac was not always as it is now, son. . . . So much has changed. . . . Now only the fountain is left."

"Where did the fountain come from?" Seth had asked his father many years ago.

"Not from Lac, son. In Elder times, Lac was not a land alone. Another land adjoined it. The Land of Mirror. The way between the two lands was called a Leak. Leaks looked like a blank spot within a house. But if you put your head or any part of your body into the Leak, you would be sucked into Mirror—a land of the greatest, unimaginable glory of colors and scents and sounds and shapes. Our family has kept the secret through many an age. According to legend, Mirrorii, as Mirror's inhabitants were called, were basically people. But whatever they imagined themselves to be at any given moment, that is the form they took. The word 'fate' was unknown to them.

"This is what most set them apart from the people of Lac. For in Lac, the wizard Cim controlled the destiny of each person. So they resigned themselves to being what they appeared to be, or rather what Cim told them to be.

"Your great-great-great grand uncle Lucius began to wonder aloud why Mirrorii could be whatever they liked and Lacii were only allowed to be whatever they were. When Cim eventually lost control of the Lacii, he blamed Lucius along with the Mirrorii.

"His fury swelled each day until it erupted into a terrible chant, a spell that took poor Lucius. One minute Lucius was sitting at the fountain, the next, there was a splash and Lucius was no more.

"Then Cim chanted out three more spells. The first called all Lacii back to their homes. It then weakened the Mirrorii and allowed him to force them back into their own land.

"The second spell made the Leaks impenetrable so the creatures were locked into Mirror and out of Lac.

"The third gave the Mirror people the task of mimicking the actions of the Lacii on the other side of the closed-up Leaks—what we now call 'mirrors.'

"But imagination holds more powerful magic than any the wizard could work. Little by little, the Mirrorii will regain their old ways. They will break through the barriers. I fear they will reenter Lac with anger in their hearts, prepared to do battle with those they have been forced to mimic. My bones tell me the time is near. Your destiny is entwined with theirs, Seth, and you need to prepare. A fish will appear to swim through the Royal Mirror, announcing the Mirrorii's return."

Seth had been unable to understand what difference he could possibly make in a struggle between a wizard and these strange creatures called Mirrorii.

"As the Appointed One, it might be your responsibility to protect the town."

Seth had been frightened and fascinated by this tale. The retelling of it over and again through the years had not lessened the wonderment and anxiety which filled him each time. *Responsibility* his father had said. But Seth wasn't sure what that really meant. And how was one boy to protect an entire village?

Because the Seatons had no mirror in their tiny home, Seth's fascination had grown. Like forbidden fruit, he could not shake his desire to touch a mirror; to have a mirror. Even as a young boy, Seth had seen the Royal Mirror from time to time and had looked into his own reflection, furtively, studying the two different colors of his eyes while trying to hide his curiosity. Hamlin's stories seemed almost absurd when Seth faced his perfect reflection. Had he actually been looking at another person, locked behind the glass?

"If I were a Mirrori and had to mimic someone, I would be so furious I'd smash through that mirror-door." Seth realized that he had been staring at his reflection in the water. A fish surfaced, did a little flip-flop, and dove to the bottom of the pool. The fish had a silvery stripe running down its back, just as the legend described great-great-great-grand uncle Lucius the fish. "Hello, Lucius," Seth whispered. So many strange things hid beneath the surface of this world. The appearance of this fish Seth accepted as one of them.

The one question his father had never been able to answer was why their house had no mirror.

"Why are we different?" Seth burned to know. It wasn't exactly that he wanted to be like the other Lacii. Their lives seemed so meaningless.

Yet, he was lonely. No Lacii ever talked to him. When they bought produce from the Seatons' market stall, they looked askance at Seth, as though his oddness would wear off on them if they came too close. He heard their whispers about the uncomely lad whose face was too rounded, whose eyes were too bright. He saw them sign themselves against the "evil eye" which some feared when they discovered the blue and brown. Some wore an almond strung around their neck when they came to buy from him, hoping to protect themselves from any evil magicks his eyes might cast. So he had learned to keep his eyes lowered, shielded from their view, hiding his strangeness.

"This legacy, is it so much more important than I am myself, that it does not matter if I am happy now?" he had once asked his father.

"Oh yes, Seth. So much more important than you alone. You must put the greater good ahead of your own happiness and desires."

One recent day, when he glanced up at the palace from his fountain perch, he caught a glimpse of a figure in a vaulted window on the third floor. The figure appeared to be a maiden and Seth could feel her gaze upon him. It felt different from the cold stares of the market shoppers: full of curiosity, but in a friendly way, as though she might almost reach out and touch his shoulder. She didn't smile. Lacii never did. But Seth felt radiating from her a wistfulness, a sad longing—reflecting his own. After the third day that he saw her watching, Seth began to pretend they were friends. But this made him lonelier still. He wondered who she was and if she was as lonely as he.

Seth's visits to the fountain were no longer casual. During the past month, he had tried to spend at least a few minutes there every day. He had loved the marble fountain boy and the sound of the water splashing into the basin from the moment he had first seen it as a baby; but this was different. Now he had a reason for being there.

It was exactly one full moon ago that Seth had encountered the fish with the silvery stripe down his back. And it was exactly two days after that, on his next visit to the fountain, that he had seen *her*.

"Just a wave would do," he said to the fish. His curiosity about the maiden in the turret window was like a flame burning him from within. "Who is she?" Gazing up at the turret window, he thought how like a hummingbird she was. Yes, there she was, like every other day of this entire moon. Motionless. Gazing back down at him. Turning toward the fish, Seth said, "She's wearing a mask, you know. But one of these days, Lucius, she's going to let it fall. Then I'll know who she really is.

"I wonder why she's up there." Seth sighed. "And why she doesn't come down. Perhaps she's a princess. No, she doesn't have the look about her. Not that I know what a princess should look like. Just . . . not like her. Even at this distance . . . oh, I don't know." Seth trailed off in his thoughts as the fish flipped into the air and splashed into the pond, sending a series of ripples over Seth's trailing fingers. The boy glanced down at the water and when he returned his attention to the window, she was gone.

"She has a spark of . . . I don't know what, Lucius. Curiosity?—try though she might to hide it." Even at this distance, he could tell that she had a different look about her. And Seth knew by now that she watched, waiting for him to come, then covertly studied him while feigning indifference.

Looking away from the window at last, Seth bent toward the fountain. "Goodbye, Uncle Lucius," he whispered. "I'll be back tomorrow." The fish flipped its tail out of the water, splashing Seth. Seth almost forgot himself and laughed, but at the last instant tightened his mouth into a straight line and assumed his mask of anonymity. He turned away and headed down the path which skirted the village market.

Shortly, he realized he had forgotten his basket and had to return to the fountain. Looking up, he caught a glimpse of her, peeking from the side of the window. His heart skipped a beat and inside, his smile returned.

Once Seth had made his way out of the village and was beyond the wall, he breathed deeply of the fresh, scented air. He filled his lungs with it and dispelled the stale air of Lac within the wall. "The girl in the window must smell like this," he thought. Why did he feel such a kinship to this maiden? Other maids made him feel nothing but discomfort. This maiden, though . . . this one tormented him with her staring eyes and fascinated him with her falsely blank face.

"That's it! The mask. No one else disguises themselves that way." Seth was sure the maiden masked her true self as she looked out at him, even though she had never revealed another. In the village, Seth did what he needed to blend in, to keep the Lacii from discovering that he was not like them. If the maiden also blanked out her personality, then she too must have something to hide.

Seth had sat too long at the fountain. The shadows cast by the honeysuckle and goldenrod were lengthening and blurring and it would soon be dusk. The faint, purplish-red glow now tingeing the clouds was so beautiful it almost made his heart ache. *Could she see the sunset,* Seth wondered. He hoped so. He wished he could share it with her. "Soon, I'll know her secret and then maybe I can coax her out of the palace."

From her window, she could see the boy. Aldys moved cautiously, careful not to disturb the curtain. She did not wish him to see her.

But he must have sensed her presence anyway, because no sooner had she peered over the window sill than he turned his face upward and gazed in her direction. A small gasp escaped her lips, but she remained motionless.

For a month, now, she had watched him, the month she had been in confinement in this room of the center turret. The turret was a boring place to be. The wizard had taken away her embroidery and stitchery. She had tried using a piece of coal to draw pictures on the pale slate floor, but had received no meal that night. Music had become her only entertainment. Very quietly, she would sing or hum, but each day, she had become more creative in her accompaniments, sometimes adding the delightful ting of her hair comb on the bed frame, or the clear ringing of her spoon on the window glass, along with a sharp heel-toe click.

This was how she had first spied the boy, on the second day of her imprisonment. Having twirled and danced her way across the room from the door to the window, Aldys had just added a tiny ting to the window as she whisper-sang. She stopped in mid-beat to stare at the fountain. A boy sat at the edge of it, looking even more sad and lonely than she felt. But almost immediately, he looked up at her and smiled.

Aldys had not responded. Not the slightest motion of her hand or face gave her away. She had, however, warmed in the sun's glow at that moment.

Aldys had stood locked in the midst of her dance until the boy finally looked away, back to the fish swimming around the fountain. Only then did she dare to drop her hand to her side, whispering, "who are you lad who talks with the fishes?" and still pondering this, she had stealthily slipped away from the window and gently sat upon the edge of her bed. "A friend?" she pondered. "Why have I never noticed you before? I know you were not there yesterday. Will you be there tomorrow?"

Truthfully, Aldys had been frightened by the encounter. The display of sadness, the smile—they were not Lacii. Slipping her hand into the secret inner pocket of her gown, Aldys had felt for the relic and immediately some of her tension eased. The scrap of fabric had once been stiff and shiny, but the fondling of untold years had made it as soft as the fur of a baby mouse, and it warmed instantly at her touch. For a moment, she sat on the edge of the bed, rubbing the satin between her thumb and forefinger. Then, quietly, she got up and glided to the door. Stooping, she peered through the keyhole. When she was satisfied that no one could see her, she withdrew her hand, still holding the scarlet patch, and brought it to her lips. As she returned to the bed,

Aldys gently kissed the satin and then caressed her cheek with it. It was napped and nearly threadbare in places, but the color still glowed like the day it was woven and cut into a fine dress for her majesty the queen. And Aldys handled it reverently, as though it still belonged to the queen, because it was red and because it was the last scrap of red in the entire kingdom of Lac and had been the last for ever so many years. And besides that, it had once been held by Aldys's mother, the queen's dressmaker, whom she was missing very much right now.

She had stayed awake many hours, that night a month ago, thinking about the boy, exploring one possibility after another. "He could be the wizard's spy." It seemed a lot of trouble to watch an ordinary maiden, but the wizard did not think she was a very ordinary maiden, did he? "Thou art creative," he had shouted at her. "And that is forbidden!"

"My name is Aldys, daughter of Orilla, royal seamstress," she had replied. "I must be creative to do my task."

The wizard had hissed at her, thrown his left hand up in front of his face, horror twisting across his features like surging waves. "NO! No, that cannot be! That one was taken care of long ago." Then he bade the palace guard seize her and shut her in this turret. Neither wizard nor king had come near her since. Everything but the necessities was removed from the room. But the mirror was tightly fastened to the wall, seemed indeed to be a part of it. The guards could not budge it. And so it remained. *How ironic*, Aldys had mused. The mirror was the one thing of which she had no need.

At least they hadn't blocked the window. If they had, she never would have seen that boy. That boy! If he wasn't a spy for the wizard, then who was he? As miserable as she was, the boy looked more miserable still. His had not the blankness she saw on the faces of other people. This lad's face held the same inquisitive light her mother had cautioned her to hide from her own face. "Mask your spirit," her mother had always warned. "Let no one see your inner fire. It is not of Lac and you will regret the discovery of it." So she did as her mother said. Most of the time.

Unfortunately, Aldys had let the mask slip more than once. Then she had completely forgotten herself one day and embroidered a pattern on the king's new robe with the most succulent shade of threads which she had secretly dyed using beet juice. The wizard was livid when he saw it. Indeed, he turned nearly the same color as the threads, which looked lovely on the robe but hideous on the wizard's face.

Now look what the lovely color had gotten her.

Aldys had crept back to the window that first day, craning her neck so that she might see out without being seen, but the boy was gone.

She knew of no one else in the entire kingdom who had that hidden spark. Until him. Was it possible that she was meant to see him? Was that why she had ended up in the turret? After all, she was much too busy with her stitching ordinarily to be looking out at the fountain. Or perhaps he had arrived from some far-off place to rescue her? Aldys thought this possible, in a wishful kind of way. More likely he was an ordinary boy from Lac who only looked special because the sun was beginning to set and sent a false cast across his face. Still, no one else ever sat there, talking to the fish. For she was sure he was talking to them. Perhaps that was why the other people gave him a wide berth and did not look his way. Perhaps he was mad. "And I shall surely go mad if I have nothing more to occupy my thoughts than a boy at the fountain," she had thought.

Before finally drifting to sleep, Aldys had tucked the scarlet scrap back into her secret pocket. And when she slept, she dreamed of the boy. "Don't be afraid," the boy in the dream had said to her. "We're here to put the world right." Aldys had awoken feeling calmer than she had since she had been locked in that room. Yet she remained afraid of the boy and intensely curious about him.

So every day thereafter, she crept quietly to the window to observe him. She knew it was rude and a little cruel when she did not return his smile. Her gaze remained steady, but she gave no hint of warmth. Even still, the boy came every day now and he never failed to look up at her with longing in his eyes.

Amy Schiffman

The Past Decade

SPRING 2000

This morning I did not sit at my computer. I did not read a script, nor flip the pages of a manuscript. I did not read the newspaper nor take a power walk. I just sat in my office and stared into space. And in that space were two children. My children: Sadie and Eloise.

It is now seven a.m. Sadie is wearing a pull-up and putting on a puppet show. Her audience is me and her six-month-old sister. Eloise, the baby, is on a mat on the floor. Sadie prances behind the portable proscenium and sings a song. Loud. The tune is "THIS LAND IS YOUR LAND," but the words are her own. The child development specialist says that she still needs to wear a diaper to prove that the poop is her own.

Eloise has just learned to roll over. She has maneuvered herself onto her stomach on the pad with the appliquéd puppies. Now she is stuck in this position, her arms and legs waving like an inverted beetle. However, she's not complaining, Eloise is happy just to be there, in the early morning, waving her arms and legs in time to her sister's song.

And I am happy, too, except when I sob uncontrollably. I went back to work when Eloise was just three months old. I got an offer from a wonderful firm, and I had to take if, for many reasons, not the least of which was health insurance. Going back to work pre-empted post-partum depression, or so I thought. I'd just be too busy to be depressed. Instead I just feel overwhelmed. All the time.

So I get up early, because Eloise wakes me up to nurse, and this is my special time with her. Except when Sadie wakes up, too, and is jealous. Once Sadie climbed up on my lap and tried nursing the other breast. If I stop nursing Eloise to pay attention to Sadie, I feel that I am cheating Eloise. If I try to get Sadie to watch TV and put Eloise down on her pad so that I can read a manuscript, I feel that I am neglecting both girls. If I nurse the baby and read a script at the same time, my arms ache. I shouldn't worry about paying more attention to one child than the other. I shouldn't worry about loosing my job if I get behind in my reading. I shouldn't worry about my arms, they won't always ache. I should just enjoy these blissful moments with my children who are very young. I should live in the moment. I should, I should, I should.

I was somewhat relieved when Eloise began to lose interest in the breast, preferring the sweet and sticky formula that flows easily from a bottle. One less thing to feel conflicted about. Now anybody can feed her, at any time. When I finally get around to packing up the nursing bras and the ugly blouses, I realize how nice it would feel to start wearing lingerie instead of utilitarian underwear with trap doors over each breast.

WINTER 2000

Sometimes I don't believe the baby in the crib is the same one I carried in my body for nine months. She is a year old now. She's so substantial. Breast feeding seems a mere memory. But I have evidence. There is a container of breast milk in the freezer. Once such a precious commodity, now I don't really know what to do with it. These days Eloise sits in a highchair and feeds herself grown up foods like pasta and pizza. She uses both hands. Sometimes she waves a spoon in one hand while stuffing banana into her mouth with the other. She loves all food, especially cake.

Maybe I could bake the breast milk into a cake for her first birthday. Or into the elaborate dessert I'm planning to take to a Christmas party. Then one day I find a pamphlet in a pile of new-mother literature that says that breast milk, even stored in the freezer, only lasts six months. Technically, this breast milk has expired. I start to cry. I cannot throw it out. It's just going to have to stay in the freezer until Eloise goes off to college. I need that little plastic bottle as evidence of where she came from. Like the breast milk, Eloise originated inside me, but unlike the breast milk, she will have a life beyond our kitchen. A life for which she is gradually being prepared.

DECEMBER 2001

It is that precious moment. Both girls are asleep. My partner is happily watching the news—at low volume. I clear a place among the unpaid bills and unanswered pleas for contributions on my desk. I switch on my computer. I cannot remember the password to get into my e-mail. Or maybe my computer has forgotten me, as it's been a year since I looked at my writing. So I skip past the e-mail, it's just a distraction, and open a folder named "personal writing."

I open a file that was written on New Year's Day 2000. A year ago, the issues were pretty much the same: What to make the kids to eat? How to find more time to be with the kids? But a few things have changed:

Work is good. I'm fitting into the corporate culture, while piecing together a wardrobe of size 12–14 clothes, because I still haven't lost the "baby weight." Twenty-five pounds is now down to 20, but I haven't returned to my pre-baby figure. My shrink would probably say I'm reluctant to let go of the weight, just the way I'm reluctant to throw out the breast milk. I loved being pregnant. I felt more efficient with one child on the inside and one on the outside. These days I'm always being pulled in opposite directions, by partner, work and kids.

Sadie is finally pooping in the toilet, although it's still a struggle for her on some level. For the second child, developmental changes come more easily, completely out of her or our control. One day she figures out how to crawl, the next thing we know she is walking. Soon she has learned to talk—a new language, without a single Berlitz class. In two years they accomplish what it takes adults a whole lifetime to learn.

I look up from my computer and stare through the wall in my study, past the walls of the girls' bedrooms and try to imagine the shapes of their sleeping bodies under the covers. Sadie is long: her knee and hip and shoulder joints define an already athletic frame. Eloise is long, too, no longer a logroll of baby, she now has distinct parts: head, arms, trunk, just as she has distinct ideas about what she wants to eat, what she wants to wear, in which direction she chooses to walk.

I'm loathe to spend any more of my rare spare time writing. But perhaps my writing doesn't really take me away from them. Maybe it helps me look at them more clearly, see them and record them. They are changing so fast. When they are asleep, or when I am in my office, the writing is a way to draw them towards me again. Remaking and remembering. The Sadie and Eloise on the page will always be a part of me, even as their flesh and blood counterparts grow up, become more independent, and eventually let go of me.

Susan Shopmaker

Steak-Night 1978

*One-Act Play Written for and Performed at the 2007
All-Kirkland Reunion*

A COLLEGE DORM SUITE. COMMON ROOM. A WALL OF WINDOWS
UNDER WHICH IS A BUILT-IN WOODEN COUCH. MARIMEKKO
FLORAL FABRIC OF BLACK AND PURPLE AND ORANGE COVERS
THE COUCH. STANDING IN THE CENTER OF THE ROOM IS A
YOUNG GIRL ABOUT 17 YEARS OLD, HOLDING TWO PIECES OF
LUGGAGE. SHE LOOKS LIKE A DEER CAUGHT IN THE HEADLIGHTS.

GIRL: Hello? PAUSE Hello? PAUSE Anyone here?

A DOOR OPENS AND SMOKE COMES POURING OUT. FROM THE
HAZE A WOMAN OF ABOUT 20 YEARS OLD APPEARS, FOLLOWED
BY ANOTHER. THEY ARE EATING LARGE CRISP APPLES.

NAOMI: Oh heyyy. We didn't hear you. Welcome.
ANNIE: I'm Annie. This is Naomi.

ANNIE THROWS HER ARM AROUND NAOMI AND KISSES HER.

ANNIE: We're your suite-mates. Welcome to 'B' dorm. That's nice
luggage. Isn't it heavy? It looks heavy.
GIRL: Ummm. Sort of. I thought I'd put it in my room?
ANNIE: Which one are you?
GIRL: What. Oh um. Tracey.

189

NAOMI AND ANNIE LOOK AT EACH OTHER.

NAOMI: As in 'Dick'. Ha?
ANNIE: Hey Dick. THEY CHUCKLE.
NAOMI: Well your room is over there. Why don't you put your bags away and come back and have a toke or two.
ANNIE: Is that Tartan?
TRACEY: Ummm. What. Oh this. Yeah. Uhhh Yeah I think it is. Yes.
ANNIE: You may wanna burn that thing before your first class. THEY CHUCKLE.
NAOMI: No! Don't! I could use that in my performance piece. What size is that.
TRACEY: Ummm. I'm not sure. I can look.
NAOMI: No no no. It'll fit. I could probably stress the hem a little.
ANNIE: Y'know what would look radical?
NAOMI: What.
ANNIE: Pentacles. Upside-down pentacles painted on it.
NAOMI: Oooooo I like it—good idea. A Bold statement about our place in the Universe. Tracey do you have a camera?
TRACEY: Ummm. No. Ummmm. No I don't. I think I'm going to go to my room and put these down?
NAOMI: We'll be out here.
ANNIE: Waiting.

TRACEY LEAVES. NAOMI AND ANNIE LOOK AT EACH OTHER. BEAT. THEY GO BACK TO THE ROOM THEY CAME FROM. "LOVIN' YOU" BY MINNIE RIPERTON STARTS TO PLAY . . . YOU CAN HEAR ANNIE AND NAOMI SINGING . . .

TRACEY COMES BACK INTO THE COMMON AREA. SHE IS WEARING JEANS AND A SWEATER.

THE DOOR OPENS AND NAOMI AND ANNIE EMERGE. AGAIN PRECEDED AND FOLLOWED BY A CLOUD OF SMOKE. THEY HAVE STARTED TO EAT NEW APPLES . . .

NAOMI: Where's my skirt.
TRACEY: Uhhh. I I I -
ANNIE: Wannaapple? PAUSE Want some Cider?
NAOMI: Oh. YOU'RE Tracey! You got a package. You got a package from Kansas. That is so crazy.
ANNIE: Kansas is claustrophobic.

NAOMI: What's in Kansas.

TRACEY: My parents.

ANNIE: Ohhhhhh. Wow. That is so farrr out . . . there. No water. Claustrophobic.

NAOMI STARTS AN INTERPRETIVE DANCE WHILE SING-SPEAKING THE PATTI SMITH SONG:

I-I walk in a room, you know I look so proud I'm movin' in this here atmosphere, well, anything's allowed and I go to this here party and I just get bored until I look out the window, see a sweet young thing humpin' on the parking meter, leanin' on the parking meter oh, she looks so good, oh, she looks so fine and I got this crazy feeling and then I'm gonna ah-ah make her mine ooh I'll put my spell on her . . .

ANNIE: Wanna bong hit?

TRACEY: No thank you. I mean. No. Not yet.

NAOMI: Woah. Check it out. It's snowing.

OUTSIDE THE PICTURE WINDOW, IT HAS BEGUN TO SNOW. HEAVY FLAKES. LIKE PIECES OF PAPER.

ANNIE: Excellent.

NAOMI: I'm not so sure about the pentacles anymore. They'll bring to the forefront a Wiccan sensibility that I'm not so sure is really relevant to the piece. I'm really trying to define Deviancy through Movement, that which is Deviant, in a Post Vietnam era and I'm not sure it works. . . . That! Is really coming down.

THE SNOW IS PILING UP OUTSIDE THE WINDOW.

ANNIE: I really wanted to wear my Birkenstocks.

NAOMI: I'm hungry. You hungry Little One?

TRACEY: A little. It's coming down really fast. I've never seen snow like that before.

ANNIE: You'll get used to it. Jesus it looks like 2 or 3 feet already. What's in the package from Kansas.

TRACEY: I think steaks.

NAOMI (GRIMACING): Ohhh that's too bad. I am getting sooooooo hungry.

TRACEY: We can cook them if you want that's what they're for—for my roommates.

NAOMI: No meat. No meat. No meat.

A SOPPING WET 20-YEAR-OLD MAN COMES IN THE ROOM WEARING NOTHING BUT A TOWEL AND L.L. BEAN DUCK BOOTS. HIS LONGISH BLOND HAIR IS HANGING OVER HIS EYES.

NAOMI: Chip! Yay. You're back.
ANNIE: And clean, clean is gooood. Yummyyummy.
NAOMI: I knew I was hungry. Just this once we'll make an exception.

AS NAOMI, ANNIE, AND CHIP GO INTO THE SMOKE-FILLED ROOM

CHIP: It's snowing. Wow.

BEFORE THE DOOR CLOSES AN APPLE ROLLS INTO THE COMMON ROOM.

DOOR SHUTS.

OFFSTAGE LAUGHING—"BRICK HOUSE" STARTS TO BLARE— TRACEY SITS AND STARES OUT THE WINDOW AS THE SNOW PILES UP—IT COULD BE 5 FEET—SOMETHING OMINOUS IS HAPPENING OUT THERE.

Maria Stadtmueller

Taking Francis Hostage

Strip naked in the center of town in broad daylight. Declare that from now on you will own nothing and will trust in everything holy that it will all work out. When your dad—rich, influential, mortified—finally unlocks the basement a few weeks later and lets you out, start again, giving away all your swanky stuff in the name of love. Neighbors, family, friends, strangers—think you're nuts. But you are happy—gleeful, even. Stripped down to feeling a dying man's hot, dry breath and the mountains' cool, moist breath, hungry unless the merciful feed you, and how many of those do you meet?

You were on to something. We might still have a chance.

It took just a few years for six thousand people to join you, longing to give up everything to live as you did, your call spreading at the maximum thirteenth-century land speed of a guy on a horse on a rutted road. Salvation was an understandably sharp hook back then, but even those numbed by luxury or power had to have wondered who all these people were, these penitents, flooding in to see you. Their unruly tide surged against the rising islands of finely appointed villas and the brocaded brokers inside. Soon tens of thousands of believers swore peace, refused to bear arms, refused to take oaths of fealty. How could the nobles of Assisi raise an army against the bellicose nobles of Perugia, or Perugia against the insulting nobles of Siena, if their grunts and foot soldiers balked in order to favor their souls? Who could force them once the pope protected these legions of simplicity seekers with a papal bull? Who could have imagined that the steep stone stairway of feudalism would erode under the shuffle of dusty, sandaled feet?

Eight hundred years later, here we are. Many of us believe in your god and some of us don't.

It doesn't matter. It is common knowledge that you are loved by Catholics, Protestants, Jews, atheists, Buddhists, agnostics, Muslims. Yes, you are more popular than Jesus. Just an average October Tuesday, and we can still taste the morning's first espresso, but tour buses, cars, and motorbikes pack the parking lot. Taxis and city buses unload arrivals from the train station at Santa Maria degli Angeli and thread back through the city walls. We are mustering. Cameras, bags, maps at the ready. Tour guides hoist their colored pennants, gather their troops, brief them in English, Italian, German, Korean, Japanese, Spanish, Portuguese, Swedish, Chinese. We begin our march up the hill.

Eleven thousand of us will come today, and eleven thousand tomorrow, and five million every year. We will swarm your cathedral; we will all circuit your steep, narrow streets; we will occupy that piazza in the center of town. You could ask us. Better yet, you could insist, in this same square where you made such a show of relinquishing. We would put down our gelati and panini and cappuccini and listen, quiet as the birds. You could begin by telling us why we're really here.

We might think we've come to view Giotto's honeyed frescoes; to imbibe some "mystical" experience hawked in a tourist brochure; to say the prescribed prayers of the Assisi Pardon and be granted a free pass from purgatory (Jesus and Mary appeared, offered you a favor, and that's what you chose on our behalf. Could you ask again?). Or we're here to put a face on faith (we have nothing verifiable of Jesus', but these are your shabby sandals, your letters, the rags you held to your oozing hands). Or we are here to pay homage to a man who would not sit at the holy table unless he could set places for birds, wind, water, wolves, and herbs; or to spend an afternoon in this town built from pink stones and then check it off our lists. Five million of us a year, even though there are more Giottos in Florence and Bologna, we can be pardoned in Rome, and Umbria holds other hill towns that will blush and serve us truffles.

You were a warrior once—surely your fellow soldiers joined up for different reasons. Weren't some adventurers, runaways, lovers of hot blood and battle, idealists, avengers, careerists of the heaved sword, all forged into something new and invincible once someone with conviction pointed to the target and gave the spur?

Five million of us, and here is the extent of our instruction: you must all stay together, you must wait until four to shop, you must be back at the hotel at seven, announce the tour guides. You have to pick up some of those cute Francis refrigerator magnets for the grandkids, insists the American matron to another. You must stop a moment and let the Franciscan spirit surround you, says the tony British voice on the digital basilica tour, as each of us is surrounded by others instructed to stop a moment and let the Franciscan spirit surround them.

We are wandering, and there is no sign of where to go. You know you could take us there.

Which is why I have shoved you head-first into this coffee mug of pebbles (the four-inch plastic you, available everywhere in town). To get your attention—your intercession, if we need to be formal about it. Nothing personal, just the formula. If I were selling a house, I'd bury St. Joseph the carpenter on his head; if I were looking for a husband, St. Anthony of Padua, the finder, would be my upended hostage. You are the patron saint of ecology, the last pope said. I can't pray anymore, but this people's witchcraft of the religion I once shared with you makes as much sense. So as long as I'm here, with your bones just up the street, your sweat no doubt baked into the pores of some brick nearby, you and your non-biodegradable congregation of tiny plastic birds will remain upside-down on the sink of this disturbingly deluxe tiled bath of my monastery guest room.

Not that I think you're uncomfortable. Italy is full of rocks where you lay your head and slept. Days and weeks on end you prayed in stony clefts and fissures. Your medieval geology, or was it your personal one, told you those rocks split open during the biblical earthquake that marked the crucifixion. To you they rang with a saving sound.

An earthquake is always the death of something and the birth of something else. Ten years ago here, the force that birthed these hills pushed again, hard. Roofs, roads, collapsed. In the basilica, birds hearing your frozen sermon crumbled and alighted on the ground, an oak beam returning to earth brought with him a soft brown monk. We know now that earthquakes come from a power below and not one above, and that their echoes ring through a chasm of deep time you thought reserved for heaven or hell. What you heard reverberating in your stony hermitages was a holy sound, yes, but not of some unnecessary redemption. You heard our creation. It was the labor that delivered us into the holy family of Mother Earth, Brother Sun, Sister Water, Brother Fire, the marrow-deep bonds you sang about. It was the love song of the trilobite as she gave herself up for the limestone that cradled the aquifer that fed the Umbrian chestnuts that surrendered their fruit to the grinding stone to feed your blood.

What are the stones chanting now, down there in your mug? Can you hear the sigh of Sister Water passing through? She is still useful, and humble, and precious, but she is far from pure. Ask the stones to sing to you of glaciers they have ridden, of icecaps you couldn't have known in your time, of continents and creatures unfathomable to you, and of the measurements and thresholds we've devised to mark how we silence them forever.

Reach back and remember your rage—written in the old sources, not available in gift shops—how you ripped into your monks when they succumbed to comfort. How you threw sick brothers out of a too-posh house; how you ordered a library in Bologna burned—monks can't own anything, not even books, you ranted. How you cursed the monk who loved the books, refused his brother monks' pleas for mercy, and sent a burning drop of sulfur to bore through his skull.

If you can work miracles—and some here believe ruined crucifixes talked to you, and I'll believe anything if it works—come out from under your stifling cloak of mildness and try again. Preach to us of poverty, because if we were poor we wouldn't be here. Stare down your failure and ours—that insistence on heaven at the expense of earth. You're the only one who can, at least here. You went alone out into the winter woods and embraced the feared she-wolf of Gubbio because you knew she killed from hunger. So do we. Dare us to strip off our wrinkle-resistant travel separates in this same piazza, cast us to our knees, not to pray but to feel our flesh and bones hard against the terrifying stone and wet, saving dirt. "All which you used to avoid will bring you great sweetness and joy," you said. We will chant it. Then send us home to keep stripping away, to reveal our naked, joyful animal bodies.

Now that our vision must adjust to the frescoes' seismic cracks, it could well be the birds were preaching back.

Constance Stellas

Building

A One-Act Play Written for and Performed at the 2007
All-Kirkland Reunion

Scene 1
Stage is bare and two workmen walk on and start clearing away rocks.
They are just doing their job. A young student walks on and looks at
the workmen for awhile:

STUDENT 1: What are you guys doing?
WORKMAN 1: Don't know exactly, clearing this land for something,
maybe a college or something like that.
STUDENT 1: WOW, right here.
WORKMAN 2: That's what they say.
The student and workmen freeze for a few minutes

Scene 2
Three more people students and workmen come and begin moving
rocks around, building and banging, measuring.

WORKMAN 1: Maybe we should begin over here.
STUDENT 3: These apple trees are so beautiful we should keep them.
WORKMAN 2: How about over there?
STUDENT 2: I'm not sure we have all the plans clear.
STUDENT 4: I think we should use these rocks here and paint them
chartreuse.
WORKMAN 1: Not a practical idea.

A professor with a cap and gown walks on.

197

PROFESSOR: What are you doing?

All of the workers and students stare at him. With a tone of excitement they say:

STUDENT 1: We are forming an ad hoc committee to examine how, with the help of these excellent professionals, to create a college.
STUDENT 2: We are also forming another ad hoc committee to decide how the students and faculty with the help of these excellent professionals would run the college.
STUDENT 3: And learn a lot.
STUDENT 4: And create a beautiful place . . . maybe with chartreuse furniture.
PROFESSOR: Chartreuse?
STUDENT 4: Oh yes, Chartreuse.
WORKMAN 1: I said it wasn't practical.
WORKMAN 2: I suggest mauve.
PROFESSOR: Hmm, Chartreuse?? In this mud?
GROUP: Why not?
PROFESSOR: Yes, why not. Sounds good.

Professor exits

Tableau of students and workmen

Scene 3
More students and workers and professors building a whole tower very carefully, adding one rock at a time so that the whole thing looks like a pyramid. This is done quickly and there is much admiration and congratulations from all the workers.

Then the professor enters:

PROFESSOR/PRESIDENT: What is this? Very interesting. *(He picks up a block and plays totally innocent as if he hadn't been involved in the other scenes.)*

STUDENT 1: This is the college we created out of Mud and Brains.
STUDENT 2: And Ad Hoc Committees and Joy. What do you think?
PROFESSOR/PRESIDENT: It is beautiful. It needs something, something . . . a final touch. *(From under his hat he pulls out an apple and dark green cloth.*

HE puts the apple at the top of the pyramid and drapes the green scarf.)
STUDENT 4: Couldn't the mantle be chartreuse?
STUDENT 2: I don't want to stand in the way of anyone who feels strongly about Chartreuse but I think the dark green and the apple look strong and good.
STUDENT 1: Maybe we could rotate and use the Chartreuse on a bi-semester basis.
STUDENT 3: Yes, that could work . . .
GROUP OF STUDENTS: Yes, that could definitely work.
PROFESSOR/PRESIDENT: BEAUTIFUL. We have all made an excellent college. Let's all have a picnic . . . there is a little place I know, just waiting for us, down the road.

All Freeze in Tableau

Then there is a drumbeat that beats faster and faster.

Scene 4
A man or woman in a three-piece suit, monocle, clip board, and whistle starts motioning the students and workers to dismantle the pyramid and move the rocks and put them back into the piles that they were in at the beginning of the show. Soon all the workers, students, and professors are standing on one side of the stage and the SUIT on the other side.

The Kirkland group looks sadly at the piles says GOOD-BYE and exits

The SUIT marches off.

Then the professor and a student come on and unfurl a beautiful piece of rainbow-colored material and toss an apple up and down.

STUDENT 1: We created a place with all the colors of the rainbow.
STUDENT 4: Look at that magnificent chartreuse.
WORKMAN 2: And lots of good, sturdy buildings.
PROFESSOR/PRESIDENT: Ideas, and learning, and our students go out into the world more powerfully than blocks, mud, and committees.

At first the PRESIDENT, STUDENT 1 and STUDENT 4 start throwing up their apples and catching them like tough guys throwing and catching a coin. Then the PRESIDENT says think fast and a game of catch ensues, all the actors in the play come on and continue playing catch with their apples.

Billie Jean Stratton

White Welkin Rafting

Wild Ezekiels at the weirs,
warlocks of the water wheels,
and seers seeking storms, say
rivers of vapor in vast, rippling ribbons,
larger than the Amazon,
sail round the earth's vault.

Meridians of moisture,
streaming north for port,
they stitch astral's cellar
to heaven's floor
on the high sky ride.

How clever
changing water's form
for the thronging
pole ward transport,
thrusting ice bolts
like armies rain arrows
into the cold ponds.

Isn't that how the gods would be?
Is an angel landing ever really seen,
hiding in the atmosphere,
like a bride kept in the dark
of a dim, distant century?

Walk the thought barriers, darling.
Let shattered glass and broken dreams
sharpen your small, white feet.
Play the nine pine pins.
Visit me in sleep.

How much more must I see?
How much longer must I be
sheeted with this body?

I thought I would die when you left me behind,
but now the mountain is so easy to climb.
I hardly need these hands anymore.
I simply flatten with the wind
listening to that hymn's refrain,
"love lifted me," and the saints
in all their pain insisting
we simply must love again.

Epitaph For Every Zipped Fly Who Once Stood At Hoot's Bar

(Dedicated to their ghosts who still stand stalwart and tall)

Part 1

One afternoon, Hoot began to shed,
  and when the last drop of sweat
    from his swollen forehead met
      the whiskey stains beneath his lips,
        like some summer pond
          sucked into surrounding dry fields,
Hoot was dead.

We all knew what Hoot's death meant
  gathered in his bar that night.
The old men mourned nails and hair
  grown out gaskets of wood.
The young men mourned chassis
  they couldn't afford.
The coach's wife just moaned,
  her swaying head looped under a Chevy,
peering at imaginary smoke.

Even Hank, the ex-drunk, mourned

                    at home.

Hank, the drunk with a daughter,
  liked Hoot so much he slipped him
    100 dollar bills like some honky card trick,
past the bank and feed store's nose,
  sniffing the wind after his soul
    even though they owned it.

Hoot just laughed and
  paid the milk truck driver
    10 bucks to deliver his milk check home first.
    "Hoot! No goddam bill collector
      is gonna steal my money!"
        Hoot's face never changed.
He just said,
  "Yup."

Part 2

One night, so cold the pipes froze,
  Hank and his daughter finished hauling water
    to the heifers across the river on the Butts farm.
Heading towards his second fifth,
                    he slid
alongside Hoot's.
          "Just one,"
he said, and left her in the car.

Half an hour later
  he might have felt guilt,
    but Jack Daniels slowly thawed
      the chill of reason away,
leaving his brain filled with the warmth
  of naked flesh under a heat lamp.
He might never have remembered
  if a cold draft hadn't
    reached for him across the room,
      if Jenny hadn't
followed in its wake.

He watched her head move
  like a milking machine
    suck-squish, suck-squish,
nodding to Fatty, Bruce,
  Delmar, Leonard and Jake,
    all eyeing her body
      rigid with fear,
ever since the man called Monroe
  threw her on a bale of hay
    and wouldn't let her go.

Hank wished his daughter was home.

Part 3

She took soda in a beer glass
  shaped like Mae West's chest,
on one foot, then the other,
  rocking with Hank's shouts
    buying the house
      another round,

and just before boredom
   sank her like a stone,
      she noticed a suited gray "Canadian"
         a long way from home.
He was good looking, and as far
   as she could tell, just passing through.
Her attention could have proved
   helpful to a kindly stranger,
      but this one wasn't dumb
         and even three years older
was "jail bait."

He wasn't flattered.

Hank watched her
   out the corner of his eye,
      pull fourteen up to fifteen
         fifteen up to sixteen, sixteen
            up to seventeen, and turning just
as she passed legal, sidled up
   a little cocky
                  for a conference.
"You like that man?" he asked,
   and she, a little bold,
      because a drunk's about as good for sense
as a blatting calf, answered,
                              "Yes, I do."
He nodded real easy and said,
   "I bet you'd like to bed
      right down with him, wouldn't you?"
         rubbing his manure caked coveralls.
She held solid at eighteen
   and shaking with the slap
      he could deliver
                        didn't answer.
Hank never pressed anything trapped.
   "Well, you need someone older,
      I'd teach you myself if I could.
         Want me to go over and ask him for you?"

Jenny turned
   a "bastard" on her breath
      and sat down in the corner.

Part 4

Hoot's wife slammed the bar door shut,
  tighter than the brass coffin's lid.
    She hated the place so much there was nothing she'd touch
      'cept the window and she covered it
        with meat packing paper, the color of shit.

When Jenny came home for Christmas,
  Hoot's body was hardly even cold.
Everyone supposed Hoot's daughters
  were still in shock when they heard
    about the party on New Year's Eve.

Just inside the door, Jenny
  felt her stomach begin to roll.
    The stale corners still held
      shame's nameless back end.
        The booth's ripped plastic
          loosened new pathways for pain.

She smelled the same old sickening smell,
  that bathroom's rotting beer well.
    Everyone smoked pot and drank booze.
      Hoot's eldest wasn't talking 'bout
        the baby she'd had in 10th grade.
Jenny wasn't gonna ask.

Their fathers, long thought lost,
  still sleighed their best hands
    in ghostly sleights of bluff.
This wizardry was such
  these jaded Judys
    and faded Punchinellos
never even felt the tug.

Behind that brown paper, the town cop just sat.
  His car was parked front and center, but well,
    you know how the story goes in those little home towns.

He never even checked the place out.

Shed Song

Now that we are still and forever apart,
the moon steams a red that seems
to weave a funeral wreath around my heart.
Heavy rain overruns the stream.

This summer, the sun was so bright,
I fell onto my own hands twice,
slowly searching the tangled weeds
for strawberries on my hands and knees.

Down in the feral smell of plant rot,
I crumpled to the ground white hot,
When fantasy and reality intertwined
I pranced past all sense of time.

There were no short nights in July.
Hours before dawn, I sat naked on the lawn,
my long skirt covering it all, the heat
Beating down into the cool ground.

August, and I see my breath.
The woodshed bat, halfheartedly flaps,
a turn or two and creeps
back under the rafters to rest.

Outside the crickets rub their legs
in a rhythm that resembles mine.
The clicking sounds like castanets.
It gives the stillness life, a breath.

I've died daily to hold you
all these years, to kiss: your lips
your hips, your finger tips, anything you wish.
How dare you make love to me over distance?

Now that I am here and you are there.
The moon steams red and silently stares.
Heavy rain overruns the stream.
A cold, rising mist is all that remains.

Jane Summer

Mrs. Chretien Listened to Elgar

I

June was still in its infancy, the crickets scritched in the basement and the days were bruised with the broad promise of summer, when Sarah Chretien awaited her eleventh birthday. Something big would happen, she was sure, upon turning eleven. The other turnings had been fairly unconscious events that came upon her like dusk and which she recognized only when her grandmother stepped off the train; presents sat at her feet bursting with the desire to be unwrapped, and candles were lit with joy, not mourning.

Eleven had to be different.

Kids had been invited and on Sunday came, for cake and orange soda and a kind of French ice cream no longer manufactured in America. Her grandmother with her carton of cigarettes and nougat was met at the train by Mr. Chretien and his authoritative automobile. Most of the children still dressed for birthday parties, clip-on bowties for the boys and ruffled things for the girls—anklets, sleeves, hairbows, petticoats. Everything on the outside was very pretty. Polaroids were taken.

But their slippery party shoes were as hazardous as their suburban days, which boys spent playing war, girls baking brownies.

Sarah did both, detesting both.

II

I'm going to tell you something ugly not because it explains what Sarah did. I'm telling you because no one else has the guts to. I'm telling you for my own good. I'm telling you for Sarah's sake.

Why was it so difficult for Sarah to say no? Why did her tongue curl up and tuck itself in? Because she didn't want anyone to see she could be ravished? A slender, blondish kid, shortsighted and game—it had been obvious.

Because Buck's father owned the bowling alley in town, which of course had a refreshment counter, Buck always had a carton of chocolate bars in the playroom, 24 bars to a carton. That was the sole enticement to Sarah, the abundance of chocolate in her neighbor's house.

Storytellers who draw this part out to make it arousing should be refused an intelligible language for the rest of their days.

Not a Halloween went by when Buck didn't dress as a slender G.I. Obsessed with World War II, he would spend his life looking for someone to kill. But while he was still a third grader he would remain content to watch TV war movies and play D-Day with his classmate Sarah Chretien.

He and Sarah crawled on their bellies from backyard to backyard and ate raisins out of their ill-fitting football helmets. But Sarah couldn't bring herself to aim her stick rifle at the women hanging wash and babies in sandboxes. She couldn't throw the wormed-apple grenades at the Germans hiding in the cathedral of the oak tree. So Buck came up with a new attack plan.

Had she known, Mrs. Chretien would not have approved of Sarah playing war with Buck. Not Mrs. Chretien, who made her husband disassemble and dispose of the hunting rifle he'd kept by the bed of his first wife for five years. She'd have done it herself but refused to touch the thing. In the days when she was still invited to dinner parties, she'd interrupt the fish course and the male discourse on Vietnam with something like, "Honor and duty my big toe!" She was a woman who, whenever requested, rose before dawn in a drafty house, stepped into her long underwear and dressed for a Women Strike for Peace gathering at the state capitol building while her husband snoozed on undreaming. A pacifist who exchanged her bedroom crucifix for a LIFE Magazine photo of Gandhi, she was not to be disturbed when listening to the Baptist preachers or the music, especially Elgar's E minor cello concerto, which strengthened her antiwar resolve.

She was a righteous woman. But where did her principles get her? It was Mrs. Chretien who had encouraged Sarah to play with Buck—she'd known him since he was in diapers—Mrs. Chretien who had taught Sarah the folly of violent behavior. And it was her maternal impulse which led Mrs. Chretien to impose Sarah on Buck's mother, who was home with the vacuum all day while Mrs. Chretien rang up potted plants at the garden store.

A curse on the planet, a foul shadow rose, when Buck and his damn chocolate bars came upon the breath of life.

What happened was this: Buck considered Sarah's refusal to participate in the heightened violence of his game. His knuckles went white as he clutched his tree-limb rifle. "Okay then. You can play a captured German spy."

A spy, why not? Sarah had always admired James Bond's inviolability. "Do you want to be tortured or stripped?"

Buck had to be kidding.

Buck tied her to a pipe in his parents' basement. He interrogated her. He threatened to strip her. All the while Sarah, desperate for excuses for the game to stop, whispered, *"My mother is expecting me home, I promised to help with dinner, I have to go home, I think your mother's calling you."* When it was clear Buck was not going to stop until her parts were showing pink and tender as raw chicken, why didn't she scream her head off?

She was eight, that's why. Trying to resist the enemy in the most profound way, Sarah suddenly stopped up her tears and envisioned the carton of chocolate bars on the other side of the wall.

"Wanna stay for dinner?" Buck asked when the war was over. He never offered her even one stinking piece of chocolate.

Sarah burst out of the house and cried all the way home but unlike the wee little pig, she cried in tremendous choking sobs that were part tears and part wordless outcry.

Sarah hoped no one would notice her as she made her way home, it was just a short distance, but an older boy she knew as Kenny was bouncing a basketball in his driveway. He played the cello in the high school orchestra. Mrs. Chretien had taken Sarah to the school concerts, all of which began with the Pledge of Allegiance.

Kenny was aghast at the sound of Sarah, and hearing her he stopped, basketball cradled on his hip. "What's wrong, little girl?" But Sarah could not stop. Kenny listened helplessly as the saddest part of the Elgar—not the cello solo he'd been practicing all week but the wailing protest of the whole damn orchestra—flowed from the girl's mouth. He listened as she continued, a troubadour on a plague-ridden course.

Sarah Chretien never forgot the sandy-haired Kenny. She knew he was God, God in disguise, and she would have waved to him in her most friendly way except the long passage of tremolos was coming up and that was no time to lose control of herself.

III

The children had crossed some threshold—there were fewer pinafores and tulle party dresses, already some boys were fuzzy-faced—and Sarah hated them. Why'd she throw this party anyway, why'd she agree to put herself in the vortex of trouble?

Mrs. Chretien and Sarah's grandmother were busy in the kitchen putting the last touches on the cake. The rest of the attending mothers offered no protection but instead observed dispassionately as a few kids paired off and girls got felt up in the corners and under the stairs. The mothers, excepting Buck's mother, who sucked on her infinite supply of red licorice, simply pulled on the L&M cigarettes and, between furtive glances in the foyer mirror, swallowed one more cup of coffee. At night their toenails would turn brown from all the coffee. That's why they painted them opaque red.

When the celebrating was over, Sarah tore down the streamers and, with the party hats and soggy plates, buried the sweet mess in the paper tablecloth her mother had bought at the stationer's.

"Did you have a good time, birthday girl?"

"It sucked," Sarah answered, thinking of how the kids had nicknamed her Cretin, Sarah Cretin, at her own birthday party and of the buttercream rosettes they defiled with their indifference to her grandmother's pastry-bag mastery.

In bed that night the Happy Birthday! lettering that had been printed on all the party goods mocked her. Happy Birthday! was stenciled over everything, including her mother's forehead as she bent over to kiss her daughter goodnight. Sarah turned to the wall to avoid the kiss but there it was, Happy Birthday!, the stupid phrase, projected on her wall. It was even on her own tongue, in silver letters, and wouldn't scrape off.

Mrs. Chretien took out the garbage in her bare feet while her husband stealthily turned the radio dial away from the Beethoven sonata and the war news and didn't stop turning until he caught Tom Jones' latest hit, "What's New, Pussycat?" Sarah could hear the radio from her bedroom. The song and her father were a complete and distasteful mystery.

IV

What constitutes a normal day? Is it a day without disaster? There's no such thing, there's a little dying in each and every day, a little more ash in the lungs, a little more shame in the face.

Sarah had school the day after the party. A normal day by everyone's recollection. The bullies made fun of the fat girl and her bologna sandwich. Sarah's class saw a filmstrip on personal hygiene. The school bus ran over one of the twins' clarinets. At least the end was near, only one more week of schoolwork and then summer vacation. But it would be the same the next year, maybe worse, and increasingly worse as the boys grew darker and the girls nastier and the former kindergarteners would dive too deep and a thresher would take an arm and no one from this town would become famous though one would work in local television.

But that's out of the realm of Sarah's story. Sarah's days depend on what's on your bedroom wall, be it Jesus or Gandhi or the Star of David. Some say her world is filled with golden light, others say it's blacker than the world of the blind mice.

Sarah sat at her bedroom table, where she had convened so many tea parties for her dolls, and completed her homework. She shut her spiral notebook. On the back cover she drew her formulaic daisy. And another. She capped the pen and slipped it into the notebook's wire coil.

With the hammer she had taken from the toolbox under the sink in the kitchen where she paused to munch half a donut, Sarah banged a nail as high above her head as she could reach. This was the hardest part. She kept missing the narrow head. Her arms grew tired. More than once she nearly toppled off the stepstool.

Her left thumb would blacken at the nailbed where she'd accidentally hammered it. "You incompetent Cretin," she mumbled to herself and then swung the hammer onto her hard skull. Lights flickered. The eleven-year-old wobbled. Then she returned to her task.

Sarah's grandmother had given her a red patent leather belt for her birthday. She threaded it through the buckle then hung the belt onto the nail at the last punch hole. Sarah slipped the noose over her head and stepped off the stool. And that was that.

V

Not until the war ended was Mrs. Chretien able to visit Sarah. It had taken many years for her to recognize that the monster she'd encountered in her daughter's closet was her own flesh, her lovely Sarah. By the time she was released from the hospital, her daughter's body was boxed and buried, and though she'd attended the burial, Mrs. Chretien could not remember much other than the earsplitting sound of the crickets rubbing their greedy legs together on that bright June day, while somewhere off in the distance the Good Humor man jangled his bells, his change-maker, and the world went as white as his uniform as she turned her gaze to the sun.

"I can't forgive her," Mrs. Chretien said to Gandhi. "Don't ask me to," while Mr. Chretien deferentially lumbered out of the marriage bed like a bear in the night and began to learn how to be more of a father to his wife than he had been to his daughter. He can't be blamed. He was afraid of Sarah, of his love for her.

Mrs. Chretien was denied her music for years. Too melancholy, her husband and physician concurred, and her collection of symphonic records was donated to the Salvation Army along with two boxes of Sarah's clothes. "Take it," Mrs. Chretien had shrugged. "Take it all." But Mrs. Chretien had put the Elgar in her head long ago, when Sarah had been young enough to seek comfort in her lap and they'd lain on the couch together, in silence, understanding the way of the world in that first hopeless movement.

This is what the dead rumble from their graves below our feet, from their thrones above our heads, this earth-moving requiem, and Mrs. Chretien lies in the warm grass beside her daughter's bed and together they listen, one breath keeping the tempo, the other offering a cold breeze from the old battlefields.

Zan Tewksbury

Last Train to Bhutan

A One-Act Play Written for and Performed at the 2007
All-Kirkland Reunion

AN INTERLUDE FOR THREE CHARACTERS AND THE COLOR RED
CHARACTERS:
ZIGGY, 50-something, an offbeat lawyer who attended Kirkland College
in that school's twilight years
NORA, 17, Ziggy's precocious, college-bound daughter
THE SPIRIT of HARRY KONDOLEON, fashion and decor cop; also
beloved "Kirkland male," and later acclaimed playwright whose
tragically early death in 1995 cut short a brilliant career, and who is
lovingly and respectfully brought back to life to comment on the current
culture, and on Ziggy's life now and then, in his inimitable manner.

MUSIC: Pat Metheny's "Last Train Home" [*play from before the lights
come up until Harry Kondoleon begins speaking*]

SCENE: The master bedroom of Ziggy's condo-loft in Portland, Oregon.

*Center stage, ZIGGY, full-bodied from a life (perhaps too) well lived,
is propped up on her teak opium bed, dressed in a too-short, red
silk, slip-dress, an eye mask shoved up above puffy, bespectacled eyes,
mussing her short, once-hennaed, and now graying hair. The remnants
of a large glass of red wine sits on a teak bedside table. The wall behind
the bed is painted deep maroon, and the bedding consists of sheets,
blankets and pillow shams in hues of garnet, coral, and ruby. An eastern
decor theme is evidenced by a Red Tara thangka over the bed, and by*

alabaster statues of eastern deities (Ganesh, Kwan Yin, and Reclining Buddha) placed for maximum spiritual support around the room.

ZIGGY is reading a thick transcript and taking notes on a yellow legal pad. She looks up from time to time, putting the end of her pen into her mouth, and gazes into the compassionate eyes of Kwan Yin downstage right, as if seeking wisdom and insight she is too weary to summon for herself. A pair of diminutive, curly-haired, Wiener dogs are nestled like sausage links next to Ziggy's right hip on the bed.

The sound of water running from a sink faucet comes from offstage right.

HARRY KONDOLEON holds court over this monotoned scene from his perch on an elevated ledge in the corner, stage left.

HARRY KONDOLEON: [*looking around at the space*] Condo-loft, what the heck is that? Leave it to the 21st century to bring us a hybrid residence for the artiste wannabe! And what's this music? A jazzy raga? Fusion/confusion, like Ravi Winston, or George Shankar . . . [*snaps left fingers while dancing right hand and waggling his head . . . looking down at Z, right finger points*] Okay, I'd call that dress "slutty-tasteful." I'm thinking Fredricks of Hollywood . . . hmm . . . doesn't go with the rest of the stuff in here; must have come from the ill-advised *lis pendens*[1] Neopolitan boyfriend . . . why's it so tattered, though? Like a Tibetan prayer flag left flapping on a mountaintop . . . hmm . . . now I'm intrigued.

ZIGGY [*pen cap in mouth, reading from transcript*]: "Please identify all conduct of your supervisor that you claim constituted retaliation for your complaints of sexual harassment" . . . [*groaning in disgust as she quotes her own objection*] "Oh, come on! Asked and answered like five times already, plus, calls for a legal conclusion." . . . Frigging defense attorneys; there oughta be a law against deposition harassment!

HK: [*gesturing toward wine glass*] Lush! Well, at least the grapes are organic and locally grown . . . So, I guess the Pendleton blanket she's under tells us we're in Portland, "Orygone"—not a "real" city by any means, but if Gus Van Sant didn't totally abandon it after high school, how bad can it be? But, Dios Mio! Was there a fire sale at Neiman Marcus, or something?? [*In a mocking high voice*] "Oh, I'm losing my *jing*,[2] so ka-ching ka-ching!" [*imitating sound of old cash register ringing*] How does the girl even sleep in this crimson tsunami?

[*Chuckling*]
Still, it's a vast improvement over that monastic room in Minor Dorm with the cotton gauze Tree of Life bedspread and the Desiderata poster on the wall. [*Looks out*] Oh, come on, the only reason I was in Ziggy's dorm room was because I wanted to see her decorating style, as part of the audition process for my senior project film, so stop imagining things already! Anyway, we both already had boyfriends . . . [*next moment*] Oh God, what's come over me? Why do I feel like meditating? [*assumes lotus position with eyes closed, middle fingers touch thumbs*] Ohmmmm. . . .

Offstage left, the water turns off, and Nora comes out of the master bath with a towel on her head, wearing plaid boxers and a white tank top. She is taller than her mother, and slimmer, with large brown eyes and thick hair that she has just dyed blackish brown.

ZIGGY [*looking up at the sound of the bathroom door opening*]: Did the hair dying go okay, Poodle?

HK: How very precious! She refers to her kid and her dogs by the same term of endearment . . . but, those dogs aren't even poodles, they're . . . what are those dogs, anyway . . . mini doxies?! Gasp, they're about the size of that Hamilton professor's teacup Yorkie that used to run around the campus looking like an ornamental squirrel [*head in hands, shaking it in mild disgust*]

NORA, *her voice high and breathy*: I think so Mommy, but can you take a look to see if I got the color on evenly? [*She crawls onto the bed, removes the towel from her head, and shakes out her wet, chin-length hair, offering it to her mother*]

ZIGGY: Here, lemme see [*she inspects her daughter's head, turning it and looking underneath the locks like she's seeking out nits*] . . . hmm, pretty good job, I think. [she collapses back against the pillows] Sorry I couldn't help you with the actual dye job. I just had to get through this deposition tonight so I can start writing my client's trial testimony tomorrow . . .

NORA: Hey, Mommy, can you help me study for my French test?

ZIGGY [*lowering the depo transcript and pad, and patting the bed, beyond the canine yin/yang, and Nora leans back on the pillows beside her mother*]: Sure, I'm pretty much done with this, and *really* tired of reading answers given to carefully crafted defense questions that try to make what my client's supervisor did to her look like no big deal. Poop! [*tossing the thick transcript onto the wooden floor beside the bed, startling the two dogs, who jump to their tiny feet and start yipping fiercely*].

NORA [*in a lilting baby voice*]: Oooh, Ku and Qetz, it's okay, don't bark . . . [*the dogs look at her adoringly, whimper a bit, and then settle back down on the bed*] . . . you scared 'em, Mom!

ZIGGY: Sorry, poodles [*she pats them both with one deft pat of her hand, so small are they*] . . . go'sleep [*she gathers them into her hip, snugly, and they sigh contentedly*] . . .

HK: There it is again. . . . so affected, but in a kind of endearing, motherly way . . . [calling over to Z] Hey, where's my pat and cuddle, my tuck-in? [*Z appears to be hearing things, but there's nothing there*] No? Oh, alright, I'll just self-soothe [*hugs self and rocks on his ledge*] . . . Mmmm, Mmmmm . . .

NORA [*whispering, so not to hurt the dogs' feelings*]: You know, Mom, they're not what I call "real dogs." . . . I mean, German shepherds are real dogs . . .

HK: Uh-oh, a difference of opinion here . . .

ZIGGY: Yea, that's what Beto says he wants us to get after these guys "pass" [*whispers last word in Nora's ear*] . . . C'mon, you know we had to get "condo-sized" dogs . . . Plus, they're hypoallergenic . . .

HK: Of course! Why didn't I think of that? "Get the right dog for the right space." That Ziggy always had a knack for coming up with logical solutions that fit only her own sense of logic!

NORA: Okay, so the test is on past tense. Tell me if this is right: "*Quand j'etais une jeune fille, j'habitais en Australie.*"

ZIGGY: [*pausing to conjure up her rusty French*] Hmm, I don't know. Maybe you should say, "*J'ai habité[3] en Australie,*" because it was just a short-term living situation, not an ongoing thing.

NORA: Six months, right? Damn, I wish I hadn'ta been a baby . . . I can't remember squat about what it was like living in Australia.

HK: A stint in Australia? So very Kirkie! I can almost see her out in the bush, pretending she's re-enacting scenes from *Walkabout*.

ZIGGY: I loved Aus! Especially my three-day walkabout in the Red Centre. Your dad didn't want to take a baby to such a wild place, so he stayed home with you and your brother in Sydney. He was just so affected by that "*A dingo et my baby*" movie. I was alone for the first time in many, many years. Not that I didn't miss you, big time!

HK: As I was just saying . . . but you know, this is getting freakier by the minute! She even *travels* to red places. . . . Then again she always did take themes to their logical extreme, like dressing in that "oh, this old thing?" style, but you could see it was all perfectly coordinated, right down to the cocktail umbrellas in her hair . . .

NORA: God, I can't wait to get high school over with and go away to college and go traveling by *my*self . . . [*getting too excited, she stops*] . . . I mean, I'll miss you, and Dad, and [*putting her face down on the dogpile*] you lil putchkums, but I need to get out of Portland . . . I wanna see Cuba before it gets ruined . . . and not on some stupid tour, either. I mean the *real* thing.

HK: Holy Fidel! Like mother like daughter. . . . You can't get much redder than Cuba [*winks*].

ZIGGY: Hmm, Cuba, eh? [*Eyebrows raised skeptically*] But, I know whatcha mean, Poodle. [*Reaching for the glass of wine and sipping while she looks off into space*] . . . one place I'd really love to take you to is Bhutan, the last Buddhist kingdom on Earth . . . maybe when you graduate from college . . .

NORA: Yeah, travel sounds great . . . but gotta go to college first! . . . So, I'm down to my top three, what do you think: Sarah Lawrence, Bard, or Hampshire . . .

HK: Choosing where to go to college was really a very simple matter for me; I just chose a school that matched my initials [*holding out one hand at a time*] H-K, Hamilton-Kirkland! Ta-da! [*shrugs shoulders*] Such a pity Kirkland isn't still around for Nora to apply to . . .

ZIGGY: Hmm, those are all good, progressive schools . . . too bad Kirkland isn't still around, it would be perfect for you . . .

HK: Is there an echo in here? [*cups hand to ear*]

NORA: I even put down Hamilton as a place to send my ACT scores, but I understand it's not the same as when it was Hamilton *and* Kirkland . . .

ZIGGY: Too true. We had this motto during the times before the merger "et" my school, *"Living together is better than marriage."* We even wore it on tee shirts. For us Kirkland students, it was all about having choices, and. . . .

HK [*speaking for Ziggy*]: . . . *"You know how much I love choices!"* . . .

ZIGGY: Well, even though we lost our fight and the merger happened, I still like having choices: like choosing whether to go watch telly with Beto down in his photography studio, or stay up here with you, in our testosterone- and TV-free zone.

HK: Uh-oh, was that a metaphor for the Hamilton-Kirkland experience that just blew by me here?

NORA: [*Flopping back on her pillow, makes face*] Yuck, Beto's always watching *Antiques Roadshow*! I like our living arrangement, especially when you disappear because Will is coming over . . . [*Ziggy shoulder nudges her daughter and they smile knowingly*]

HK: [*singing*] Someone's got a boyfriend . . .

ZIGGY: So what did you guys do today after school?

NORA: Welllll . . . after we hung out at Anna Banana's and "drank coffee," we had a pretty good band practice . . . The guys loved my new punk ballad, and it was all going great, until Will and I got in a fight over the dumbest thing . . .

HK: . . . Ziggy's daughter's a singer in the band: no surprises there . . . I can still see Ziggy up on stage in Minor Theater, bleating out Sondheim songs like fingernails scraping on a chalkboard. [*Raises invisible highball glass and rasps drunkenly*] "Here's to the ladies who lunch!"

ZIGGY: What's up with old Willy boy?

NORA: Oh, I don't know. He was just being randomly aggressive on the drums. I swear he's been doing this distant, macho act ever since he started reading *On the Road*. It's like he's trying on this new persona, just for the hell of it.

HK: Now, that novel will make anyone want to take a road trip, see the world, get really wasted, and beat up girls . . . naw!! [*Looking out at audience*] Remember, kids: ART CAN'T HURT YOU.

ZIGGY: [*Chuckling knowingly*] Guys sure do seem to need their freedom, or at least seem to *think* they do . . .

NORA: I'm okay with giving him all the space he wants, it's just . . . [*beeping sound*] Oh, I'm getting texted . . . [*She digs a cell phone out from under the doggies and flips it open*] . . .

ZIGGY: What's it say?

NORA: "Anorable" [*typing a text reply with insanely fast fingers*] How sweet! [*flips phone closed and sighs*].

HK: Love in the electronic age, can you dig it? Text message make-ups and such. Before we know it, humans will return to communicating via telepathy [*Solemnly pronouncement-like*] People, I do believe we are coming full circle!

ZIGGY: Wish I could snap my fingers, Poo, and make everything be trouble-free in your relationships. Sorry, but it looks like you'll just have to go through the fire, like I did. . . . Well, hopefully *better* than I did . . .

HK: Ziggy never had that healthy fear of fire when it came to relationships . . . [*a la John Belushi*] Ohhhh no! She would just put on the kevlar catsuit, and jump right back into the red pit of flames. . . . Who could stop her? [*Shrugs*]

NORA: [*Fanning self as if overly hot*] Whew, why's it feel so warm in here? I thought *you* were the one getting the hot flashes . . . So where the heck is that place you were talking about wanting us to go to? Bhu-whaaa?

ZIGGY: Bhutan. It's in the Himalayan mountains.

HK: Ah yes, Bhutan. [*As if quoting from book*] *"A tiny bean of a country wedged between northern India and southwestern China."* What, do they measure progress by gross domestic blissfulness, or something?

ZIGGY: The well-being of the country is measured by its Gross Domestic Happiness, which I totally love. [*HK throws up hands*] And, there are these drinking establishments called chang houses, where you can do whatever you want as long as you are acting out of selfless service to another person. If you're caught acting out of self-interest, though, you are basically chopped to pieces. Sounds uber-romantic . . . and a bit dangerous . . . just my style . . . [*said with a faraway look as she swills down the last of the wine*]

HK: Hmm, this National Geographic-like fascination of hers might explain the militantly non-Western decor, but I still wonder what's with the threadbare thingy she's got on? Looks like *it's* been to a Bhutanese mountaintop.

NORA: Sounds cool. How do you get there?

[Last Train Home *comes up again, more toward end of song, just before the vocals come in*]

ZIGGY: Right now you can only fly a small plane into a very narrow valley between the mountain peaks, but they are talking about building a train line in India to the border with Bhutan, where you can change to a small bus. I think we should wait to go til we have a choice about how to enter the country . . .

HK: [*dramatically*] Give me choices or give me [*Feigning exasperation*] Oh, give me strength! The fabric of this metaphor is stretched so thin it needs seamless panties, in fire engine red, natch . . . !

NORA: I'd love to go with you, someday! [*gets up off the bed and goes to her mother's side, arms out*] C'mon, let's dance! [*ZIGGY emerges from her blanket and starts flailing her limbs about the stage as Nora cooly bops, while the two dogs stand on the bed and look on quizzically*]

NORA: Hey, awesome red dress-thingy, Mom! Where'd you get it?

HK: [*Perking up, eyes wide*] Finally! I'm all ears . . .

ZIGGY: One of my sassy girlfriends gave it to me for a joke birthday present a couple years ago. It's what I had on when I met Beto at Burning Man. . . . Yep, wearing just this, my Johnny Fluevog cowboy boots and my Mexican leather hat . . . ! [*Nora pulls a black brimmed hat from a nail on the wall and plops it on her mother's head. Ziggy fishes chunky black cowboy boots from under the bed and gives them to NORA who dons them*].

HK: Now I see! A week of screaming 90 mile-per-hour winds in the desert is all it takes to ruin a perfectly good silk baby doll! But there it is: Walkabouts, Bhutan, and Burning Man! She's now officially a full-on Kirkland cliché . . . Stick a fork in this scene, folks, it's so very overdone!

NORA: [*Boogying in her boots*] You are totally weird, Mom, but I like it—most of the time!

ZIGGY twirls in a circle, arms outstretched, dervishlike, to the rising vocals in the song, while NORA gets down on her booted feet. The dogs start yipping excitedly.

HK [*fairly shouting to be heard over the melee*] Bedlam, utter bleeping bedlam!! And this is one Kirkie who wouldn't have it any other way . . .

LIGHTS DOWN as music fades . . .

[1] *lis pendens*: "during litigation proceedings"; in this case, a divorce.
[2] (Pron. "*zhing*"): Chinese medicine term for kidney essence or life force.
[3] Pronounced "ahbitay."

Ellie Tupper

Ping

For want of a nail, the shoe was lost
Hoofs clattered on the rocky path, harness jangled. Dust rose and clung to the dark stains on the horses' legs, the riders' boots. Behind the last few horsemen, corpses dragged, banging and flopping over the stones. There wouldn't be much left of them to dangle from the Palace walls when the Imperateur and his Riders got back to Couronné.

The dust drifted across the track and settled on a girl who crouched in hiding, staring after the company in despair. It didn't matter where the troopers had been. Someone had let slip a word, out of spite or foolishness or torture, and the Imperial Riders had been sent. So there went the traitor, whoever he was, at the end of a rope—along with everyone who knew him. Let the country be at peace, every citizen loyal to the Imperateur. Tears traced the dust on her cheeks.

The rattle of hoof on stone moved past and away. Then, just as silence fell, Bella heard the slightest clear note, a *ping* of metal. She waited another moment, till the dust cloud hid her from anyone who might look back, then crept out to see. A lost harness buckle might buy a handful of olives for supper.

The fallen object lay right in front of her. Not a buckle but a horseshoe nail: square, sharp-tipped and dully dark. Bella knew nothing of farrier-work, horses were for rich folk, but it seemed awfully long, stretching across her palm. She couldn't imagine what sort of man would hammer it into a horse's foot.

She stood up to watch the dust float away behind the imperial troop. It struck her suddenly how this shard of iron seemed to sum up the Imperateur's domination of her beloved country: purposeful and brutal, inflicted on beings who could not resist, by men who cared for nothing but obedience.

Bella's hand clenched around the nail. This could go on no longer. People were dying—men at the hands of the Riders and their spies, women and children from starvation. Yet the people were terrified. Betrayal lurked in every shadow, the steel-handed troopers a constant threat. How could her land be saved?

An old saying came into her mind. "For want of a nail . . ." How did it go?

> For want of a nail, the shoe was lost
> For want of the shoe, the horse was lost
> For want of the horse, the knight was lost
> For want of the knight, the battle was lost
> For want of the battle, the empire was lost
> And all for the want of a little nail . . .

The nail seemed to grow hot in Bella's palm, matching the sudden intense purpose that gripped her. One little lost nail. But it symbolized an enormous thing: Barassonne I, Imperateur of Sillon, was not invulnerable. This tiny defect, just perhaps, could represent the first crack in the shackles that fettered the Sillonais.

~

For want of the shoe, the horse was lost
Summer again. The day's heat throbbed from the dusty stones, even now past midnight. The little band of saboteurs crouched in a cluster of thornbushes as Pierre, their sentinel, crawled flat as a snake to survey the Imperial outpost. A lone Imperial guard stood stiffly down below, scanning the empty desert.

There was no moon tonight. The stars cast a witchy silver glimmer, the perfect light to bewilder the sentry's vision, while Bella and her companions had planned their route for days and could have walked it blind. As Bella waited, her hand crept to the bosom of her blouse where the horseshoe nail rested in its leather sheath, as it had for the past year. This little metal symbol had hundreds of copies now, passed secretly from hand to hand as a token of solidarity against the Imperial tyranny. But the original was hers, and as always she felt a surge of strength and purpose when she touched it.

It was time. Pierre twisted back and beckoned. In the hot still darkness, bored and weary, the sentry had finally begun to nod. Moments later, Pierre's cudgel granted him a deeper sleep.

In trained silence the dozen patriots fanned out among the barracks huts. Gloved hands strewed thorns across the stableyard; others dumped scorpions into the boots that stood freshly greased in regimented rows. Bella herself slipped into the barracks kitchen, where she stirred handfuls of sand into meal sacks, wildspice into the breakfast gruel that simmered over the banked fire. The wildspice was her own, last-moment idea; the troopers would have an exciting morning when the herb reached their bowels.

In less than a hundred-count they were finished and had vanished back up among the rocks. Bold Pierre waited behind till everyone was clear. His task was the most dangerous, the most audacious: that of heaving the sentry's unconscious body into the camp well. Rescuing him should distract the other troopers long enough for the patriots to escape, but the well was deep and the noise could not be muffled. Bella held her breath.

The splash of water rang like victory bells in the silence, and Pierre sprinted for the rocks as the first shouts of alarm rose up. A naked Rider, more alert than the rest, scrambled out to loose a flight of arrows after him. But they only clattered off the boulders of the hillside as Bella and the others yanked their comrade to safety. The saboteurs took to their heels, breathless with laughter and triumph.

The Imperial Riders—those who were fit to ride, anyway, and whose horses had escaped the thorns—would burn the closest villages as they always did. But they'd find no villagers there to wreak their vengeance on; only hovels, stripped and empty. And the news would spread to the other towns, to Couronné, to the Imperateur himself, that his power was crumbling.

~

For want of the horse, the knight was lost
The sun of a third summer blazed down, and the people's joy blazed up to meet it. Bonfires had kept the past few nights as bright as the days. Sillon had a new future, as golden as the sunlight.

Bella's heart filled as she gazed from her balcony across the Grande Place of Couronné. Only two weeks ago the Dreamers of Freedom—the Imperateur's mocking nickname for the rebels, adopted with defiance— had marched into this very plaza with bold faces and beating hearts. Scores of them, clutching makeshift weapons and indomitable courage. And met, far from the massacre they dreaded, a welcome. Barassonne's minions had thrown down their swords and cheered their deliverers, while the few remaining collaborators had vanished into the shadows like the vermin they were.

Now thousands were gathered here, jammed into a solid exultant mass. Some clusters of folk were trying to dance, trampling their neighbors' toes and getting only laughter in return. Others drank, sang, or just howled in exuberance.

Beside Bella, Pierre stood at solemn attention—but his smile kept breaking out uncontrollably. He slanted his eyes at Bella. "A great day, my lady. A great day."

"Ha! Never 'my lady,' Pierre my brave!" But Bella grinned. "A wonderful day for Sillon."

On the parapet above them, the trumpeters rang out a brilliant fanfare. Pierre's smile returned, broad and proud. He took a step back, and Bella moved forward to the balcony railing. The Imperial crown was so heavy she couldn't look down or she'd lose her balance, but she knew that every eye in the Grande Place was on her.

"People of Sillon!" she cried, and everyone hushed to hear her. "Sisters and brothers! Today we build, together, a new future for our dear country! No longer will we fear, no longer dread the morning. I greet you now with the same joy you feel, the same pride. You have honored me with your trust, your patriotism, in asking me to become your Regent. I shall always honor you in return. My people, today Sillon is free!"

Their response thundered like an earthquake. *"Bella! Bella! Mira-Bella!"*

Late that night, Bella sat in her chambers alone, listening to the distant merriment that still rang through the city. Her women had helped her out of her gold-embroidered gown; the immense crown had vanished back into the treasury. She sat now in a silken robe finer than any she'd ever seen, on velvet cushions each worth a villager's house, and fingered the horseshoe nail in its sheath between her breasts.

A tap on the door, and Pierre entered. He had a wine jug in one hand, two goblets in the other, and a smile on his face. "A nightcap, my lady?"

Bella lifted her head sharply, then returned his smile. "How many times must I tell you, don't call me that. You'll make me vain."

"My Bella, then?" He set down wine and goblets and pulled a cushion off the divan to sit at her knee. "Ma belle . . ."

She smiled down at him, cupped his strong brown face in her hands, and pulled him up to her. "My consort . . . "

But she felt restless. Soon she pulled away from him, rose, began to pace. "What is it?" he asked.

"The Imperateur," she said. She spun in her tracks to face Pierre. "He worries me. How can Sillon be free if Barassonne still lives?"

"He's in the deepest dungeon in the Palace. And we know the dungeons here are very deep," said Pierre with satisfaction. "I like to think of him meeting the same rats my father and yours did. But we all agreed that your plan was best. Mercy is far better than vengeance. A few days to give him a taste of what others have suffered, and then accept his parole and banish him—a solution worthy of my wise and gentle Bella."

Bella drew her robe tight around her. The little leather sheath jabbed her breast, and she imagined the nail felt hot. "I have to see him tonight."

Pierre smiled. "You're so eager, my love. He's probably still too proud to accept your clemency. But you may be right to present your offer soon, so he can think about it in his prison. Yes, let's see him."

The dungeon was horrific: cold, stinking, silent. It took two guards to haul open Barassonne's cell door. Bella signed to them to leave, including Pierre with a turn of her head. They left a torch for her, and she stepped into the cell alone.

Blood smeared the face of the man huddled on the cot. Bruises blackened his arms and legs, what she could see of them under the heaps of chains. Her men had obeyed her thus far: he'd not been killed, but they'd had their time with the hated tyrant. He looked up at her with eyes sharp with recognition. "La Bella," he mumbled, and grinned a broken grin. "I knew you'd come."

In her fine robes, she stood over the former oppressor. "I'm not here to gloat, Barassonne."

"Oh, no. They tell me you plan to offer me amnesty. How noble." He gave a low, terrible chuckle. "Do you have that nail with you? Of course you do."

Bella touched the sheath, through her robe. "It's the sign of the revolution. Of your weakness, Barassonne. It's inspired the Sillonais for two years, and brought you to the ruin you deserve."

"Oh, it did that. And I suppose I do deserve it. But you should know, I didn't at first.

"Oh my, yes, I was as noble and high-minded as you." Bella stared, and the battered ex-Imperateur gave an amused grunt. "Hmm, hmm. You're too young. You don't remember how things were under Andruyen the Mad. He called himself the Césare. Blood ran in the streets daily; he was worse than I was. The people finally rose against him, and I at their head. And my inspiration was the tiniest thing imaginable: a horseshoe nail."

Bella gasped. "That's impossible."

"Oh no." The huddled man gave a wheeze that Bella suddenly realized was supposed to be a laugh. "Ah, damn these ribs—you dreamers are tough, I'll give you that. No, all I wanted was to save my country. Too bad I had all my old comrades executed afterward, they'd have told you it's the truth. I found the thing in the dust one day, and was never the same again."

"I'll hear no more of this," she commanded, her voice shaking. "You're making it up."

"Ah, ma belle, I wish I were," and all sign of laughter was gone. "It's probably too late, but I want to warn you about that thing. It's evil."

"My nail?" Bella demanded. "It's saved countless lives by bringing you down."

"I had a dream," Barassonne continued, as if she hadn't spoken. "A nightmare, one night about a year into my reign. A demon appeared by my bed. It stood so tall its head brushed the ceiling beams—brushed clear through them, as if they were the spirits, not it. It was broad as a wall, with a naked hide as black as a winter night that shimmered with a foul green light. Hmm, it doesn't sound that bad, but I promise you, ma belle, I wet the bed like a child. Then it spoke to me, and my bowels went too. It said it wanted the nail."

Bella clutched the sheath between her breasts. She couldn't speak. The man must be demented.

"Of course I said no," Barassonne mumbled on. "And the demon laughed. My, if I hadn't crapped everything already— It told me the horseshoe nail wasn't what it seemed. That it was one of the demon's own claws—and it showed me the gap in its huge paw, where one of its filthy black talons was missing. It said it had dropped the nail here among us humans for a game, just to see what we would do with it. Well, I wasn't going to just hand my nail back, demon or no demon. It had made me Imperateur! Besides, I was witless with terror. All I could do was gape at the monster and of course hold onto the nail—just as you're doing this moment."

Bella snatched her hand away from her bosom. "What—what happened?"

"Ah, you're interested now? Well, that's all. The demon laughed again and said it could wait. That the talon would destroy me, as it had Andruyen, and it planned to enjoy the show. And then it vanished.

"I had to tell my chambermen I'd been taken by a fit of illness, to explain the bedding, but I never let go of that nail. Until . . . until one day I discovered it was gone." For the first time, the man's voice wavered, and the chains clinked. "It turned my heart to sand. You think your Dreamers won you this revolution? I tell you, girl, it was the nail. The demon's Talon. It found another soul to feed on, and dropped me like an empty wineskin."

Bella's head was swimming. The horseshoe nail was her inspiration, yes, but it was she and her friends whose dreams and daring had won freedom for Sillon. Had brought her to the throne. "You're lying. My nail, magic? Impossible! We worked for this, all of us together. We freed Sillon from your tyranny. Your evil!"

"Oh, I don't argue that. But it's *you* that's, what, Regent now. Not anyone else." Barassonne snorted. "Girl, you'd still be chasing goats in the hills if it weren't for that nail."

"No!" A terrible heat was rising in Bella's breast. "You lie," she snarled. "I know what you want. You want to ruin us, ruin me with these lies! I won't have it. You're insane, raving. But you'll never tell, I'll never let you tell!" She was gasping, sobbing. "Never! Never!"

She heard Barassonne laughing again, laughing. But his laughter sounded wrong. It bubbled and broke. Then her vision cleared, and she saw that he lay amid the piled chains, bleeding from face and eyes, his throat a ruin. But still he laughed. "Ah, ma belle. It has you now. This is more like the amnesty I expected. Best . . . of luck . . . my dear . . ."

She realized she was clutching the nail in her hand. It flowed with Barassonne's blood. Horror skewed her sight so that the nail seemed impossibly long, jutting from her fist like a spike. Her robes were darkly spattered, her hands stained.

The blood seared her skin, roared in her brain. The vague dissatisfaction she'd felt in her chambers, only minutes ago, vanished in a burning certainty. Amnesty? Absurd! They never could have trusted him to keep these ravings to himself. Far better to silence him now.

The guards had left a bucket of water by the cot. Bella rinsed her hands and sheathed the nail. Calm now, she could see she'd foolishly imagined things: it hadn't grown, it was still only a simple nail. She summoned the guards and met their shocked faces boldly. "I have saved Sillon from a terrible mistake," she said. Pierre, blank with dismay, kept looking from her to the body and back. "The traitor Barassonne has rejected my mercy," said Bella. "He is ill, unfortunately, but we will give him a fair trial. Then we shall 'execute' him under the law. And none of you will speak a word of tonight. Am I understood?"

The guards bowed aside, and Bella swept past them, up into the night, to the haven of her chamber. Pierre stumbled behind her. She turned her head, "Oh, and Pierre. I don't think the title 'Regent' has quite the right dignity for the Lady of Sillon. Let's just use 'Imperatrice.' Everything's got Barassonne's monogram on it anyway, BI. Bella Imperatrice has a nice sound."

~

For want of the knight, the battle was lost
The peasants had been arguing for an hour now. The same excuses: the hot summer, the drying wells, the swarming flies and the sickness they brought. Bella stood up abruptly from her throne. "Enough." The peasants and their podgy spokesman gaped at her. How the devil could the man be so plump if his goats were all dying the way he said? "Enough. The taxes are due. They will be paid. If you don't have enough olives, I'll take the goats. Away with you."

Sniveling idiots. Bella turned with a flutter of silk and strode back through the curtains to her shady courtyard. A clap of hands brought maidservants with iced wine, sugared nuts, soft bread. Bella collapsed onto a cushioned bench and took a long drink of wine.

"My lady." It was Pierre. Bella studied him over the rim of her golden cup. His tanned face had paled over the past year, here with her in the Palace. He looked pasty and anxious. Even his broad shoulders and curly black hair looked tired. The dashing boy who'd plotted raids with her, dared death for her, had faded away.

"What is it?"

"Your ceremonial sword. You left in such haste . . ." He held the long sheath out across both hands.

"Ah. Thanks, Pierre. Bring it here." He obeyed, bending low so she could take it easily. Bella grasped the gold-studded sheath and slipped the sword out a few inches. The Great Sword of the Imperatrice of Sillon. She'd had it commissioned last summer, right after her coronation, and it had only been finished a few months ago. The blued steel gleamed and the gold initials *BI* sparkled along the blade.

She'd had the artisans embed the horseshoe nail inside the crystal hilt. Beneath the gold filigree that wrapped the crystal, the rough black iron was clear to see, dark and potent. Bella closed her hand around it and felt the strength shiver through her body.

"My lady," Pierre said again.

Bella opened her eyes, annoyed. "Yes?"

"I wonder— Might I have the favor of a few moments' speech with you?"

He sounded so damned timid these days. "Yes, of course. What is it?"

Pierre perched cautiously at the end of the bench. "I was thinking, my dear— My lady— That you might have been a bit hasty just then." Visibly bracing himself against her disapproval, "They were telling the truth, you know. This summer's been terrible. Wells are going dry. There's nothing to irrigate the crops with."

229

"Summer's hot every year in Sillon. That's why we make such good wine." Bella took a sip from her goblet, and bent her stare on Pierre. "Why don't they just grow vines instead of barley?"

"They—the land they have isn't right for vines," said Pierre. "But that's not it. Bella, you've been, well, pretty harsh with the people lately. Those executions last week—"

"Were perfectly justified. Don't speak to me of it. Traitors, all of them. How dare they speak ill of Sillon, their own homeland!"

"It's not Sillon they're unhappy with," said Pierre, so quietly she almost couldn't hear. "It's you."

Bella's voice matched his in softness. "What did you say?"

Pierre straightened, facing her. "I said, Bella— I said, the people are disappointed in you. You've grown hard. You were kind, before. You loved them, they loved you."

"Hmph. People's love can turn to hate like that!" with a snap of her fingers. "Am I right? See how it has! The best ruler is both loved *and* feared—it's the only way to control a country. But if you can't be both, then—" and she looked him in the eye, "fear is better."

"Do you know what they call you?" Pierre asked.

Bella's face softened to a smile. "Mira-Bella. The miraculous Bella. I've always liked the sound of that."

"It doesn't sound like that any more. Your name is Sangui-Bella, now. Bella, please hear me—"

She roared to her feet. "Sangui-Bella! Bloody Bella? How dare they! How dare you!" The sword in her hands was light as a feather. Through the crystal hilt, the horseshoe nail seared her palm. *"How dare you!"*

Screams brought her back to herself. "Shut up!" she raged at her women. Pierre's body lay there, legs still slowly twitching, his blood running over the white flagstones like wine. She tried to drop the sword, but the hilt clung to her hand, the nail filling the crystal with blackness . . .

She dreamed that night. Pierre came to her, the tanned, youthful Pierre she remembered from so long ago. Had it been only a year? Impossible. He stood at the foot of her bed and smiled at her.

Bella sat up with a cry and reached for him. "Pierre, my brave!"

And Pierre's smile twisted into a snarl. The warm dark eyes narrowed to a brutal black gleam, the face became a leering mask. His clothes faded away to obscene nakedness as his body swelled like a cloud of filthy smoke to loom over Bella.

"You stupid little bitch," rumbled the demon, and laughed.

A murky aura filled the chamber, dirty greenish-gray. Through it her rich surroundings still glittered faintly, dimmed and polluted. Bella clutched the covers to her breast, too petrified with fear even to reach for her Sword, lying on the table by her bed.

"You still have my talon, don't you?" the demon grinned. At its words, the Sword's hilt suddenly flared up, a foul green blaze that glittered off the demon's hide. "He warned you," the monster purred, "that greedy thug who had it before you. But by then its grip on you was too strong . . . and to give it up now would tear your guts out. Ah, it was a fine thing when I first thought of leaving my little bait among you weak-willed humans. It's been delightful to watch you tear each other to shreds over it like starving dogs.

"Little whore, keep the nail, at my pleasure. For now. When your soul is ashes, when you become wholly mine, it will move on to its next victim. In the meantime, I will watch, and be amused. Live long, little fool—if you can."

∿

For want of the battle, the empire was lost
The people never came out to see her processions any more. Medruche, her chief advisor, said it was because they feared to foul her divine form with their lowly gaze. Bella knew that was ridiculous, but he amused her with his compliments. The lazy worm was probably sitting in the shade back at the Palace right now, sipping iced sherbets. But Bella chose to ride out often, even in the summer heat, with her gilded armor blazing and the Great Sword of the Nail at her side. Just to remind them all who she was.

Her spies reported regularly on all the secret midnight gatherings, the plots against the throne and stability of Sillon. The commandant of the Imperial Riders was swift and efficient at following up on these rumors. Bella had ridden today to view the results of last week's cleansing. The troopers led her stallion carefully upwind of the ruins, and a perfumed scarf took care of most of the stench of burning. They'd had no luck with the villagers, who'd scattered like desert rats, but the troopers had torched their hovels as a warning against treasonous muttering.

The commandant sat his steed to Bella's left, properly a pace or two behind her. A vile man; if she weren't Imperatrice she might be afraid of him. But she knew that his lieutenants—she'd chosen them all—would kill him before he got within arms-length of her. They all

231

watched each other because they feared each other. And she was the one they feared the most.

Bella smiled.

"Well done," she said, and turned her stallion back toward Couronné. The Imperial Riders hastily spurred their horses into line. She required a strict order of precedence, punishing mistakes with demotions, floggings, whatever came to mind. It was amusing to change her direction unexpectedly, then watch forty armed and mounted men falling over themselves to suit her. On a whim she decided to execute the last man to reach his place, just as an example, and paused idly to see which it would be.

Abruptly amid the confusion came an instant of utter silence, as if Bella had been stricken deaf. In it, the slightest sound rang out. A small, metallic *ping.*

For a moment Bella didn't understand why it sounded so familiar. Then her eye lit on a thornbush a few paces away. In its shadow crouched a young boy, staring up at her with huge, hate-filled eyes. On the sand in front of him lay a long black horseshoe nail.

Bella seized her sword. The crystal hilt glittered: unbroken, but empty. The Nail had left her. "After him!" she screamed. But the disorganized Riders took too long to untangle, and the boy escaped.

That night Bella lay awake in her luxurious bedchamber. Lamplight wavered over the gilded furnishings, but she saw none of it. Words returned to her:

"I found the thing in the dust one day, and was never the same again . . ."

"The people are disappointed in you. You've grown hard . . ."

"I will watch, and be amused . . ."

Beside her bed, the empty crystal hilt of the Sword glittered mockingly in the lamplight. The Nail was gone, and with it all the fierce purpose that had driven her to the throne of Sillon. Losing it was tearing her guts out, just as the demon had said.

She'd walled herself in with toadies and brutes. She was alone. How much she would give to see Pierre again, bold and proud! But all that was left was the demon's mocking illusion. Tears filled Bella's eyes, and she flung herself among the cushions and sobbed.

At last she could only lie exhausted, the tears still silently flowing. She felt as drained as the wineskin Barassonne had spoken of. Without the Nail, she was nothing. How was she to live without its strength? The mere thought of her reign, the foul things she'd done so ruthlessly, set every nerve crawling with horror and shame. *There* was the true evil of the Nail, the demon's Talon. It had snared her by her own compassion, her yearning to rescue her beloved Sillon. Its insidious venom had twisted her ideals into atrocities, innocent Bella into Sangui-Bella. *Pierre* . . . The remorse was unbearable. All these years, it had never once occurred to her to cry; she'd never wept since the day she first found the Nail in the dust. Yet tonight she couldn't stop.

And from the seed of that simple fact, as Bella lay there desolate, a stunning realization slowly blossomed.

The Nail was gone. But not just from her sword. From herself.

Bella sat up, clutching a cushion to steady her suddenly trembling hands. She was not bereft. The Talon had abandoned her, yes, and taken all its brutal power with it. But the simple strengths she'd begun with—justice, conscience—still remained. Reviving and breaking her heart . . . but *she still had a heart.*

Across her opulent chamber, Bella began to see not a hideous black specter, but a glimmer of her old companion, hope.

How could this be? When Barassonne, Andruyen before him, had acquired the Nail, they'd lost their souls forever. Why should Bella's be restored once the evil had slunk away? Was she stronger, purer?—no, that was arrogance as bad as the Nail's! Or just that the Talon had owned her for a mere four years, while the others had ruled under its power for decades?

Perhaps Pierre could have told her. It might be as simple as love.

But guessing was a waste of time, and already Bella was planning. Even with the Nail, it had taken two years to depose Barassonne. The Talon's new victim was only a boy, no leader yet. With luck, Bella would have time to act. Time to purge her court, one by one, of the corrupted villains she'd encouraged. To find honest men among her troops and slowly, carefully, raise them to command. To set her spies against each other instead of against the guiltless. They feared her—ha, now she'd give them a reason.

Her rapacious followers wouldn't surrender their privileges easily. The Nail's disappearance could not be hidden. Any doubts of her authority must be quashed, yet without harming the innocent. It would be the hardest, most dangerous work of her life.

But if she succeeded, the revolution that Talon-possessed child was even now dreaming of would wilt before it flowered. Sillon would finally, truly, be free.

How *dared* that monster play this game with her land, her countrymen, for its own amusement! To free Sillon—to atone—yes, Bella would willingly face even a demon.

Now, she might even win.

And all for the want of a little nail.

Julie Weinstein

Train

I
What an exciting moment,
living totally for what
may happen.
There is a herring gull. We could perhaps
catch up to it.
Perhaps not, this train.
A river. I will
follow that river to its mouth,
swallow
whatever it is that is
waiting for me there,
I can make no distinctions now:
I am tied to nothing
this perpetual forward motion.

II
A woman looks out
the window of a train.
The passengers are not
a part of her vision.
A wooden house sags into the river.
The river, diamond-backed,
that she seems to be riding.
A duck also
rides the river.

There is the old stone manor, ruined,
on the little island.
She has passed it many times.
She would like to get out and
touch it.

III
The motion of the train,
non-motion, a lull.
The sound of mute voices,
pages turning words.
Going against
the river now. The birds
take off at this sound that passes
and leaves an empty silence.
And faces look out the train.
They are seeing,
or perhaps not,
their own passing
run before them
in the ruffled river, at the edge.

3/21/75–4/13/75

Abigail Wender

Thanksgiving

i. Engagement

The fall my brother announced his plans
to marry again, across your table we watched him
slip and nod, his eyes close
and we sat—twelve or fourteen of us,
family and friends—beneath the chandelier,
passing gravy and cranberry
and saying things, whatever
it was, while he began to die.

Bless our ignorance
for we can never be forgiven
for choosing not to see him.
No, he couldn't help himself.
When he turned to us in illness,
we turned away.

ii. Transplant

What happened had nothing to do with drugs, my brother answered.

Barely moving, he lay under a white sheet, his eyes open and clear.

The nurse brought methadone in a tiny cup like a paper hat.

Tell me more about us, he said, falling back to sleep.

iii. Coda

We were wrong, not evil.

I assumed death would reveal a moral—
for his loss to equal something.

That proved false.
All that is left
is to speak of how he'd hold his head

to one side, rapt,
as if he were pondering every word.

The Winter My Runaway Brother Returned

He came back wearing a Salvation Army coat
and a ponytail to his waist.
Watch him, you said.
Find him, Domina said.

Had he let me
I would have kept him, hid him, fed him.
That winter I followed him,
jumped subway stiles and guard rails,

at 3 a.m. we skidded and shrieked.
I thought we would burn
with the stars, our cries
thinning to lace, lace becoming ice.

Waking up
in his one-room studio, he lit a pipe,
smoke unfurling, unraveling his mind.
An ember flew up, I was unhinged

watching his eyes
under the closed thin lids,
the pipe slipped to the quilt.
A flare opened a dark hole.

Yellow Balloon

This time I won't answer the telephone
so no one's girlfriend
never hands me a small packet,
no dope tied up in a yellow balloon
never to hide in my purple sneaker.
She never stands at a door
naked but for no towel wrapped
around her, no one laughs
unseen behind her and I won't think "Slut,"
no riding to Riker's,
no dope in my shoe.
In the prison no waiting room,
no concertina wire at windows,
no guard touches my shoulder,
never saying, "Why so scared?"
This time I won't fear my brother
with hair not shorn, eyes not stung.
This time he never looks
and I never flinch,
never shudder like no camera lens,
no asking if I have it,
I won't have it.
I never have to deny him,
never renounce him,
he never loses me.

Valerie Worth

Crows

When the high
Snows lie worn
To rags along
The muddy furrows,

And the frozen
Sky frays, drooping
Gray and sodden
To the ground,

The sleek crows
Appear, flying
Low across the
Threadbare meadow

To jeer at
Winter's ruin
With their jubilant
Thaw, thaw, thaw!

Acorn

An acorn
Fits perfectly
Into its shingled
Cup, with a stick
Attached
At the top,

Its polished
Nut curves
In the shape
Of a drop, drawn
Down to a thorn
At the tip,

And its heart
Holds folded
Thick white fat
From which
A marvelous
Tree grows up:

I think no better
Invention or
Mechanical trick
Could ever
Be bought
In a shop.

Mushroom

The mushroom pushes
Its soft skull
Up through the soil,

Spreads its frail
Ribs into full
Pale bloom,

And floats,
A dim ghost,
Above the tomb

Where an oak's
Old dust lies
Flourishing still.

Contributor Biographies

Nin Andrews, Kirkland Class of 1980, is the author of several books including *The Book of Orgasms; Why They Grow Wings; Midlife Crisis with Dick and Jane; Dear Professor, Do You Live in a Vacuum?; Sleeping with Houdini;* and *Southern Comfort.* She also edited a book of translations of the French poet, Henri Michaux, entitled *Someone Wants to Steal My Name.*

Natalie Babbitt (nee Moore) grew up in Ohio. Her mother, an amateur landscape painter, provided early art lessons, for in the beginning, Natalie wanted only to become an illustrator. She majored in studio art at Smith College and married Samuel Fisher Babbitt right after her graduation in 1954. They spent the next ten years in Connecticut, Tennessee, and Washington, D.C., with Sam building his academic career, and she raising three children. In 1964, she urged Sam to collaborate with her on a children's book, *The Forty-Ninth Magician* (Pantheon, 1966)—he the author, she the illustrator—but then came the move to Clinton, NY, and the creation of Kirkland College. Sam didn't have time for more story writing, so Natalie decided to try becoming her own author and found that writing provided a challenge equal to that of illustration and is equally satisfying. Natalie is the author of seventeen children's books, including *Tuck Everlasting,* and her illustrations appear in nine volumes of poetry by Valerie Worth.

Samuel Fisher Babbitt was born in New Haven, CT, in 1929. He entered Yale, with the largest freshman class on record, in fall 1946. He enlisted in the US Army at the end of his sophomore year, but instead of the contracted two years, he served an additional year, most of it with the infantry in Korea, being discharged as a master sergeant. Graduating (finally) in 1953, he stayed on at Yale, working and studying part-time, and was married to Natalie as soon as she graduated from Smith. He was dean of men at Vanderbilt University for four years, served briefly with the Peace Corps' administration in Washington, and then returned to Yale to complete his doctorate in American Studies. In 1965, he was appointed president of Kirkland College.

After Kirkland, Babbitt worked in New York City as a fundraiser for the Memorial Sloan-Kettering Cancer Center, and then as senior vice president for development at Brown University in Providence, RI. Technically in retirement since 1994, Babbitt has been active in the Providence theater scene, as administrator and board member, and, increasingly, as a professional actor. The Babbitts plan a move within the next few years, back to the New Haven area.

Nina Bogin was born in New York City in 1952 and grew up on Long Island. She studied at Kirkland College and New York University (BA, 1975). She moved to France in 1976 and lives near the Swiss and German borders. She has received a National Endowment for the Arts grant and published three volumes of poetry, *In the North* (Graywolf Press), *The Winter Orchards* (Anvil Press Poetry), and *The Lost Hare* (Anvil Press Poetry). Her poems have appeared in literary magazines and anthologies in the United States, Canada, the United Kingdom, France, and Poland. She teaches English at a technological university and translates art history and literary criticism. She is married with two adult daughters.

Michael Burkard taught at Kirkland College from 1975 to 1978. He is the author of eleven collections of poetry, including *In a White Light, Ruby for Grief, Unsleeping, Envelope of Night: Selected and Uncollected Poems 1966–1990,* and *lucky coat anywhere*, and his three books of drawings and text are available at blurb.com. He has received numerous awards, including a Whiting Award and the Alice Fay di Castagnola Award. He currently teaches at Syracuse University.

Selma Burkom

THEN: One Side of the Lectern
Miss Jones's School; Pimlico Elementary School, #223; Robert E. Lee Junior High, #49; Western High School; Towson State College; New York University; University of Minnesota

:The Other Side of the Lectern
Forest Park High School, University of Minnesota, Kirkland College (1969–72), San Jose State University—Tutorials in Letters and Science, English Department, Women's Studies Program, American Studies Program, Humanities Department

:Out of the Classroom
The Union, Grievance Representative
Management, Associate Dean of the Faculty

NOW: Lectern-less
San Francisco Towers

Leslie Cook graduated from Kirkland in 1978. Leslie's poems are a wonderful gift to all who knew her. Each is a moment in time observed with remarkable insight by a barely mature young woman. In 1974, our family did celebrate Thanksgiving at a condominium on the Hudson across from New York City, and the barn and county marker were as she described them, down the dirt road from our recently acquired homestead in western Massachusetts. Leslie was not especially happy there after the freedom she had experienced living in inner-city New Haven. Thankfully, at the end of her third year in high school, she was accepted by Kirkland College. There she thrived with a double major in art and creative writing, working at various jobs including the college switchboard and running a country music show on WHCL. Encounters with Tanya Tucker and Patti Smith expanded her horizons. By her senior year she had fallen in love, adopted a kitten, and was living off campus. Those four years in Clinton, NY, were the best she had. She died as a result of an automobile accident on March 15, 1979, in Cambridge, MA. She was 21 years old.

Nancy Avery Dafoe, Kirkland Class of 1974, holds a master's in teaching in English from SUNY Cortland College and teaches English at East Syracuse Minoa Central High School. Nancy is a published poet and short story writer and also has written two novels, a screenplay, and a full-length book of short stories. Her book *Breaking Open the Box: A Guide to Creative Techniques to Improve Academic Writing and Generate Critical Thinking* was published by Rowman & Littlefield Education in 2013. She is married to Daniel Dafoe and lives in Homer, NY.

Nicole Dafoe is a 2004 graduate of Hamilton College and a 2007 graduate of Northeastern University School of Law. She is a lawyer working for the US Department of Labor in Washington, D.C., where she lives with her husband Adam Naill, a lawyer. Nicole is the daughter of Kirkland College graduate Nancy Dafoe and Daniel Dafoe.

Kathy Durland Dewart graduated from Cornell University with an MFA in Creative Writing in 1971. She taught at Kirkland from 1972 to 1975 and wished she had been able to stay longer. During the next twenty years, she did what she could to improve the lives of children and animals and raised her daughter, Tess. In 1994 her dear friend/sister-in-law, Constance Saltonstall, was dying of cancer and asked her to use her inheritance to establish an artist's foundation and colony. The Constance Saltonstall Foundation for the Arts is still thriving in Ithaca. Kathy was the director in the early years and on the board until 2011.

Rachel Dickinson was in Kirkland's last class and was the first and only woman from Kirkland to win a Thomas J. Watson Fellowship. She is a freelance writer and author (*Falconer on the Edge*, 2009) whose pieces have appeared in numerous publications including *The Atlantic, Smithsonian, The Hamilton Alumni Review,* and perceptivetravel.com.

Linda Dunn (cover art) is an artist, teacher, and collector of abandoned linens. Born in Philadelphia, PA, she graduated from Kirkland College in 1977 and received a BFA from the Rhode Island School of Design in 1991. She is a founding member of Lowell Fiber Studio and lives in Cambridge, MA. Linda's work begins with discarded hankies, sheets, and table runners: tactile artifacts of past lives. She transforms these with personal imagery, and then combines them with paint, collage, and stitch to explore memory as it changes over time. Her work is in several private collections and has been exhibited nationally.

Carol G. Durst-Wertheim, Kirkland Class of 1974, has taught and served in the administration of several New York metropolitan universities in culinary, food studies, hospitality, and tourism programs. She was the first director of the New York Restaurant School, owned a catering business, and is the author of *I Knew You Were Coming So I Baked a Cake* (Simon & Schuster, 1997). She served on the Board of Women Chefs and Restaurateurs and co-chairs their Scholarship Committee. Carol is creating an oral history of the New York Women's Culinary Alliance and leads "Menus at the Movies" at a local library. She completed her doctorate researching women in the food industry, has consulted for numerous community-based organizations, and has worked on national cookbook awards and baking contests.

Stephanie Feuer's, (Kirkland Class of 1977) articles and essays have appeared in *The New York Times, The New York Daily News, The Boston Herald, Sojourner, BettyConfidential.com, The Mom Egg,* and many other publications. She's read her work at KGB, The Bowery Poetry Club, The Cornelia Street Café, The Museum of Motherhood, and in the "See Me, Hear Me" show, and is a creative nonfiction editor of the literary magazine *Conclave*. She lives with her husband and teenage son in New York City, where she manages a healthcare website. Stephanie recently completed a young adult novel.

Elizabeth A. Fletcher, Kirkland Class of 1974, lives in Swarthmore, PA, with her husband Fred Tinter and sons Evan, 21, and Alex, 13. She is a project manager for a company that develops assessments of physicians and other healthcare professionals. She does outreach to medical schools and sometimes travels to interesting places like Prague. She also writes for the company website and develops marketing materials. She says, "Family life is always busy. Both my sons are avid soccer players and our younger boy plays baseball, so we watch lots of games. In my spare time, I read and write both poetry and fiction. Currently, I am working on a middle-grade fantasy novel."

Doris Friedensohn was dean of students and associate professor of American Studies at Kirkland from 1970 to 1973. She is Professor Emerita of Women's Studies at New Jersey City University and the 2003 winner of the American Studies Association's Bode Pearson Lifetime Achievement Prize. Among her publications are *Cooking for Change: Tales from a Food Service Training Academy*, Full Court Press, 2011 and *Eating As I Go: Scenes from America and Abroad*, University Press of Kentucky, 2006. Kirkland College published two of her books on innovative teaching and learning: *242: Education and Social Change*, with Daphne Petri, Kirkland College Press, 1972 and *Action Studies: American Attitudes and Values and the Struggle for Social Change*, with Gwynn O'Gara, Kirkland College Press, 1973.

Elias Friedensohn, who died in 1991, was chair of the Arts Division at Kirkland from 1970 to 1972. He joined the Queens College (CUNY) Art Department in 1959, took a leave of absence to work at Kirkland, and retired as Professor Emeritus of Art in 1987. A figurative artist and a passionate humanist, he worked in several media—from epoxy sculpture and oils to watercolor and charcoal. In addition to more than forty one-person exhibits, Friedensohn's paintings and sculpture appeared in major national shows at the Whitney Museum, the Art Institute of Chicago, the Smithsonian Institution, and many others. He is represented in a variety of permanent collections including the Whitney Museum, Sara Roby Foundation, Walker Art Center in Minneapolis, and Los Angeles County

Museum. An illustrated booklet on his work, *Secrets of Elias Friedensohn*, can be obtained by emailing doris.friedensohn@verizon.net.

Tess Gallagher taught at Kirkland from 1975 to 1977. Her *Instructions to the Double,* published in 1976, features an etching by Laura Battle, Kirkland Class of 1978, based on a photograph by Helen Morse, Kirkland Class of 1977. Tess' ninth volume of poetry is *Midnight Lantern: New and Selected Poems* (Graywolf Press). Other poetry includes *Dear Ghosts, Moon Crossing Bridge,* and *Amplitude.* Her short fiction includes *The Man from Kenvara: Selected Stories, Barnacle Soup—Stories from the West of Ireland,* a collaboration with the Irish storyteller Josie Gray, *At the Owl Woman Saloon,* and *The Lover of Horses.* She spends time in a cottage in Lough Arrow in the West of Ireland and also lives and writes in her hometown of Port Angeles, WA.

Judy Silverstein Gray, Kirkland Class of 1978, has authored one book and has a compilation of short stories in process. An award-winning journalist for seventeen years, she is also a Poynter Institute for Media Studies contributor. Mostly, she finds inspiration in the narratives of everyday people. She has also juggled a strategic communications career for more than three decades, working with clients on parks, agriculture, historic preservation, and healthcare. As a longtime US Coast Guard reservist, she has documented the organization's rich history—including hurricanes, rescues, and marine environmental protection. She and her husband Rich live in Tampa, FL, where they enjoy kayaking and bike riding.

Susan Hartman, Kirkland Class of 1974, was twice awarded the Watrous Prize for poetry and received an MFA in writing from Columbia University. She is the author of two books of poetry, *Dumb Show* and *El Abogado,* and a chapbook, *Satyr.* She has written cover stories and profiles from places as different as Northern Ireland and Queens, Las Vegas and Brooklyn for *The New York Times, The Christian Science Monitor,* and *Newsday.* She teaches journalism and nonfiction at New York University and is also on the faculty of the International Center of Photography (ICP) in New York City.

Constance (Connie) Halporn (text design and technical support) graduated Kirkland in 1978 with a major in media studies and stayed on as assistant director of Audio-Visual Services at the merged Hamilton College. In summer 1980, she returned to New York City and joined Columbia University's Biomedical Communications Division at the

College of Physicians and Surgeons. While rising to the head of medical photography, Connie was still coaching and photographing judo. She was an official photographer for US Judo team at the 1992 and 1996 Summer Olympics games. She and her husband, Frank Colonnese, still coach judo at NYU Polytechnic University in downtown Brooklyn, New York.

Martha Hawley was born to US-Canadian parents, raised in New York suburbs, and is now a US-Dutch dual national and resident of Amsterdam. Her 1973 Kirkland Bachelor of Arts in Languages and Literature was earned on the Hill; in Bogotá, Colombia; and in New Haven (Modern Chinese at Yale). Ramona Macfarlane Marroquín Hawley is her daughter. She has produced work in print journalism and narrative nonfiction, teaching, and international radio production. Her articles have appeared in *Songlines*, UK; *Silk Road*, Taiwan; *IPS (Inter Press Service)*; *Mixed Magazine*; *Eindhoven*; and other European and North American publications.

Alice Aldrich Hildebrand graduated from Kirkland in 1973, with a major in creative writing. She graduated from Bangor Theological Seminary in 1987 with a Master's of Divinity. She is an ordained minister in the United Church of Christ, currently employed as a chaplain at Maine Medical Center in Portland, ME. She has received numerous awards for poetry, including the Watrous Prize, 1973. Her work has been published in *Puckerbrush Review* and *Killick Stones, an Anthology of Maine Island Writing*. She is married and has three sons.

Ellen Horan graduated Kirkland College in 1978 as a history and studio art major. She has participated in art shows and worked as a photo editor for magazine and book companies, including Condé Nast and Hearst. She published a novel, *31 Bond Street*, about a legal drama unfolding in New York City before the outbreak of the Civil War and is working on a new novel.

Elisabeth (Liz) Horwitt, Kirkland Class of 1973, has written fiction since the age of 10. She majored in creative writing at Kirkland and won a Watrous Prize for a short story. She currently lives in Newton, MA, with her husband and Welsh Corgi. Her son Jeremy is pursuing a career in 3D video game animation. Liz writes articles for the business information technology press. She has completed one novel, *Lucia and Susan*, and is currently working on a novel for middle graders, about an adolescent artist who feels like the world is against her and bonds with her curmudgeonly Nana.

Deborah Pender Hutchison, Kirkland Class of 1973, lives in a small log cabin in a "holler" at the base of a forested ridge in the surprisingly rugged hills of south-central Indiana. She shares the space with her singer-songwriter retired Episcopal priest spouse (Jonathan, Hamilton Class of 1974) and assorted critters, some tame, some wild. She's been a singer-songwriter, a flutist, a lay pastor, a mother to two sons, and a spiritual director—sometimes all at once. Writing poetry grew out of a growing desire to "eff" the ineffable.

Lynn Kanter, Kirkland Class of 1976, writes: "What good is a degree in creative writing from Kirkland College? I learned to read and think from Nancy Rabinowitz and Peter Rabinowitz. Bill Rosenfeld and Tess Gallagher introduced me to the craft of writing." With that firm foundation, she has had two novels published by Third Side Press (*On Lill Street* and *The Mayor of Heaven*), as well as numerous short stories and essays. She has made a living as a writer, working for the past twenty years for a national social justice organization, the Center for Community Change. "Mature fruit from a vanished orchard."

Peggy Dills Kelter, Kirkland Class of 1978, is an English as a Second Language teacher at Mid Valley Elementary, a rural school in northwest Oregon. She entered the teaching profession in her late forties, following lengthy stints as a bookseller and an artist. Her monthly column, "Cascade Observations," grew from an occasional assignment writing book reviews for her hometown newspaper, *The Hood River News*. Peggy is married to Jim Kelter, a brewmaster for Full Sail, a local brewery. She is the mother of Rose, a graduate of Linfield College who currently works in public health. Peggy lives in Hood River, OR, in the heart of the beautiful Columbia River Gorge.

Naomi Lazard was poet-in-residence at Kirkland College and has also taught at the University of Montana, SUNY Purchase, and the 92nd Street Y. She is the author of the poetry collections *Cry of the Peacock* (Harcourt Brace), *The Moonlit Upper Deckerina* (Sheep Meadow Press), and *Ordinances* (Ardis Press). She also has published a children's book, *What Amanda Saw* (Greenwillow), and a book of translations, *The True Subject: Selected Poems of Faiz Ahmed Faiz* (Princeton University Press), which was republished by Oxford University Press in 2012. The recipient of two NEA Fellowships, Naomi has published in *The New Yorker, Chicago Review, The Nation, Harper's, The Paris Review,* and other newspapers and literary journals.

Denise Levertov (1923–1997) was born in England and moved to the United States in 1947 with her American-born husband, Mitchell Goodman. She was the author of more than twenty books of poetry, including these from New Directions Press: *To Stay Alive, Footprints, The Freeing of the Dust, Breathing the Water, A Door in the Hive*, and *The Sands of the Well*. She taught at Brandeis University, MIT, University of Washington, and Stanford University. From 1970 to 1971, she was a visiting professor at Kirkland College at the height of Vietnam War protests and taught some contributors in this anthology.

Kathryn E. Livingston's (Kirkland Class of 1975) articles, essays, and reviews have appeared in *Parenting, Publishers Weekly, Redbook, Country Living, Family Life, Edutopia, Working Mother, American Photo*, and other magazines. She is the author of several books on photography, a self-published book of essays, *All About Motherhood* (iUniverse), and the co-author of two parenting titles, *The Secret Life of the Dyslexic Child* (Rodale) and *Parenting Partners* (St. Martin's). She lives in Bergen County, New Jersey, with her husband and three sons, and is currently penning a memoir about how the unlikely pairing of yoga and breast cancer changed her life.

Donna French McArdle graduated in 1976 after studying with Tess Gallagher and Michael Burkard, and, for one semester in her junior year, with the poet Richard Shelton at the University of Arizona. In 1978, she attended the Bread Loaf Writers' Conference on a scholarship and then entered the MFA program at the University of Iowa, graduating in 1980. She has published in *Antioch Review, Prairie Schooner, Coe Review*, and *Cutbank*. In 2003, the Massachusetts/Boxford Cultural Councils gave her funding to create *Essex County Harvest*, a book that follows the local growing season. She now works as a writing coach in a public elementary school.

Victoria Kohn Michels, Kirkland Class of 1980, has published poems in *Under 35: The New Generation of American Poets, Open City, The Quarterly, Hanging Loose, River Styx, Rolling Stone, The Bad Henry Review, Maine Life*, and *Red Weather*. She was the editor of *Red Weather* (1979–1980). For many years she worked as a photo editor and reporter for publications including *The New York Times, LIFE, People, Fortune*, and *Entertainment Weekly*. She has published articles in *The New York Times, LIFE, Elle*, and *Premiere*. She conducted the interviews for *A Cry For Help: Stories of Homelessness and Hope* with photographs by Mary

Ellen Mark and has done interviews for commercial and nonprofit film projects with Oscar-nominated director Martin Bell (*Streetwise*). She lives in Brooklyn with her husband and daughter.

Jennifer Morris, Kirkland Class of 1972 (marketing and promotion), was led into the emerging field of multimedia production by Kirkland's Electronic Music Studio. She helped found a laser engineering and entertainment firm in 1979 and participated in high-profile extravaganzas such as the 1986 Liberty Weekend. Her work was also featured at corporate events, trade shows, and music festivals for more than twenty years, in diverse venues ranging from Las Vegas casinos to Boston's Symphony Hall. She exited the firm in 1995 to focus on family commitments and became a consultant and communications strategist. She and her spouse of thirty years have three adult sons who are active in the performing and graphic arts.

Liz Morrison, Kirkland Class of 1978, is a San Diego writer. Her work has appeared in *The San Diego Union Tribune, San Diego Jewish Journal, Living In Style, Fido Friendly,* and *Dining Out.* Her opinion pieces have been featured on several websites including *Washington Blade, Houston Voice, Southern Voice,* and *Generation J.* Liz's short stories have been published in *Sinister Wisdom* and in the following anthologies: *Testimonies, From These Walls, Storied Crossings,* and *Mentch—Queer Jews Speak Out.*

Ilene Moskin graduated from Kirkland College in 1976. She earned an MFA from the University of Iowa Writers' Workshop in 1979 and an MSW from Wurzweiler School of Social Work in 1989. She is the clinical director of a community mental health clinic in Brooklyn NY, where she has worked for the past twenty-one years. She lives in New York City.

Isabel Weinger Nielsen, Kirkland Class of 1976, began writing poetry at the age of 7 and decided then that she would always be a writer. She attended Kirkland College because of its creative writing program and did public relations for the Arts Division while there. Her senior project "Portraits and Self-Portrait" included "She Might Break," which won the Watrous Award for fiction in 1976. Isabel decided not to pursue writing as a career but expanded her creative horizons and is now a freelance photographer living in Northfield, Vermont. She and Lars Nielsen (Hamilton Class of 1977) married in 1982 and have two sons, Ari and Noah.

Barbara Elizabeth Nixon, Kirkland Class of 1976, is an Episcopal/ Anglican priest living in northern California. She loves the mountains, the ocean, the arts, traveling, and spending time with friends. She loved the glen, the coffee house, the apple trees, the cows, fields, and forests at Kirkland where she majored in religion and dance. Her spirit still dances, and she continues to serve her Lord Jesus Christ today as she did during her years at Kirkland and Hamilton.

Gwynn O'Gara, Kirkland Class of 1973, is the author of three poetry collections, *Snake Woman Poems* (Beatitude Press, 1983), *Fixer-Upper* (d-Press, 2007), and *Winter at Green Haven* (Word Temple Press, 2008). She has taught with California Poets in the Schools for twenty years and was selected as Sonoma County Poet Laureate for 2010–2011. Her poems appear in *Calyx, Beatitude* Golden Anniversary issue, *Sage Woman*, and *What the World Hears*, the California Poets in the Schools 2009 Anthology. She lives in Northern California with her husband, dog, and apple tree.

Joanne Papanek Orlando graduated from Kirkland in 1974 as a sociology major. In the fall of her senior year, contemplating her future plans, she realized that she had committed significant energy to her home church and the Kirkland/Hamilton religious community. She graduated from Harvard Divinity School in June 1978 and was ordained as a Unitarian Universalist minister that same month. Discovering that parish ministry was not for her, she worked as a hospital chaplain. In December 1974, she married Rocco Orlando III (Hamilton Class of 1974), and they have two sons: Rocky and Alex.

Jo Pitkin, Kirkland Class of 1978, founded the Hamilton/Kirkland literary magazine, *Red Weather*, in 1976 and served as its editor through her senior year. In 1977, she won the Watrous Prize for "The Lakehouse." Jo earned an MFA from the Writers' Workshop at the University of Iowa and is the author of *The Measure* (Finishing Line Press), *Cradle of the American Circus: Poems from Somers, New York* (The History Press), and *Commonplace Invasions* (forthcoming from Ireland's Salmon Poetry). She has won numerous awards and is published in journals and anthologies including *Little Star, The New York Review of Books, Crab Orchard Review, Nimrod International Journal, Quarterly West, Ironwood, Stone Canoe: A Journal of Arts and Ideas from Upstate New York, Riverine: An Anthology of Hudson Valley Writers*, and *Vanguard Voices of the Hudson Valley.*

Rebecca Pressman (copyright and permissions) graduated from Kirkland College in 1978. She then received a JD from Catholic University, an MLS from Rutgers University, and a PhD from Florida State University. She is currently employed as a law librarian for Legal Services of New Jersey and lives in Nyack, NY. Her article, "Fair Use: Law, Ethics and Librarians" was published in the *Journal of Library Administration* in 2008.

Clare Guzzo Robert, Kirkland Class of 1973, lived in Cambridge, MA; Washington, DC; and Geneva, Switzerland, before settling in Orange, CT. She is a graduate of the Yale University Divinity School and is ordained in the United Church of Christ. Currently, she is serving as interim associate minister at the First Congregational Church of Guilford, CT. Clare's essay is based on her experience of mindfulness meditation, learned at Insight Meditation Society, Barre, MA. As a pastor, Clare teaches Christian Meditation, combining a Buddhist and Christian approach to mindful living. Clare is married to Patrick Robert, and they are grandparents of Lila, born in June 2011.

Irma Rosenfeld has taught English and creative writing at Hamilton, Utica, and Baldwin-Wallace colleges, and the 1969 Inter-Arts Seminar at Kirkland. Writing her own fiction and poetry has been a lifelong occupation, along with those involving music and travel, the latter, most ambitiously, realized by full years in Brazil and Macedonia, where husband Bill had Fulbright lectureships. Dominating all these interests has been the challenge of raising three children, all enticed into the pursuit of arts and letters.

William Rosenfeld, now retired, taught at the college level for forty years, twenty-six at Kirkland and Hamilton. He has written a few poems that he admits to and still enjoys writing fiction (both long and short), creative nonfiction, and currently a play. His historical novel based on Giuseppe Garibaldi's military experience in Brazil was published in 2013 by Branden Books. He maintains a gratifying correspondence with former students and with winners of the annual chapbook prize awarded in his name.

Deborah Ross, Kirkland Class of 1975, came to Hawai'i in 1980, first to teach English at UH-Manoa, and then at Hawai'i Pacific University, where she has been professor of English for more than a decade. Inspired by John O'Neill at Hamilton and Ursula Colby at Kirkland, she has published on various aspects of gender and narrative, ranging from Shakespeare and Frances Burney to Disney, as well as her own "women's stories." She is a single mother of two teenagers, two rabbits, and a cat, who inspire her to look for humor in the frustrations and sadnesses of daily life.

Betty Sarvey Salek, Kirkland Class of 1978, said *The Fish in the Mirror* was first born as her senior project at Kirkland. She feels she was fortunate to have Natalie Babbitt as one of her readers, since writing for children was no longer offered as a class. In the many years since then, the story has undergone several transformations. Although she was unable to live the dream of being a full-time writer, creative writing has been an ever-present aspect of her life, sandwiched between jobs writing for newspapers, caring for a daughter and twin sons, and her current job as a substitute teacher, which keeps her in touch with children and is highly rewarding in itself. For the past thirty years, she has lived in rural central New York State, not far from Clinton.

Amy Schiffman graduated from Kirkland College in 1978 and soon began working as a magazine editor and columnist in New York, for *American Photographer Magazine, GQ,* and *Diversion.* She moved to California, where she ran the Literary Properties Department at the William Morris Agency and sold (among many others) the novels *Friday Night Lights, Apollo 13, Sleepers,* and *Primal Fear,* all of which became feature films. Today she is a partner at Joel Gotler and Associates, where she continues to represent literary properties to film, television, and stage. Her client list includes Dennis Lehane, Don DeLillo, Daniel Woodrell, Dan Savage, and screenwriters including Peter Filardi and David Murray. She lives in Santa Monica with her partner, Claudia Eller, and their two children.

Susan Shopmaker, Kirkland Class of 1978, is a casting director for film and television in New York City.

Maria Theresa Stadtmueller, Kirkland Class of 1977, started writing long after leaving Kirkland. After years working in classical music, she was a stand-up comic based in New York City; that career morphed into writing essays. She then earned an MFA in literary nonfiction writing at the University of Iowa and has published in *Utne Reader* and in *The Iowa Review, Dark Mountain Journal,* and other literary journals. She lives on a permaculture homestead in Vermont, works for Middlebury College, and contributes radio essays about her conviction that this whole techno-industrial sticky trap is headed for the cosmic trash heap.

255

Constance Stellas was a charter class member of Kirkland College and since graduating has pursued a variety of careers. She is an actor and writer, with four published books and several short stories. Currently, Constance is an astrologer. A profile of her "unusual" profession was featured on Hamilton's e-newsletter. She can be heard on Sirius-XM radio twice a month, and her astrology column is featured in the magazine *Prestige*.

Billie Jean Stratton, Kirkland Class of 1974, a farm girl from a very small town in Chenango County, came to Kirkland with an inquiring mind. For various reasons she was unable to write a paper and without knowing it, too attention deficit to read. Nevertheless, Kirkland gave her the foundation for overcoming adversity and going on to succeed. She has always used her life as a staging ground for her work and her work as an instrument to survive her life. She remains dedicated to the idea that a truly free woman's college is necessary for women to understand their rightful position in this life and that this reality needs truly free women to help solve the problems that are intrinsic in this life.

Jane Summer, Kirkland Class of 1976, after working extensively in magazine publishing and then among the elderly as a creative arts facilitator, is earning her MFA at Goddard College. Her prose and poetry have been widely published, most recently in *The Spoon River Poetry Review, North Atlantic Review, North Dakota Review*, and *Ploughshares*. She maintains many Kirkland friendships. Summer has a niece, one remarkable young woman.

Melanie Sutherland (stage director and event producer) graduated from Kirkland/Hamilton in 1979. Melanie conceived, coordinated, and directed *Kirkland Echoes*, the four one-acts commissioned for the 2007 All-Kirkland Reunion. Her New York and regional highlights include *7 Sins in 60 Minutes* (conceived with seven women writers); *Fargo* by David Morse; *Easter in an Alley* by Michael Rispoli, featuring Tony-winner Frank Wood; a gender-bending *The Misanthrope;* and *The Love of the Nightingale* as guest director at Hamilton. Awards and Residencies: John Golden; NYSCA; four Who's Who; Atlantic Center for the Arts; NYWA board member; WAMCo past president.

Zan Tewksbury, Kirkland Class of 1980, has continued her love of theater and creative writing, first as an aspiring playwright in New York City, and later as a civil rights lawyer in Portland, OR. She met her husband, photographer Sergio Ortiz, at the Burning Man festival.

Zan's real-life daughter currently attends Hunter College in New York City and toured the East Coast with her no-wave rock band in the summer of 2011.

Ellie (Spencer) Tupper, Kirkland Class of 1972, is based in the Washington, D.C. area and is known in small but select circles for her editing, her writing, and her beer. Her greatest interest has always been in speculative fiction—members of the Charter Class were expected to be able to envision possibilities, right?—and most recently she's found success with short works. Her stories have been published by *MindFlights, Andromeda Spaceways Inflight Magazine, Every Day Fiction*, and the well-known fantasy author and editor Esther Friesner (*Witch Way to the Mall?*, anthology, Baen Books, June 2009).

Julie Weinstein, Kirkland Class of 1975, graduated with a bachelor's in creative writing. She earned a master's in psychology, worked with substance abusers, and then as a supervising social worker for Los Angeles County Department of Children and Family Services. Julie lived in Los Angeles with her partner and their daughter, and in 1997 became a single parent. In August 2009, she moved back to New York and in fall 2011 earned an MS in global affairs at NYU. She teaches general psychology at LaGuardia Community College and does volunteer work with refugees. Her daughter is at Oberlin College, class of 2013.

Abigail Wender, Kirkland Class of 1977, has published poems in *The Massachusetts Review, The New Orleans Review, Mead Magazine*, and others. She is a graduate of the MFA Program for Writers at Warren Wilson College, a contributing editor of *The Kenyon Review*, and teaches privately. She lives in New York City with her husband and children.

Valerie Worth (1933–1994) was born in Philadelphia. A poet and children's book writer, she lived in Clinton with her husband, Kirkland literature professor George Bahlke. Worth's books—illustrated by Natalie Babbitt—include *Small Poems* (1972), *More Small Poems* (1976), *Still More Small Poems* (1978), *Small Poems Again* (1986), and the posthumous *Peacock and Other Poems*.

Acknowledgments

I wish to thank Betty Sarvey Salek, the late Laurie Honors, Claire Gibbons, Judy Silverstein Gray, Jennie Morris, and Zan Tewksbury for their initial support and enthusiasm for this undertaking. Thanks, also, to Don Challenger, editor of *Hamilton Alumni Review*, Hamilton College's Archivist Katherine Collett, and Sharon Rippey and Pauline Caputi of Hamilton's Alumni Office for help in garnering submissions and contact information. I am grateful for the vision and meticulous attention of Dr. Beth Bouloukos (Hamilton Class of 2002), acquisitions editor, and her colleagues at the State University of New York Press.

I thank my Kirkland teachers Bill Rosenfeld, Michael Burkard, and Tess Gallagher for providing more than thirty years of unfailing mentorship.

The following alumnae have supported the publication of this book. I thank them for their generosity and for their invaluable contribution to perpetuating the legacy of Kirkland College: Kathryn L. Bedke (Kirkland Class of 1974), Penny Watras Dana (Kirkland Class of 1978), Carol Travis Friscia (Kirkland Class of 1977), Susan Skerritt (Kirkland Class of 1977), and especially The Susanne Marcus Collins Foundation, Inc.

Most of all, thank you to our parents, family, and friends for understanding and encouraging our connection to Kirkland—then and now.

Text Design, Scanning, and Technical Support: Constance Halporn, K'78

Copyright and Permissions: Rebecca Pressman, K'78

Copyediting and Proofreading: Zan Tewksbury, K'80

Marketing and Promotion: Judy Silverstein Gray, K'78 and Jennifer Morris, K'72

Grateful acknowledgment is given to the following sources for permission to reprint material:

Nin Andrews: "Star" in *The Notre Dame Review*, "How the Poem Dies" in *Flights*, and "The Other Girl" in *Crab Orchard Review*.

Natalie Babbitt: Excerpts from TUCK EVERLASTING by Natalie Babbitt. Copyright ©1975, renewed 2003 by Natalie Babbitt. Reprinted by permission of Farrar, Straus and Giroux, LLC.

Nina Bogin: "The Orchards" is taken from *The Winter Orchards* by Nina Bogin published by Anvil Press Poetry in 2001. "The Lost Hare" and "The Old World" are taken from *The Lost Hare* by Nina Bogin published by Anvil Press Poetry in 2012.

Carol Durst-Wertheim: "Zemel" in *Storied Dishes: What Our Family Recipes Tell Us About Who We Are and Where We've Been* edited by Linda Murray Berzok (Praeger, 2010). Reprinted with permission of Linda Murray Berzok.

Stephanie Feuer: "What Counts" in BettyConfidential.com.

Doris Friedensohn: From *Eating As I Go: Scenes from America and Abroad*, by Doris Friedensohn, The University Press of Kentucky, 2006. Reprinted with permission.

Elias Friedensohn: "My Lovely, Impassioned Students" (excerpted by Doris Friedensohn) was first published in *connections, 2: Toward a Vision of Education as Transformative Action*, Spring 1974.

Tess Gallagher: "Instructions to the Double," "I Stop Writing The Poem," and "The Red Devil" in *Midnight Lantern: New and Selected Poems* (Graywolf Press, 2011). Reprinted by permission of the author.

Susan Hartman: "In the Generation That Laughed at Me" in *Dumb Show* (University Presses of Florida, 1979). Reprinted with permission from the University Press of Florida.

Ellen Horan: From *31 Bond Street* by Ellen Horan, ©2010 Ellen Horan. Courtesy of HarperCollins Publishers.

Lynn Kanter: The first chapter of the excerpt from *Her Own Vietnam* was first published in the online literary journal *VerbSap*.

Peggy Dills Kelter: "Solitaire" in *The Hood River News*, January 2009. Naomi Lazard: "Elegy for the Twenty Skiers" in *SOLO*, and "Notes for the Recording Angel" in *The Atlantic Magazine*.

Denise Levertov: "Footprints," "Hut," "Life Is Not a Walk across a Field." By Denise Levertov, from POEMS 1968–1972, copyright ©1970 by Denise Levertov. Reprinted by permission of New Directions Publishing Corp.

Victoria Kohn Michels: "Spring in Clinton New York" is reprinted by permission of Victoria Kohn Michels. Copyright ©1984 by Victoria Kohn. "At the Brooklyn Botanic Garden" is reprinted by permission of Victoria Kohn Michels. Copyright ©2011 by Victoria Kohn Michels. "Abilene" is reprinted by permission of Victoria Kohn Michels. Copyright ©1988 by Victoria Kohn. "Abilene" originally appeared in *Under 35: The New Generation of American Poets* by Nicholas Christopher and published by Anchor Books, a division of Random House, Inc.

Liz Morrison: "The Meaning of Meat" in *Storied Crossings: 2003 Short Story Writing Contest Anthology* (Scribes Valley Publishing), http://www.scribesvalley.com/winners2003.html.

Ilene Moskin: "Poem" in *raccoon 14*, guest edited by Michael Waters.

Gwynn O'Gara: "Vagabond Sky" in *The Sow's Ear* and "Let Me Be Beautiful Like Sea Glass" in *Argestes*.

Jo Pitkin: "The Lakehouse" in *Ironwood* 16, 1980; "Loss" in *The Measure* (Finishing Line Press, 2007); "The Mollusk" in *Vanguard Voices of the Hudson Valley—Poetry 2007* (Mohonk Mountain Stage Company).

Clare Guzzo Robert: "Tea Ball Mind" in *Buddhadharma: The Practitioner's Quarterly*, Spring 2009.

Irma Rosenfeld: "Antique" in *The Chicago Review*, Volume 30, Number 4. Reprinted by permission of *The Chicago Review*. "Pavane" in *The DeKalb Literary Arts Journal*, Volume XV.

William Rosenfeld: "Astronaut" was published by Harper Square Press, Gallery Series III, 1970 and "At Shishevo" in *Antioch Review*, Spring 1977.

Maria Theresa Stadtmueller: "Taking Francis Hostage" in *Dark Mountain: Issue 1* edited by Dougald Hine and Paul Kingsnorth (2010, The Dark Mountain Project).

261

About Kirkland

Kirkland College was founded in 1965 as a result of the work of a Long-Range Planning Committee at Hamilton College, a 189-year-old, traditional, all-male liberal arts college in Clinton, NY. Under the leadership of Robert McEwen, the Hamilton president, the committee proposed that, in order to solve various academic and social issues at Hamilton and to take advantage of a dramatic increase in both men and women seeking higher education, a series of relatively small, distinctive, and interdependent colleges be formed in a "cluster" surrounding their present isolated campus in upstate New York.

Population statistics and the economic climate (which was rosy during the planning period) favored expansion. Whereas Hamilton and its alumni were not ready to accept women as students in what remained a proudly male institution, they did feel that "girls" might be a welcome addition to the social life of their rural hilltop, and so they proposed that the first of the planned colleges be a female counterpart of Hamilton. The new institution could, perhaps, offer instruction in what were then perceived as the more feminine, less traditional areas of study such as the arts and the social sciences, which were dramatically underrepresented in the Hamilton curriculum.

Plans went forward. A site was secured on college-owned open land directly across a main road from the existing campus. An architect—Benjamin Thompson—was put to work on the design of new, contemporary buildings, financed by bonds from the New York State Dormitory Authority and private gifts; a dean and then a president were hired; and the opening was set for September 1968.

But more was changing than the landscape on "College Hill." With the naming of Millicent McIntosh, former president of Barnard College, a trustee and the foremost voice in academic matters, a totally new element entered the picture. McIntosh was a seasoned educational iconoclast who believed that the new college provided an unparalleled opportunity to rethink a liberal arts curriculum. Accordingly, when she

263

Figure 1. Kirkland Trustee Millicent Carey McIntosh on earthmoving equipment at the groundbreaking ceremony for the college, May 25, 1967, *Source:* Hamilton College Archives.

and McEwen set out to hire the leadership team of the new college, they were looking for people with an open approach to the design of the new institution.

Figure 2. Opening procession at Kirkland College construction site, September 1968. *Source:* Hamilton College Archives. Photograph ©Dante Tranquille. Used with permission of *Utica Observer-Dispatch.*

At the time, new winds were blowing through both the educational and social worlds in the United States, and not the least of these was the gale of a new feminist awareness. So planning, which had originally been quite traditional in its view of women, began to take on a more contemporary cast, in which the independence of young women and their ability to chart their own course was a fundamental element. When Kirkland opened—on schedule, using a partially finished campus and buildings in which the paint was still drying—it welcomed an extraordinary group of bright, self-motivated, exploring young women, attracted to the idea that they would be intimately involved in designing their own curriculum and their own community. In lieu of grades, the college would provide "evaluations"—written critiques of a semester's work; students would determine their own "parietals" or rules of living and conduct in the dormitories; they would, in short, be given a kind of personal responsibility that signaled the college's belief that they were adults, in charge of their individual academic and social lives. Students were encouraged to take on independent work, either alone or in groups of like-minded peers, to design their own majors (or in Kirkland jargon: "concentrations"). Cross-registration with Hamilton provided a full curricular offering for all students, bringing many Hamilton students to classes in subjects never offered there before.

In terms of its promise to its students, the college thrived, and students on both campuses enjoyed an expanded and challenging set of offerings. But innovation always has two results: the new and exciting elements that enter a community, and the resentful reactions of the established order. To this mix was added two related factors—present from the beginning, but growing in intensity—which led to the college's undoing after a decade of operation. First, Hamilton College, the original incubator, became less and less supportive of Kirkland's academic and social approach. Following Robert McEwen's death even as Kirkland opened, Hamilton struggled through several rapid changes in leadership and finally elected a president who, as a former member

Figure 3. Poet Tess Gallagher (bottom left) teaching a creative writing workshop in Kirner-Johnson, 1976. Hamilton and Kirkland students facing the camera are Daniel D'Amelio, Jo Pitkin, Susanne Marcus, and Kevin McDonough. *Source:* Hamilton College Archives. Photograph ©John Hinchcliff. Used with permission.

Figure 4. Kirkland College's 1976 commencement. *Source:* Hamilton College Archives.

Figure 5. Samuel Fisher Babbitt launching the Campaign for the Second Decade in List's dance studio, 1977. *Source:* Hamilton College Archives. Photograph ©Constance Halporn. Used with permission.

of the faculty, had vigorously objected to the founding of Kirkland. Second, the economic climate, so rosy as the Hamilton planners projected budgets for the new college, became increasingly difficult. Inflation of construction costs, for example, hit 10% per year as the Kirkland campus was being built. Building bonds that had been at 3% in the planning years were at 7% when they were actually issued, placing an enormous financial burden on the new college.

Approaching the end of its first decade, Kirkland planned a major capital campaign in an effort to bolster its finances. It asked Hamilton to stand behind it financially as the campaign went forward. At the urging of Hamilton's president, that request was denied, and Hamilton announced its plans to move to a single institution under its control. Following protracted and bitter negotiations, Kirkland was taken over by a newly coeducational Hamilton in 1978.

Figure 6. Carrying the American and Kirkland College flags, two Kirkland students lead the 1975 commencement procession. *Source:* Hamilton College Archives.

Aftermath

The "merger" was difficult and messy. Although many Kirkland faculty were let go after the initial year, a group of young Kirkland faculty members was taken in by Hamilton and eventually given tenure. In time, together with more liberal members of the Hamilton faculty, these people became senior faculty leaders, and the approach to education that they brought with them became predominant at Hamilton.

Kirkland lives on in the thoughts and active lives of the extraordinary coterie of women who attended and who now exemplify the independence of thought and action that the college helped to foster. Kirkland also lives on at Hamilton College, now headed by a woman president. She leads a much larger, much more liberal and vibrant coeducational institution in which many of the hallmarks of Kirkland can be seen.

Former Kirkland President Samuel Fisher Babbitt
2012

A Note About the Title

The Kirkland College campus was built on an apple orchard, and the college's official seal featured a green apple tree with a leaf, a blossom, and an apple on a white background. The metaphor of the orchard, as reflected in the works in this volume, is perhaps not actually lost but merely fallow.

A Note About the Type

Everything at Kirkland—from the bright Marimekko fabrics covering our furniture to the architecture of Ben Thompson—was meant to convey the college's innovative, fresh approach to education. Our publications, too, had a modern look that was consistent with the college's image. For the text of *Lost Orchard,* we chose Optima, a typeface designed by Hermann Zapf in 1952–1955. Optima is a sans-serif typeface with a modern yet classic appearance. According to Kirkland's Director of Publications Jesse J. Zellner, Optima was one of the branding typefaces that was used frequently in early Kirkland publications.

For more information about Kirkland College:

- http://www.kirklandalums.org

- http://www.storychip.com/kirkland:chips

- *Limited Engagement: Kirkland College 1965–1978: An Intimate History of the Rise And Fall of a Coordinate College for Women* by Samuel Fisher Babbitt

- *Separate by Degree: Women Students' Experiences in Single-Sex and Coeducational Colleges* by Leslie Miller-Bernal

- *Going Coed: Women's Experiences in Formerly Men's Colleges and Universities* by Leslie Miller-Bernal and Susan L. Poulson

To view Kirkland Voices:
http://www.hamilton.edu/alumni/reunions/reunions-2007/kirkland-voices-part-1
http://www.hamilton.edu/alumni/reunions/reunions-2007/kirkland-voices-part-2